The Burren
and the Aran Islands

EXPLORING THE ARCHAEOLOGY

Dr Carleton Jones lectures in archaeology at the National University of Ireland, Galway and he received his PhD from the University of Cambridge. His interest in the archaeology of the Burren and the Aran Islands began in 1989 and he has surveyed and excavated in the region since. He has received support from the Heritage Council and from the Royal Irish Academy for various aspects of his fieldwork. His work has been published in both academic and popular archaeology journals, as well as being featured on national television and radio. Much of Dr Jones' fieldwork has been carried out through Burren Archaeology Research and details of current research activities including possible fieldwork opportunities can be found on **www.burrenarch.com.**

The Burren and the Aran Islands form a region renowned for its geology, flora and archaeology. Possibly the greatest interest is in its archaeology but the ancient monuments are often perceived as shrouded in mystery and beyond explanation. Recent studies, however, have shed considerable light on the functions of these monuments and the people who built them. This book presents these archaeological interpretations in an attractive and engaging manner.

After a brief introduction the book is divided into two parts, the Burren and the Aran Islands. Significant sites are highlighted within broader themes such as *The First Farmers on the Burren* and *Christianity and Pilgrimage on the Aran Islands*. More tangential topics such as *Building a Wedge Tomb* are also included and many of these are explained in concise 'panel' features such as *Contemporary Travellers' Accounts of Tower Houses* and *Cross-Decorated Stones of the Aran Islands*.

Heavily illustrated, the captions are often extensive and can be read separately or with the text. Overall it is designed to be read cover to cover or dipped into. Dr Jones' writing transforms the dry academic material of excavation reports and archaeological inventories into an engaging and understandable story.

The Burren

and the Aran Islands

Exploring the Archaeology

CARLETON JONES

To Alix

FIRST PUBLISHED 2004 BY
The Collins Press
West Link Park
Doughcloyne
Wilton
Cork

Reprinted 2006

British Library Cataloguing in Publication Data

Jones, Carleton
    Exploring the archaeology of the Burren and the Aran Islands
    1. Excavations (Archaeology) – Ireland – Aran Island
    2. Excavations (Archaeology) – Ireland – Burren 3. Aran
    Island (Ireland) – Antiquities 4. Burren (Ireland) – Antiquities
    I. Title
    941.7'48

Paperback ISBN-10: 1-903464-49-8
Paperback ISBN-13: 978-1-903464-49-6
Hardback ISBN-10: 1-903464-61-7
Hardback ISBN-13: 978-1-903464-61-8

Typeset by Anú Design, Tara
Printed in Ireland by ColourBooks
Cover and text design by Anú Design, Tara

Cover images:
Front cover: View looking southeast over the Dún Eochla stone fort from the Oghil lighthouse on Inishmore.
The other Aran Islands and the Burren are visible in the distance. Fragment of a high cross inside the small
church of Tighlagheany, part of St Enda's monastery on Inishmore;

Back cover: Knockstoolery standing stone in Doolin;

Spine: Gleninagh tower house on Galway Bay.

Yesterday . . . I saw some ruins . . . I thought again about them, and about the dead whom I had never known and on whom my feet trampled. I love above all the sight of vegetation resting upon old ruins; this embrace of nature, coming swiftly to bury the work of man the moment his hand is no longer there to defend it, fills me with deep and ample joy.

— Gustave Flaubert, novelist, 1846

I know perfectly well that I would rather paint a ruined abbey half-covered with ivy and standing among long grass than I would paint it after it has been taken over by the Office of Works, when they have taken off all the ivy and mown all the grass.

— John Piper, painter, 1941

Contents

Illustrations

Introduction

The archaeology of the Burren and the Aran Islands holds a fascination for many people and it is not hard to see why. The evocativeness of this ancient landscape, which today seems so empty but where around almost every turn one comes across signs of people who have been here before us, has captivated many. Tramping across the rugged terrain and then coming upon the massive stones of a long-forgotten megalithic tomb tilted skywards by people who have been dead for thousands of years or perhaps coming across a hidden Medieval church covered in ivy, one is brought face-to-face with both the transience of a single human life and also with the impressive length of the human story. When we visit a megalithic tomb we can touch the same stones that were quarried, split, heaved and hammered into place by other hands long before our time and it is well to remember that these monuments were built by individuals. In their time they were as real as we are today. They had children and spouses, they loved and they fought, some were ambitious, some were lazy, some were intelligent and some were dim-witted. In other words, people in the past ran the full gamut of the types of people we know today and so in some ways we are very close to those distant ancestors. But it is also well to remember just how much time separates us from them. About the same amount of time has elapsed between the very last time a megalithic tomb was built and the birth of Christ as between the birth of Christ and our own lives. So while in some ways we may be close to those ancient tomb builders, in many ways we are far removed from them. It is perhaps for this reason that these ancient monuments are often perceived as shrouded in mystery and beyond explanation. Recent archaeological studies, however, have shed considerable light on both the monuments and on the people that built them, and I wrote *The Burren and the Aran Islands: Exploring the Archaeology* in order to bring these advances in our understanding to as wide an audience as possible.

The book is designed so that it can be read either cover-to-cover or dipped into as you make your way around the sites. Read cover-to-cover, the book provides a chronologically ordered account of the people and their changing societies over the past 5,000 to 6,000 years. As an on-site guide, the book provides a detailed explanation of the key sites for each period. The location of all the sites discussed in the book are shown on the maps contained in the book. If you are visiting the sites in the field, however, I strongly recommend that this book be used in conjunction with one or more of the many detailed maps of the area that are available. For a single map that covers both the Burren and the Aran Islands at a scale of 1:50,000 there is the Discovery Series No. 51 produced by the Ordnance Survey of Ireland. A more detailed map covering just the Aran Islands is also produced by the Ordnance Survey at a scale of 1:25,000. Two separate maps, one covering the Burren, the other covering the Aran Islands, have been produced by Tim Robinson. Robinson's Burren map has a scale of approximately 1:35,000 and his Aran Island map has a scale of approximately 1:28,000. These are all excellent large-scale maps which is why I decided not to duplicate the effort by producing maps of equivalent detail within the book. All the sites discussed in the book can be located on these large-scale maps by using the grid reference numbers which I have given with each site description. The grid reference consists of a letter followed by two three-digit numbers, the first is the Easting and the second is the Northing. As an example, the grid reference for Black Head on the north-west corner of the Burren is M 154 122. To find Black Head on the Discovery Series No. 51 map first find the section of the map which is identified by the letter 'M'. A small graphic in the right-hand margin of all the Discovery Series maps shows how the letters relate to map areas and the letters are also printed as large blue icons on the map itself. On Map 51, the letters appear in the ocean just south east of Inisheer. It can be seen that letter M on Map 51 refers to the large, upper right-hand quadrant of the map. The next step is to find the Easting – these are the blue grid numbers that increase as you move to the east (to the right). Move east from the M icon until you find the vertical grid line '15' (the first two digits of your Easting). Now, staying on the vertical '15' line, move north (up) until you find the horizontal grid line '12' (the first two digits of your Northing). You will now find yourself at the south-west corner of the grid square that contains Black Head. The final digit on the both the Easting and the Northing is used to determine where in that grid square Black Head is located. If you visualise the space between vertical grid lines '15' and '16' as being divided into tenths, the final '4' of the Easting indicates that Black Head is located $^4/_{10}$ of the way, or just under halfway, between the grid lines. Similarly, the final '2' of the Northing indicates that Black Head is $^2/_{10}$ of the way between the horizontal '12' and '13' grid lines. Although Robinson's maps also have the grid numbers marked, they are marked in a more general manner which makes the grid reference numbers easiest to use with the Ordnance Survey maps. Robinson's maps, however, do have the townland walls marked and these can be a great navigation aid if you are far from a road (the townland walls tend to be high, substantial walls).

Every site mentioned in the book is marked on the smaller-scale maps which I have provided within the book. These maps are designed so that you can see which sites are near to each other and thereby plan your visits to various sites. In many cases these maps are sufficient for finding the sites, but in cases where the sites are not signposted and are far from the road, possessing one of the larger-scale maps is necessary. All the site descriptions in this book are accompanied by icons which indicate whether the site is signposted and whether it requires a significant walk to reach the site from the road. If you're not elderly and are reasonably fit, however, don't let the 'significant walk' icon put you off. The charm of many of the sites lies in the fact that they are off the beaten track and you will never fully appreciate the beauty of the area until you spend some time walking cross country. It was difficult to quantify what a 'significant walk' was but in general it is more than a few hundred metres off the road and contains one or more of the following: rough terrain, a steep hill, fields with no path, walls that must be crossed. This brings us to the matter of stone walls. If you visit during the summer you may not see many animals in the fields and you may assume that the fields are no longer used. This is not the case and in the winter the fields are full of cattle. Both the Burren and the Aran Islands are a maze of intertwined land holdings so if you knock a gap in a wall, it's quite likely that you are opening fields onto each other that belong to different farmers. It is only common courtesy, therefore, that if you knock stones off a wall while crossing it you should replace them. Also, if you are asked by a farmer not to cross a particular field, you should respect their wishes. Mention of a site in the book does not imply that there is public access to the site so in the case of unsignposted monuments/sites permission should be obtained from the landowner if in doubt.

[P] [P̸] – indicates the site is signposted or not signposted.

[🚶] [🚶̸] – indicates a significant walk from the road is required to reach the site or no walk is required.

Only the key sites are discussed in this book and a look at any of the large-scale maps mentioned above will show many more sites. Both the Burren and the Aran Islands are remarkable for the sheer density of sites they contain. It would be needlessly repetitive to try and discuss every site. Instead, I have included sites which are either essential to understanding a particular time period or theme and/or sites which are representative of many other sites. In other words, what applies to the wedge tombs on Roughan Hill applies to the 80 or so other wedge tombs on the Burren as well. I have included all sites which have been the focus of extensive archaeological excavations.

The Landscape

Both the Burren and the Aran Islands are unique limestone regions which are distinct from surrounding areas today and would have been distinct in the past as well. They are not, however, static landscapes. The character of the Burren and of the Aran Islands has changed over time. Some of these changes were due to climatic changes and some were caused by people. Following the end of the last ice age about 10,000 to 11,000 years ago, the Burren and the Aran Islands were left with a patchy soil cover that supported a patchy tree cover. The composition of this tree cover changed over the millennia, mainly as a result of climatic changes, from an original forest dominated by birch to a forest dominated by pine and hazel.

Although there were farmers on the Burren early in the Neolithic, they did not make a significant impact on the environment until the Late or Final Neolithic when they seem to have engaged in large-scale tree clearance. The aim of this tree clearance was probably mainly to open up pastures for grazing but some clearance for cereal farming may also have taken place. Tree clearance and grazing continued into the Bronze Age and eventually led to significant soil loss on the Burren some time in the Bronze Age. In the western Burren, where the limestone is capped by a layer of shale, peat bogs began forming by the Late Bronze Age. As with the rest of Ireland, there was a regeneration of the tree cover in the Iron Age followed by a subsequent phase of woodland clearance in the Early Medieval period.

On the low-lying and exposed Aran Islands, the thin soil cover left by the retreating glaciers may have been stripped away fairly rapidly by Atlantic gales and by sea levels which were higher than they are today. This means that the Aran Islands probably always had a more patchy and scrubby tree cover than the Burren, and humans may have had a lesser role in creating a cleared landscape on the islands.

The power of the Atlantic has also re-shaped the Aran Islands during the span of their human occupation. This is seen in the dramatic erosion of their exposed southern shores and the contrasting deposition of sand on their sheltered northern shores. Forts such as Dún Aonghasa and Dún Dúcathair which are perched on the broken edges of cliffs on the south side of Inishmore have lost some of their stones to the sea while the Medieval churches of Tighlagheany on the north side of Inishmore and Teampall Chaomháin on the north side of Inisheer are today partially buried in sand. As a visitor to these regions you should not be fooled into thinking they are timeless and unchanging. They are quite the opposite.

The Archaeology

The history of archaeological research in the area really begins with the activities of the nineteenth-century antiquarians. Antiquarians is a term used to refer to those early scholars who took a scientific interest in antiquities. These antiquarians concentrated on describing, illustrating, comparing and classifying both standing monuments and smaller antiquities. They sometimes conducted excavations but more often were content to speculate and debate on what was already visible. Among the antiquarians active in the area, the name of Thomas Westropp stands out. He was not the first to record and illustrate the antiquities of the Burren and the Aran Islands but the depth of his research and the volume of publications that he produced have ensured that he is well-remembered today. Indeed, many of the illustrations reproduced in this book are his work. Not all antiquarians recorded with an equal concern for accuracy and Westropp once complained that 'the artist overpowered the antiquary' when discussing a drawing of Dún Aonghasa by the earlier antiquarian, George Petrie, where the scale of the drawing had been distorted.

The beginning of scientific archaeological excavation in Ireland was marked by the work of Hugh O'Neill Hencken and the Harvard Archaeological Expedition in the 1930s. The Harvard Archaeological Expedition was part of a wider project, the Harvard Irish Survey. This was a research programme which examined the physical anthropology, sociology and archaeology of

Ireland with the aim of establishing 'the origin and development of the races and cultures of Ireland'. Altogether, the expedition excavated fifteen sites in Ireland including two on the Burren, the prehistoric burial cairn of Poulawack and the Early Medieval cliff fort of Cahercommaun. In 1949 the Megalithic Survey of Ireland was begun by Ruaidhrí de Valera and Seán Ó Nualláin of the Ordnance Survey Office and the first volume of this extensive survey to be published was County Clare in 1961. In this survey, each known megalithic tomb was carefully recorded and the distribution of the monuments was discussed. The Megalithic Survey began the numbering system for megalithic tombs which continues in use today and which is used in this book. Each tomb is identified by a unique label which consists of a two-letter abbreviation of the county it is located in followed by a number. The Parknabinnia chambered tomb, for example, is also known as Cl. 153 because it was the 153rd megalithic tomb recorded in County Clare.

In more recent decades, several sites have been excavated on the Burren and on the Aran Islands. Some of these were limited excavations designed to mitigate damage already done to a monument, some excavations have been carried out in advance of restoration work and some excavations have been carried out within the framework of research projects. Some of the more extensive recent excavations on the Burren have been the excavation of the Poulnabrone portal tomb by Dr Anne Lynch of the National Monuments Division and the excavation of a prehistoric farmstead and the Parknabinnia chambered tomb on Roughan Hill by myself. On the Aran Islands, some of the more extensive recent excavations were those carried out at the great stone fort of Dún Aonghasa under the direction of Claire Cotter of the Discovery Programme and those at Teampaill Chiaráin by Dr Sinéad Ní Ghabhláin.

Mesolithic	c. 7000 – 4000 BC
Neolithic	c. 4000 – 2400 BC
Final Neolithic/Early Bronze Age	c. 2400 – 2000 BC
Early Bronze Age	c. 2000 – 1500 BC
Middle Bronze Age	c. 1500 – 1000 BC
Late Bronze Age	c. 1000 – 600 BC
Iron Age	c. 600 BC – 400 AD
Early Medieval	c. 400 – late twelfth c. AD
Medieval	late twelfth c. – early sixteenth c. AD

Figure 1
Prehistoric and Historic periods in Ireland.

The prehistoric period includes all periods up to and including the Iron Age. The historic period begins with the Early Medieval period when writing and literacy were introduced to Ireland.

In Figure 1 I have set out the chronology that I follow in this book. This chronology is a much-modified descendant of the traditional 'Three Age System' of Stone Age, Bronze Age and Iron Age. The Three Age System was first used in Ireland in the nineteenth century at the same time that it was becoming widely accepted across Europe. Soon after its introduction, however, people began to notice more subtle differences in the archaeology and so sub-divisions were introduced such as Mesolithic (Middle Stone Age) and Neolithic (New Stone Age). As archaeological knowledge has continued to grow, it has also become evident that 'transitional' periods between the traditional periods were often prolonged and very significant periods in their own right. Hence, in Figure 1 there is a 400-year long Final Neolithic/Early Bronze Age period – an awkward label but a significant period when societies underwent dramatic changes.

Overall, I hope this book provides a lively introduction to the archaeology of these two remarkable areas to those who are not familiar with them, while at the same time providing a fresh, human perspective on the archaeology of these areas for those who have already spent hours tramping through them.

Acknowledgements

First and foremost on the list of those I am indebted to for help and inspiration on this book is Alix Gilmer. In addition to taking many of the photographs on these pages, she accompanied me on countless days spent walking, surveying and excavating, and always interjected a welcome bit of wit into the day, as long as tea was provided. My involvement with the Burren began on a hot and dusty day on the Plano Trabuco back in 1989 when Sinéad Ní Ghabhláin asked if I would like to help out with her field work in a greener and cooler place. I traded in my sun hat for a pair of wellies and have never regretted it. Once I began my own research on the Burren, it was Paul Keane who provided the welcome and smoothed the way for our field work. Paul has since passed away but he will always be remembered by the archaeologists and volunteer workers whom he made so welcome. Many thanks also to Elinor and Carleton Jones, Snr. who through their expertise with computers produced all the maps contained in the book, the three-dimensional model of Roughan Hill, and assistance with several of the other figures. This book is based upon the work of many archaeologists and because I have written it as a non-academic book, these archaeologists are not credited within the text. To compensate for this I have arranged the bibliography according to the individual chapters so that the reader can easily see whose research was used. As always, the work and any faults are the responsibility of the author but thanks are also due to Sinéad Ní Ghabhláin, John Waddell and Claire Cotter for commenting on portions of the text pertinent to their research. Finally, thanks also to both John Waddell and Conor Newman of the Department of Archaeology at NUIG for providing photographs and drawings from their files.

The Burren

The First People on the Burren

THE FIRST PEOPLE IN IRELAND arrived around 7000 BC and subsisted by hunting and gathering. This period is known as the Mesolithic and it lasted until about 4000 BC. Most of the known Mesolithic sites in Ireland are in low-lying locations close to coasts, lakes and rivers although some upland sites are known. This site distribution appears to be related to the economy of the Mesolithic people which in Ireland seems to have been heavily reliant on fish, particularly salmon and trout. Elsewhere in Europe at this time red deer were an important source of food but there is only very limited and uncertain evidence for the exploitation of red deer in Ireland in this period. It may be that red deer had not crossed the land bridge between Britain and Ireland before the melting glaciers severed the two islands. Other animals were hunted though, especially wild pig, and shellfish and plant foods such as hazelnuts were collected as well.

The settlement pattern of these Mesolithic people seems to have been based on mobility. One possibility is that they established 'base' camps surrounded by 'satellite' camps for exploiting specific resources. In this model, the base camp might have been occupied year round or the group may have shifted between a summer base camp and a winter base camp. The other possibility is that groups shifted more frequently to avail of seasonally available resources. Although base camps should be more detectable in the archaeological record than shorter-term camps, all these sites would leave only ephemeral traces. The absence of Mesolithic sites in an area, therefore, does not rule out the possibility that Mesolithic people were in the area.

This then leads to the question, were there Mesolithic hunter-gatherers on the Burren? Given that most Mesolithic sites in Ireland are in low-lying areas adjacent to coasts, rivers and lakes, the Burren does not seem to be an ideal place to look for Mesolithic sites, particularly not base camps. As noted above, however, some upland sites are known. We might particularly expect to find upland Mesolithic sites if the upland area is adjacent to a lowland area more suited to a base camp. In this scenario we might expect to find satellite camps in the uplands situated for the exploitation of specific resources that would then be brought back to the base camp.

The question of whether or not there were Mesolithic hunter-gatherers on the Burren can then be expanded to the question of whether or not there are any Mesolithic sites in the adjacent lowlands. In fact, there is little evidence for Mesolithic people in County Clare as a whole but there are two locations with hints of Mesolithic activity. These are Killaloe and Lough Inchiquin and both are locations where we might expect Mesolithic activity, namely low-lying sites adjacent to rivers and lakes. Killaloe is located in eastern County Clare at the southern end of Lough Derg where the lake narrows to re-form into the River Shannon. Lough Inchiquin is located along the River Fergus just south of the Burren and outside the village of Corrofin. No Mesolithic *sites* are known in either area but there are some isolated finds from both areas that may be Mesolithic. From Killaloe there is a grey shale projectile point, a perforated stone that is a possible digging stick weight and several stone axes that may be Mesolithic. From Lough Inchiquin there are several stone axes that may be Mesolithic and a perforated deer antler that would have been hafted to a handle and used as either a hoe or an axe that may be Mesolithic as well. It must be noted, however, that while it is possible that Mesolithic stone axes can be distinguished from Neolithic axes, this is by no means certain and it is quite possible that the stone axes from both locations are Neolithic rather than Mesolithic.

These stray finds do, however, hint at the possibility of Mesolithic hunter-gatherers living in the lowlands around the Burren adjacent to lakes and rivers. Lough Inchiquin is very close to the Burren and if Mesolithic people stayed there for any length of time it is quite likely they made forays into the Burren in pursuit of game, to gather plant foods such as hazelnuts or possibly even to quarry chert for stone tools. What seems unlikely though is that there was any long-term settlement of the Burren in the Mesolithic. The first people to *settle* on the Burren seem to have been Neolithic farmers.

The First Farmers on the Burren

THE PERIOD KNOWN AS THE NEOLITHIC is that of the first farmers in Europe. In the preceding Mesolithic, the economy was based on hunting and gathering but with the advent of the Neolithic, the emphasis changed to the husbandry of domesticated animals and the cultivation of plants. The Neolithic way of life was introduced into south-east Europe from the Near East by around 7000 BC and it had reached Ireland by around 4000 BC.

In some areas the transition to farming appears to have been brought about by a spread of people, while in other areas it appears to have been a spread of ideas and technologies. When farming technologies did reach a new area, the transition to a farming economy did not always take place quickly. In central Europe, for example, it took around 2,000 years from the first introduction of farming to the widespread establishment of farming. A similar length of time between the introduction of farming and its widespread establishment may have taken place in some parts of Ireland. Some areas in Ireland probably had immigrant farmers, other areas may have been already well-populated by Mesolithic (hunting and gathering) natives who only slowly and selectively accepted elements of the Neolithic way of life. Different economies were probably practised in different areas, and different social organisations probably existed in different areas as well.

Furthermore, the transition to farming was probably a process rather than an event and as such it would have spanned the lives of many generations. This transition process is sometimes characterised by archaeologists as having three successive phases. An 'Availability' phase, where domesticated plants and animals were only used in small amounts and hunting and gathering were still the primary means of subsistence. A 'Substitution' phase, when farming practices developed but hunting and gathering were still relied on to a substantial degree, and a 'Consolidation' phase, when farming became the primary means of subsistence. Neolithic Irish farmers practised both cereal cultivation and animal husbandry, but animal husbandry appears to have been the more significant of the two. Cattle were the most important animals but pigs, sheep and goats were also raised, and wheat and barley were cultivated.

In contrast to the ephemeral sites of the Mesolithic, the Neolithic in Ireland is marked by the erection of the impressive megalithic tombs which are still prominent in the landscape today (mega = big, lithic = stone). These megalithic tombs have been the focus of much research and speculation and although archaeologists are certainly not in complete agreement as to their significance, at least one thing is clear: megalithic 'tombs' are not tombs in the sense of structures built solely to house the remains of the dead. They are much more than that. They were the ritual foci of local groups for generations and, in addition to funerary rituals, the rituals performed at the sites are likely to have dealt with ancestors, territory, fertility and many other concerns.

Some archaeologists have put forward the idea that one function of megalithic tombs was to serve as territorial markers. These archaeologists argue that as farming groups came into contact with hunter-gatherer groups both groups felt an increasing pressure on a scarce resource – namely land. Responding to this scarcity of land, groups began erecting megalithic tombs as impressive proclamations of the strength of their community and its attachment to that particular locale. Other archaeologists have pointed out that the many similarities in form between Neolithic houses and megalithic tombs makes it quite likely that the tombs were translations into stone of the houses of the living. If this was the case, the Neolithic people probably viewed the tombs as 'houses of the dead' or 'houses of the ancestors', an identification made very literal by the placement of the bones of their ancestors within the tombs.

These ideas about megalithic tombs show us that the transition from the Mesolithic to the Neolithic was not just an economic change, there was a change in people's world view as well. All the activities of the early farming communities – clearing forests, enclosing fields with walls and erecting megalithic tombs – would have created a landscape where the labour of previous generations would have been visible and lived in every day. This memory of past generations would have encouraged the development of several intertwined concepts: a linear concept of time, descent from ancestors, ownership and investment in a specific territory and the idea that actions in the present will affect the future – all of which are essential concepts for farmers.

It is in this period of radical, but not necessarily rapid, change that we have the first evidence for settlement on the Burren, probably as early as the early-fourth millennium BC (i.e., *c.* 3800 BC). Several megalithic tombs and the initial phase of at least one of the cairns on the Burren date to the fourth millennium, some of the traces of field walls on Roughan Hill and elsewhere may be this early and there may have been a stone axe production centre at Doolin at this time. Three important Neolithic ritual monuments have been excavated on the Burren: the Poulnabrone portal tomb, the Parknabinnia chambered tomb and the Poulawack cairn.

Figure 2
Court tomb at Teergonean near Doolin.
Grid Reference R 068 985

What we see today when we visit a megalithic tomb may be the end product of generations of use and alteration of a sacred locale rather than a single-phase construction. A monument may have begun as a timber structure, perhaps a raised platform on which bodies were left to decompose or perhaps a house where somebody had died. The timber structure may have been subsequently burnt down or left to collapse and then a stone-built megalithic tomb may have been constructed on top of the remains of the timber structure. Human bones and other artefacts may have been placed in the chambers of the tomb, rearranged within the tomb and possibly even removed from the tomb over a period of centuries. At a later time, the entrance to the megalithic tomb may have been ritually blocked, preventing any further interaction with the contents of the chambers. Still later, people may have dug into the tomb and inserted further burials.

Poulnabrone Portal Tomb

Grid Reference M 236 004

At the centre of the Burren is one of the most famous megalithic tombs in Ireland, the Poulnabrone portal tomb. In 1985 a worsening crack was noticed in one of the side stones of Poulnabrone and it was decided that to preserve the monument the stone had to be replaced. In advance of this conservation work, a team of National Monuments archaeologists under the direction of Dr Anne Lynch excavated the tomb. What they found were the disarticulated remains of at least 21 people, along with various stone and bone artefacts. These were not the remains of bodies that decomposed within the tomb, they were the remains of bodies that had been buried or stored elsewhere until they decomposed, and only later transferred to the portal tomb. Some of the bones were scorched and burnt but this was done after the bones no longer held flesh. The bones were placed in the chamber of the tomb in a jumbled mass and many had been jammed down into the grykes (cracks) of the bedrock floor.

Of the 21 people identified, sixteen were adults and five were children but only one individual appeared to have lived past the age of 40. Of the eight adults whose sex could be determined, four were men and four were women. Arthritis was fairly common and its prevalence in the neck and shoulders of these people suggests that they may have been regularly carrying heavy loads. Also evident in the teeth of the children were periods of either malnutrition or infectious illness, especially between the ages of three and six.

A series of radiocarbon dates from the bones in the chamber give a date range of *c.* 3800 – 3200 BC. It may be that the bones were placed in the tomb over this 600-year span, but because older bones were found above younger bones, it seems more likely that all the bones were gathered at one time from a different deposit and placed in the tomb together. If this was the case, this single act of deposition would have occurred some time after *c.* 3200 BC which may be when the tomb was built. Thinking about the possible uses of megalithic tombs, if one function of Poulnabrone was to act as an expression of territoriality, this may not have been necessary until hundreds of years after people had first started farming the Burren. Maybe, after 600 years of farming, populations on the Burren and in nearby regions had grown to the point where there were too many people for the land to easily support. In this situation, the people who occupied the Burren may have erected Poulnabrone as a symbol of their claim on the land and filled it with the bones of their ancestors, which they retrieved from another sacred burial place, perhaps a cave.

Mixed with the human bones in Poulnabrone were bones of cattle, pig, sheep/goat, dog, hare, stoat, pinemartin, woodmouse and bird. Although the smaller animals may be natural deposits, the bones of the larger animals appear to have been included in the deposit

Figure 3
Poulnabrone portal tomb.

There are several types of megalithic tomb in Ireland. The most common are portal tombs, court tombs, passage tombs and wedge tombs. Portal tombs are distinguished by their two large portal stones which stand on either side of the entrance and their massive, sloping capstones.

Figure 4
Finds from Poulnabrone.

The archaeologists found several stone and bone artefacts and many potsherds amongst the jumbled mass of disarticulated bones in the chamber (No.17 is a representative potsherd). Arrowheads, scrapers, stone disc beads and the head of a bone pin were all recovered. The arrowheads (No.s 2–4) would have been used for either hunting or warfare, the scrapers (No.s 5–12) may have been used for tasks such as scraping hides or working wood, the stone disc beads (No.s 15 & 16) may have been worn as ornaments or they may have been used as some sort of fasteners, and the bone pin (No. 18) may have been used to fasten a piece of clothing such as a cloak, or it may have been worn as an ornament. The small size of the polished stone axe (No. 1) found in the chamber suggests that it may have had a symbolic aspect beyond its utilitarian role as a tool. Of more certain symbolic significance are the two quartz crystals found in the chamber (No.s 13 & 14). Quartz crystals have been found within the chambers of other megalithic tombs and white quartz stones have been found incorporated into the fabric of megalithic tombs as well. The most spectacular use of quartz in an Irish megalithic tomb is the white quartz facade on the Newgrange passage tomb in County Meath. ▶

deliberately. The final deposit at Poulnabrone was placed in a small cist or portico just in front of the main chamber and was made well after the main chamber deposits. This was the burial of a newborn baby in the Early Bronze Age, c. 1750 - 1420 BC. This was a fairly common practice at the time and Early Bronze Age burials are often found inserted into earlier Neolithic monuments. Although the meaning of the monument may have changed by the Early Bronze Age, it was obviously still a significant place in the landscape and it remains so today.

◀ Figure 5
Perforated bone artefact from Poulnabrone.

Amongst the most interesting finds from Poulnabrone is a small, triangularly shaped piece of bone perforated by eleven circular holes that may have been worn as a pendant or an amulet. Regardless of how this small artefact may have been worn or used, it's likely that its overall shape and the pattern of holes in it had some symbolic significance which has yet to be discerned.

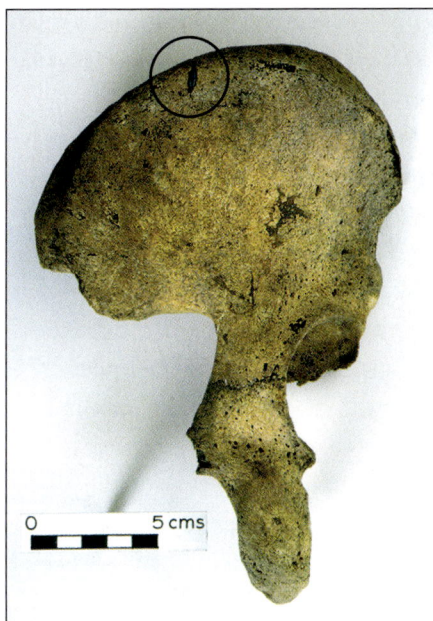

◀ Figure 6
Projectile tip embedded in pelvis from Poulnabrone.

Some of the bones from Poulnabrone showed evidence of violent attacks. A depressed fracture on the side of a skull may have been caused by a small stone projectile and another fracture on a rib may have been caused by an aggressive blow. Much more obvious evidence of aggression is this tip of a projectile point (probably an arrowhead) embedded in a hip bone. It is visible as a small black lozenge-shape at the top edge of the pelvis. Both the fracture on the skull and the fractured rib had healed showing that the people had survived their confrontations but this hip wound occurred at the time of the individual's death.

Poulawack Cairn

Grid Reference R 232 985

The monument that we see today at Poulawack is the end result of a very long sequence of ritual activities that stretched from the Neolithic into the Early Bronze Age. Although it is located a little less than two kilometres south of the famous portal tomb of Poulnabrone, it is far less visited because its complexity is hidden under a cairn of stones. The Poulawack monument is a burial cairn around 21 metres in diameter and around two and a half metres high. Within the cairn were the remains of eighteen people, the majority of which were contained in cists – boxes made of stone slabs.

Poulawack has been the focus of archaeological investigations, interpretations and re-interpretations from the 1930s to the 1990s. The cairn was excavated by Dr Hugh Hencken and the Harvard Expedition in the summer of 1934. Hencken recognised two different phases of burial in the monument but because he thought that the two phases were quite close in time, he dated the entire monument to the Early Bronze Age, based on a sherd of Beaker pottery which he found with one of the cist burials.

Much later, in the early 1980s, Dr Michael Ryan recognised that the primary, central cist in the Poulawack cairn was in fact a Linkardstown cist, a type of Neolithic burial monument that was unrecognised in Hencken's time. This revelation was then followed by a series of ten radiocarbon dates on bones from the cists carried out by Dr Anna Brindley and Dr Jan Lanting in the early 1990s. These radiocarbon dates have now shown that Poulawack actually had a very long history of use and witnessed three main phases of activity.

The monument at Poulawack began with the construction of the central cist on a small natural rise and the covering of the cist with a cairn, the outside edge of which was revetted with a two metre-high-stone wall. This first phase of the monument dates to around 3350 BC and is the Linkardstown cist phase of the monument. The central cist was divided into two compartments. The first held the disarticulated bones of a middle-aged man, a middle-aged woman, an adult female and an oyster shell. The other compartment contained the disarticulated bones of an infant along with a flint hollow scraper, a large boar tusk and two potsherds.

The second phase of activity at the site dates to well over 1,000 years after the monument was first built, some time around 2000 BC. At this time three more burial cists were inserted into the cairn which by now had slipped and settled in places. One cist contained the unburnt bones of an adolescent and a child, along with a tiny sherd of pottery. Another cist was divided into two compartments. The larger compartment contained the cremated bones of a young male along with unburnt bones of an adolescent and a child and the smaller compartment contained the bones of an adult male accompanied by a single sherd of Beaker pottery. The remaining cist contained a small number of bones from an adult and a child.

The third phase of activity at Poulawack occurred between c. 1600 BC and 1400 BC. At this time the cairn was enlarged and even more burials were inserted into the cairn. The height of the cairn was increased by about a metre, its diameter was increased by about four metres and its new outer edge was marked by a kerb of upright slabs. The burials of this phase consisted of three cist burials and a crouched inhumation that had been placed on the old ground surface, covered with a few slabs and then covered with the expanded cairn. One of the cists contained unburnt bones of an infant. Another of the cists contained a cremation, probably an adult female, along with a flint scraper and a bone point. The final cist contained unburnt bones of a young adult female.

Throughout its long history Poulawack was not an isolated monument and the various phases of activity evident at Poulawack were carried out within a landscape where other activities were carried out as well. The initial, Linkardstown cist phase of the Poulawack monument may have been roughly contemporary with the construction of the nearby Poulnabrone portal tomb and the final phase at Poulawack is also roughly contemporary with the final deposit at Poulnabrone. The intermediate phase at Poulawack is contemporary with the construction of the many surrounding wedge tombs. In this way Poulawack can be seen to embody a pattern that is emerging from other strands of archaeological evidence for prehistoric activity on the Burren. Namely, an initial phase of Neolithic activity in the fourth millennium BC, further activity in the Final Neolithic/Early Bronze Age, and a final phase of activity in the Early Bronze Age.

Figure 7
Poulawack cairn.

Figure 8
Hencken's plan of Poulawack.

Archaeologists refer to drawings such as this one, which shows the Poulawack cairn as if one is looking straight down on it, as a 'plan view'. Plan views are often combined with 'section views' such as those shown in Figure 9. A section view shows a verticle slice through the site. Cists 8 and 8A are the original Linkardstown cist. Cists 4, 5 and 6 belong to Phase 2. Grave 1, Cists 2, 3 and 7 belong to Phase 3.

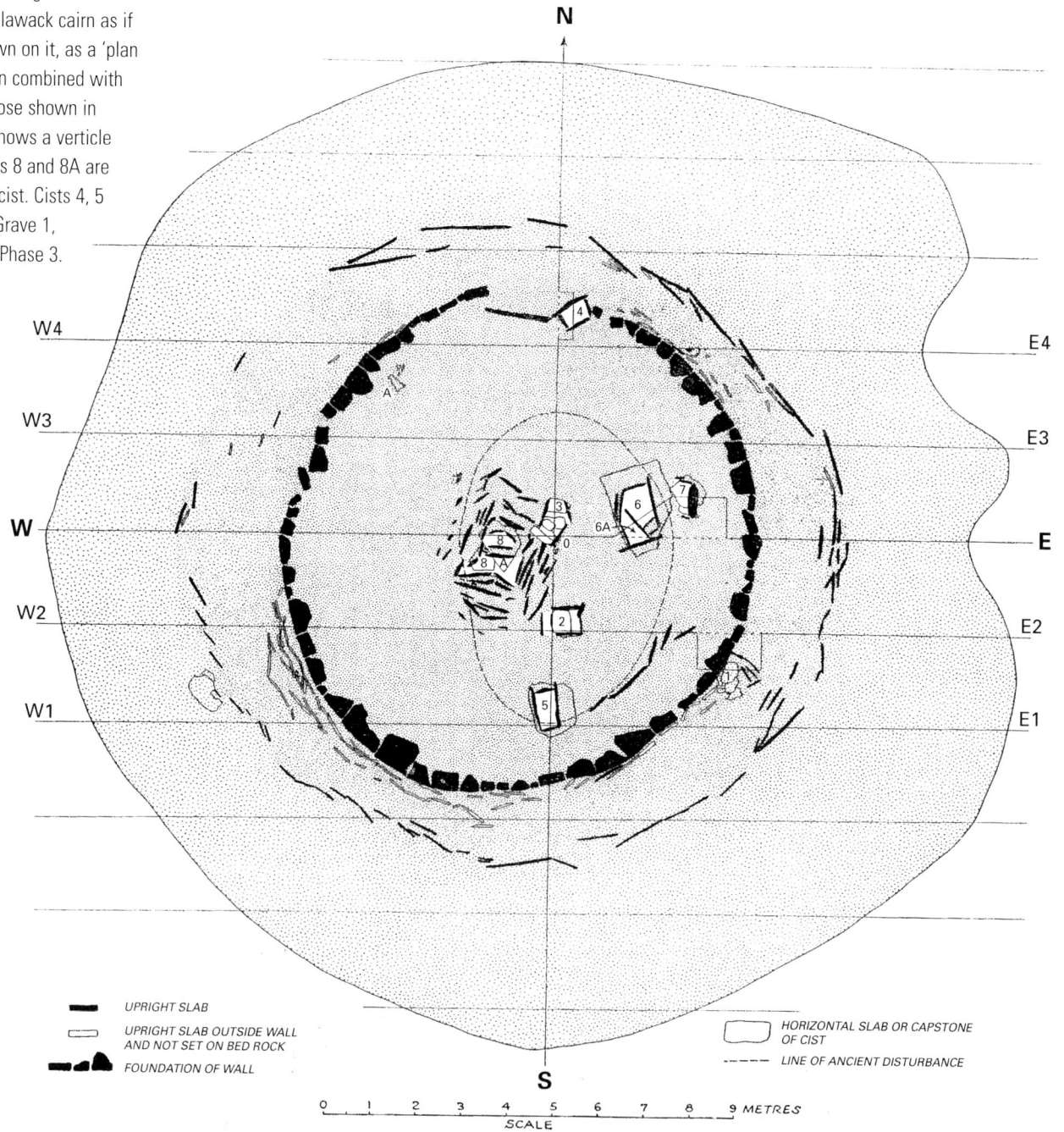

UPRIGHT SLAB

UPRIGHT SLAB OUTSIDE WALL
AND NOT SET ON BED ROCK

FOUNDATION OF WALL

HORIZONTAL SLAB OR CAPSTONE
OF CIST

LINE OF ANCIENT DISTURBANCE

SCALE

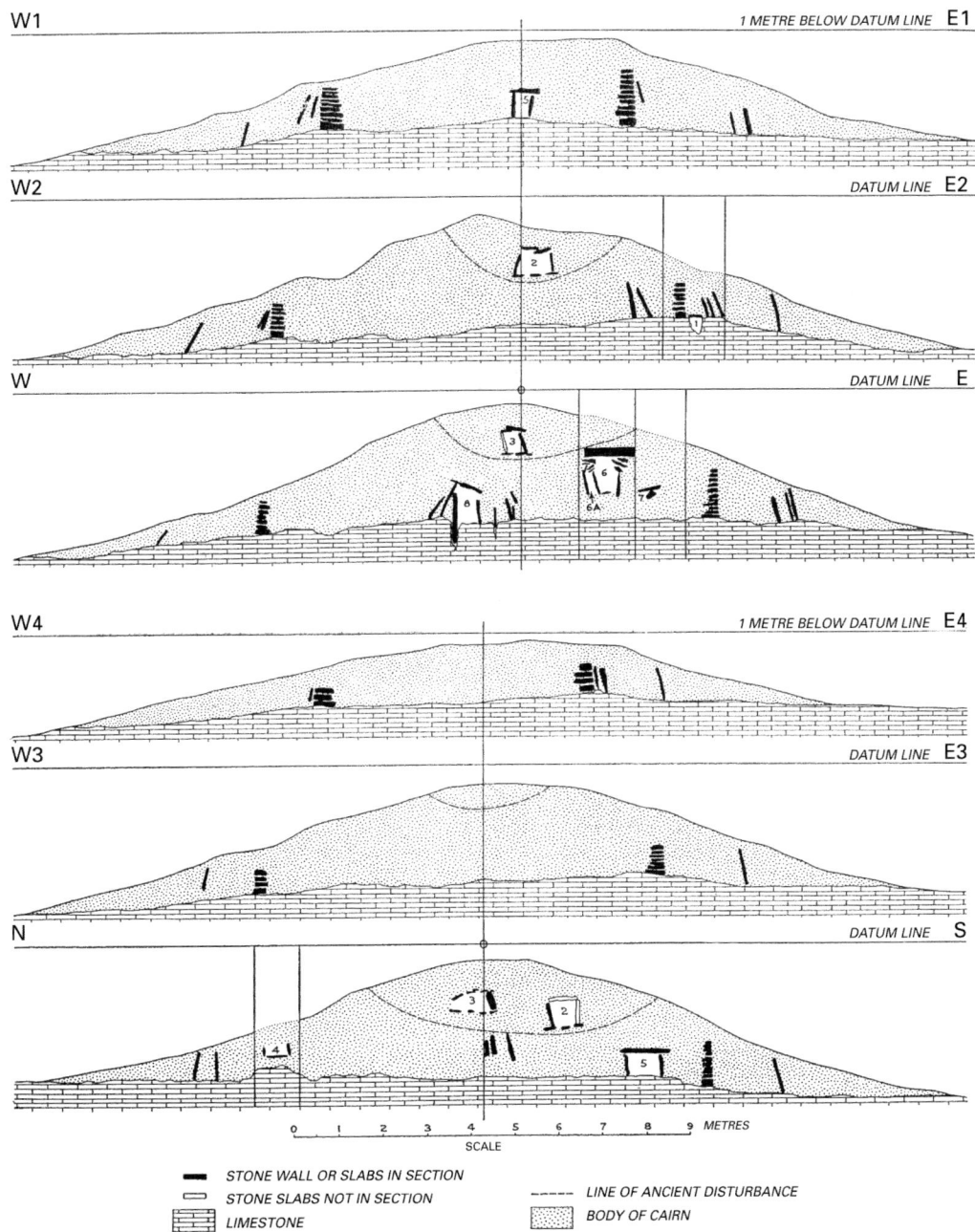

Figure 9
Hencken's sections through Poulawack.

The work was carried out between June 22 and July 10, 1934, with a maximum of fifteen workmen . . . We had previously excavated tumuli in Ireland by the method generally used on the continent whereby the mound is divided into quadrants each of which is excavated separately so as to give two cross sections at right angles. We combined this technique with the method advocated by Dr R.E.M. Wheeler, Keeper of the London Museum, who divides the mound into narrow parallel strips which are then consecutively excavated to give a series of faces at close intervals through the mound. – Hencken 1935.

These section drawings show slices through the cairn at the locations indicated by the parallel lines on the plan (see Figure 8). The labels at the ends of the sections correspond with the identical labels on the plan to show where each section was drawn.

Figure 10

Section through the central Linkardstown-type cist (Cist 8/8A) at Poulawack.

In this section drawing the shaded slabs are those which are viewed as if they were sectioned (sliced) while the unshaded slabs are those which form the far side of the cist. The bottom portion of the drawing which is filled with a brick-like pattern represents the limestone bedrock and it can be seen that two of the upright slabs have been wedged into grykes in the bedrock to hold them upright.

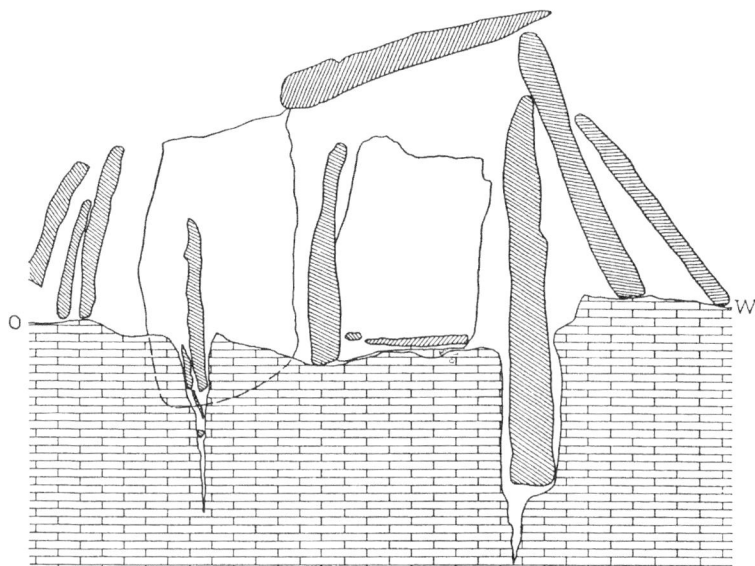

Figure 11

Section and plan of Grave 3 at Poulawack.
a – skull fragment, b – vertebrae,
c – pelvis fragment, d – femur fragments,
e – patella (kneecap), f – foot bones

In the plan view at the bottom of this figure the three upright slabs which form the sides of the cist are shaded while the five overlapping slabs which form the top of the cist are shown in outline only. The horizontal line running across the plan view shows where the section, which is shown above, was drawn. The section view shows that the top of the cist was higher on the south and sloped down to the north. The unshaded slab in the section is the slab which forms the far side of the cist.

Analysis of the bones from Poulawack allows us to make some general statements about the health of the people interred in the cairn. None of the individuals were over the age of 45-50 and many had facets on their tibia (lower leg bones) which had formed from habitual squatting throughout their lives. One middle-aged woman had arthritis in her back and pelvis and her teeth were very worn with large abscesses and evidence for periodontal disease.

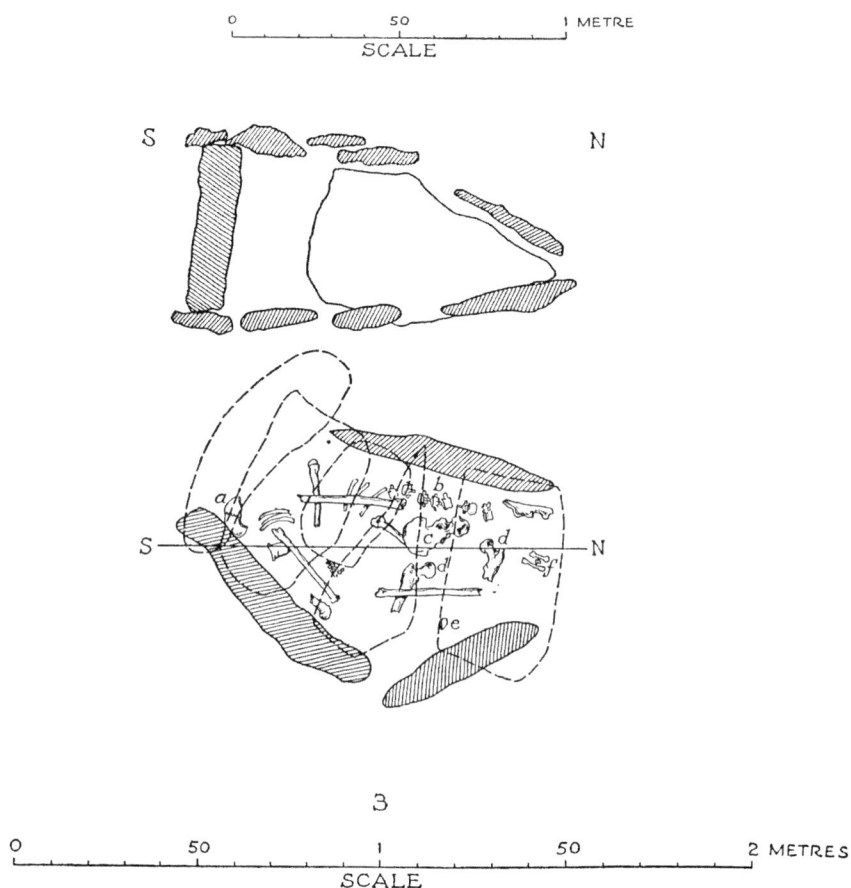

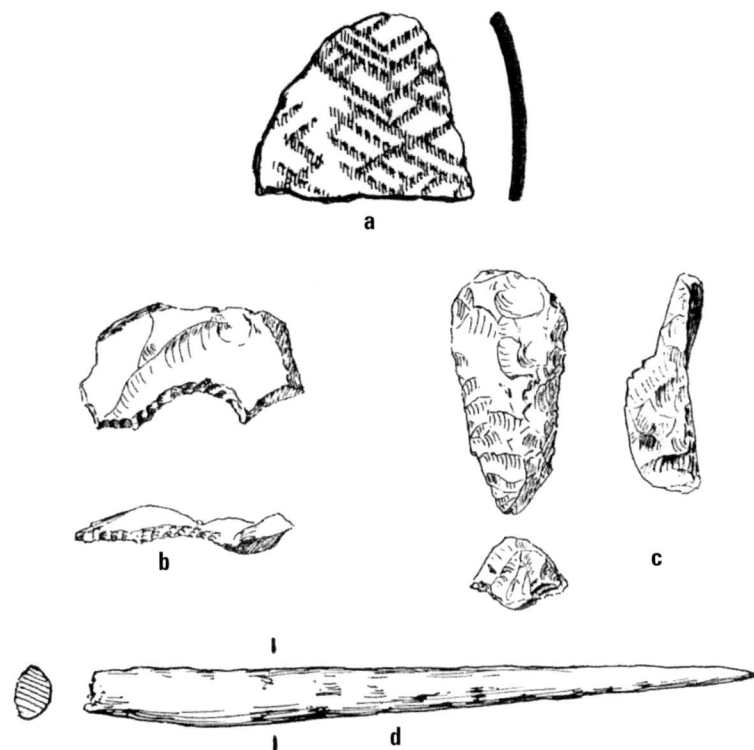

Figure 12

Some of the finds accompanying the burials from Poulawack.

a – Early Bronze Age Beaker pottery sherd, **b** – Neolithic 'hollow' flint scraper, **c** – flint scraper, **d** – bone point. Hencken excavated Poulawack before the advent of radiocarbon dating had extended the accepted duration of prehistoric time periods. Working within this short timescale, he did not view the occurrence of a Neolithic hollow scraper and an Early Bronze Age Beaker sherd in the same monument as particularly significant. Subsequent radiocarbon dating of bones accompanying these two artefacts has shown that the Beaker sherd is almost 1500 years later than the hollow scraper.

PHASE 1
'LINKARDSTOWN CIST'
3350

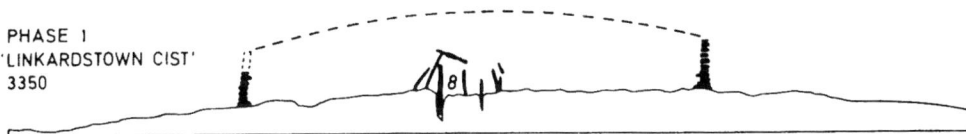

PHASE 2
CEMETERY CAIRN
c. 2000

PHASE 3
EARLY BRONZE
AGE II
c. 1500

Figure 13

Reconstruction of the phases of Poulawack.

Radiocarbon dates have shown that the three phases of activity at Poulawack took place over a period of almost 2,000 years. Obtaining many of the radiocarbon dates from Poulawack was only possible after the introduction of Accelerator Mass Spectrometry (AMS) in the 1980s. AMS allows very small samples to be dated, one-hundredth of the size required in the early days of radiocarbon dating in the 1950s. This development made it possible to date all the unburnt burials in the monument.

Doolin Stone Axe Production Site

Grid Reference R 065 964

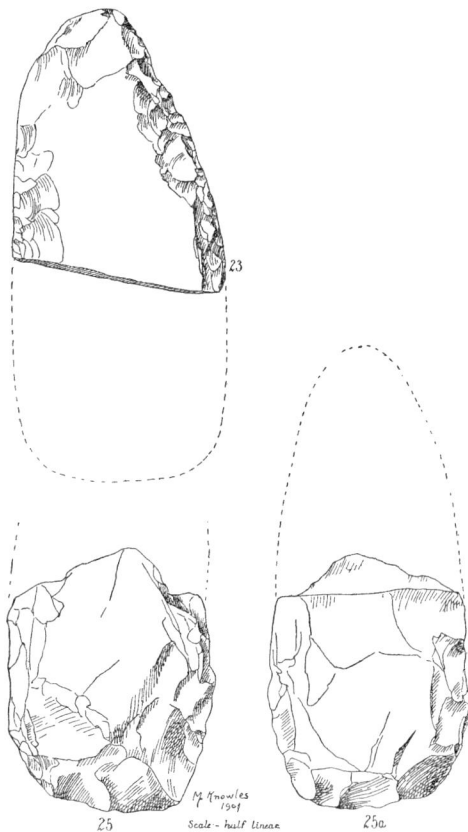

'The sand-hills lie mostly on the right bank of the River Aille, and there is an escarpment of sand from 20 to 30 feet high close to the river bed. On our first visit we only examined the higher ground, but on the present occasion Dr D'Evelyn thought it advisable to explore the foot of the escarpment, and was rewarded by finding what must have been a regular stone axe factory. Flakes, hammer-stones, and broken axes were lying all about the place in a very instructive way. The axes were probably broken in the process of manufacture, and thrown aside as useless. Some were chipped, ready for grinding, and a few had the marks of grinding on the surface' – from a report by Miss M.C. Knowles in the 1905 *Journal of the Limerick Field Club.*

Although there have been no modern investigations at this site in Doolin, the finds made by the brief antiquarian investigations of Miss Knowles and her companions have retained the attention of modern archaeologists. The area around the mouth of the Aille river near Fisherstreet and further along the rocky shore at Ballaghaline Point (where the Aran Island Ferries depart from) may have been a stone axe 'quarrying' and manufacturing site during the Neolithic and possibly into the Early Bronze Age.

Many prehistoric stone axe quarries are located on imposing mountain peaks that form striking landmarks and it seems that these locations may have been viewed by prehistoric people as sacred places, places that touched the sky and possibly, therefore, homes of the gods. The act of quarrying in these places was probably a ritual act as well as a practical labour. Archaeologists have found, for example, mountains where outcrops of the same stone are located in various areas but where the prehistoric quarrying and production took place deliberately in the more difficult location. A key feature of mountains is their location at a boundary of two worlds, the intersection of the sky and the earth, and prehistoric axe production sites have also been found in another type of boundary area, islands – where the sea and the earth intersect.

While the beach at Doolin is neither a mountain nor an island, it does share with those types of location the quality of being located at a boundary – in the case of Doolin, the boundary between the earth and the sea. It is also possible that the natural creation of axe-shaped cobbles on the beach may have added to the significance of the site. On the beach where the Aille River meets the Atlantic are millions of shale cobbles. These cobbles are battered and rolled around the storm beach until some of them resemble the trapezoidal shape of the typical prehistoric stone axe. It has been suggested that prehistoric people may have seen the axe-shaped cobbles at Doolin as gifts from the earth for the benefit of humans.

Figure 14

Artefacts collected by antiquarians at Doolin.

Illustrated are three axes broken during manufacture.

Figure 15
The cobble beach at Doolin.

The cobble beach at Doolin may have been regarded as a special boundary area between the world of the sea and that of the land. As well as providing expedient stone axes, the naturally axe-shaped cobbles on the beach may have been seen as gifts from the gods left in this shifting and dangerous boundary zone.

Turlough Hill

Grid Reference M 314 073

The massive enclosure on top of Turlough Hill is of unknown function and date but the two most plausible explanations are that it is either a Neolithic ritual enclosure or a Bronze Age hillfort. It is a very large and roughly circular enclosure with an entrance via a natural cleft on the east side and additional gaps at other points around its circumference. The gaps appear to cluster at the four cardinal points: north, south, east and west. In addition, one of the southern gaps faces the large cairn on the summit of Slieve Carran just over two kilometres to the south.

For the most part, the interior of the enclosure is bare crag. There are a few small semi-circular enclosures built up against the interior of the enclosure but it is not clear whether these are contemporary. Outside of the enclosure, but still on the summit approximately 750m to the south west, are what look like dozens of hut circles (Grid Reference M 306 069) and beyond the hut circles, another 400m to the south west, on the highest point of the mountain is a large cairn (Grid Reference M 303 068) (see Figure 55).

The Neolithic Interpretation

Although there are no exact parallels for Turlough Hill, in some respects it does resemble a Neolithic 'causewayed enclosure', a type of monument common in Britain and on the continent. Causewayed enclosures are formed by a roughly circular enclosure of ditches and banks broken by gaps or 'causeways' around their circumference. They are generally interpreted as ritual meeting or gathering places for large assemblies of several kin groups. On Turlough Hill it would be impossible to dig a ditched enclosure and so it may be that a 'causewayed enclosure' was formed solely by constructing banks of stacked stones.

Turlough Hill may have been the site of an annual gathering (probably in the summer when the mountain top was more habitable) where people came together, set up camp for a short time and participated in rituals staged in the enclosure. If this was the case, it may be that the hut circles are the bases of temporary structures that were rejuvenated every year and lived in for just the duration of the gathering. In this scenario, in addition to the rituals in the enclosure, we might imagine people engaged in other activities – gossiping, singing and dancing, arranging marriages and alliances, and bartering goods before returning to their homes.

Although Turlough Hill is located on the Burren, it is sited at the very edge of the Burren and at some distance from the likely focus of Neolithic settlement in the south-east Burren (see *Territory and Society on the Burren in the Neolithic*). From Turlough Hill one has an impressive view out over the lowlands to the east beyond the Burren and the enclosure is

Figure 16
Turlough Hill.

The massive enclosure on Turlough Hill has a
diameter of around 225 metres. The wall varies
from approximately 2.7 to 3.7 metres wide and
is generally a metre or less in height.

also sited near to, but not directly overlooking, the Corker Pass, one of the main routes into
the Burren (between Abbey Hill and Slieve Oughtmama). This location at the boundary
between the Burren and the lowlands, away from the main settlement core of the Burren,
and near to one of the main entrances into the Burren would seem to be an ideal setting for
a gathering, bringing together the people of the Burren with their neighbours to the east.

The Bronze Age Interpretation

An alternative interpretation of the enclosure on Turlough Hill is that it is a Late Bronze Age
hillfort, similar to the hillfort at Mooghaun in south-east County Clare and to the original
fort at Dún Aonghasa on Inishmore (see *The Late Bronze Age Chiefdom of Dún Aonghasa*).
Most Late Bronze Age societies in Ireland seem to have been organised into chiefdoms and
these chiefdoms typically had a large hilltop enclosure or hillfort that was a focal point for

the group. Some of these hillforts may have been the residences of the chief and his family and some may have had a defensive function as well, but their most important role seems to have been as the centre of identity for the group and as a proclamation of the group's status.

If the enclosure on Turlough Hill is, in fact, a Bronze Age hillfort, it is a significantly less impressive hillfort than either Dún Aonghasa or Mooghaun. Mooghaun has three concentric ramparts and Dún Aonghasa had at least two concentric ramparts, whereas Turlough Hill has only a single rampart. Another contrast is in the entrances. At Mooghaun, which was much less disturbed than Dún Aonghasa, excavation and survey revealed that the entrances through the ramparts were arranged with defensive measures in mind. If the multiple gaps in Turlough Hill are original entrances, they were certainly not fashioned with a concern for defence.

Unfortunately, the question of whether Turlough Hill is a Neolithic ritual enclosure or whether it is a Bronze Age hillfort is one that will only be resolved with excavation. A third possibility (although one that I think is much less likely) is that the hut circles on Turlough Hill are the result of a single turbulent episode in the prehistory of the Burren when people were so threatened that they lived for a time on top of the mountain. The problem with this scenario, however, is that it does not explain either the enclosure on Turlough Hill (which it is hard to envisage as a defensive fortification) or the large cairn which is almost certainly a ritual monument.

Figure 17

Plan of the Turlough Hill enclosure by T.J. Westropp.

The ridge is steep, bare, and fenced with continuous high terraces of rock and enormous boundary walls. Even the Gortaclare people 'did not know of any caher upon the hills'; so I did not at the time try to visit so inaccessible and equivocal a ruin. Finding, however, that a fort was shown on the map of 1899, I was led to visit, and, with the aid of Dr George U. Macnamara, examined, planned, and noted this great fort, though in stormy and bitter weather – hailstorms alternating with blazes of fierce sunshine. – Thomas Westropp 1905.

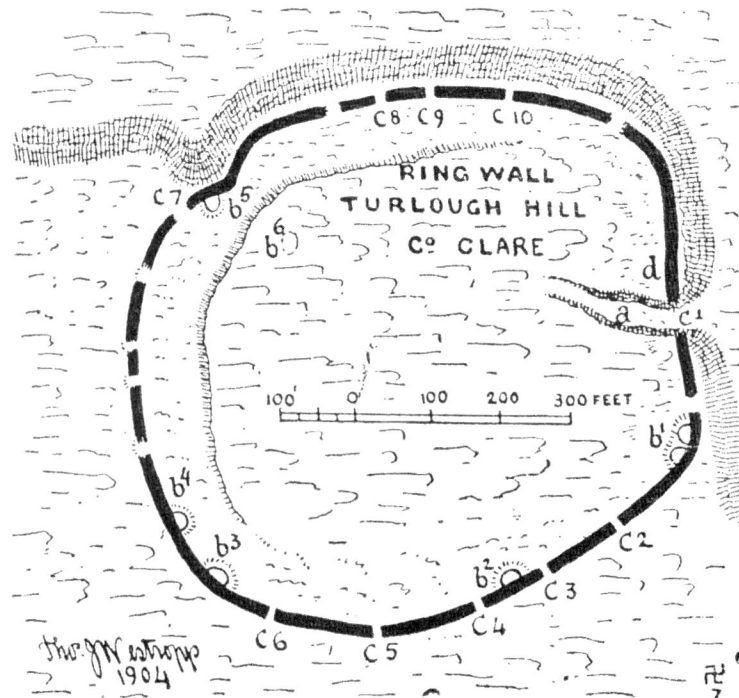

Figure 18 ▲

Slab-faced gap in the Turlough Hill enclosure.

Illustration by T.J. Westropp of one of the gaps in the enclosure. Many of the gaps in the enclosure appear to be faced with upright slabs which lends support to the idea that they are original features of the monument rather than later degradations.

◄ Figure 19

Hut circles on Turlough Hill.

The Parknabinnia Chambered Tomb (Cl. 153) on Roughan Hill

Grid Reference R 262 936

(Note: This is not the Parknabinnia wedge tomb which is signposted adjacent to the road. The Parknabinnia chambered tomb is over 400m farther west. See Figure 31).

At the south-east corner of the Burren is Roughan Hill, an area with a remarkable collection of prehistoric remains. Most of the prehistoric activity on Roughan Hill appears to have taken place in the Final Neolithic/Early Bronze Age (*c.* 2400 – 2000 BC) but there are several earlier ritual monuments on the hill and other hints of earlier activity as well. One of the early monuments, a megalithic chambered tomb, was excavated in order to answer questions about the earlier period, and the transition to the later intensive occupation of the hill evident by the Final Neolithic/Early Bronze Age (for the later activity see *Competition and Social Upheaval on Roughan Hill*). The Parknabinnia chambered tomb was selected for investigation because even before excavation, its architecture suggested it was probably one of the earliest monuments on the hill. Excavation bore this assumption out and a range of artefacts common to the fourth millennium BC was recovered from the tomb. A series of radiocarbon dates has also been obtained from the bones which were in the tomb and although the analysis of their position in the stratigraphy is not yet complete, most of the bones appear to date to the second half of the fourth millennium (i.e., between 3500 BC and 3000 BC). The radiocarbon dates do, however, extend beyond that range in both directions.

The excavation of the Parknabinnia chambered tomb was directed by myself over four summer seasons from 1998 to 2001. The excavation generated a vast amount of data which is now being analysed and synthesised, and will take several years to complete, as well as the expertise of several individuals. Some preliminary statements can, however, be made. The tomb consists of a gallery of two roughly square chambers accessed by a very narrow unroofed passage opening to the east, all of which is surrounded by a cairn. The tomb appears to be related to a type of megalithic tomb known as a court tomb but unusual features set it apart. Where court tombs have wide, U-shaped forecourts, the Parknabinnia tomb has a narrow straight-sided entrance passage (unroofed) and while court tombs typically have long trapezoidal cairns, the Parknabinnia cairn is roughly U-shaped. These distinctive features of the Parknabinnia tomb suggest that it may be a local variety of megalithic tomb restricted to the southern Burren (see *Territory and Society on the Burren in the Neolithic*).

Over 5,000 bone fragments and complete human bones were recovered from the tomb. These are the remains of at least eighteen people, the majority were adults but a teenager, a young child and an infant were also present. Most of the adults died between the ages of 25-35 but there were some who lived past 45. It is difficult to determine sex with such fragmentary remains, but there were at least two females and six males. The females appear to have ranged in stature from 4'9" to 5'2" while the males appear to have ranged from 5'6" to 5'8".

Some of the human bone recovered from the tomb was cremated but the majority was unburnt. Most of this unburnt bone was disarticulated but some appears to have been partially articulated and within the deposit of bones and stones that filled both chambers there were discernible concentrations of bones. In the north-east corner of the first chamber a group of leg bones was clustered near an upright pillar-like stone that may have been a roof support. The bones in this cluster consisted of a largely complete pelvis with a sacrum, two proximal femur ends, two distal femur ends and two tibias, along with some other bones. Other concentrations consisted of a pile of disarticulated bones topped with a partial skull, a group of arm bones, a group of bones containing several articulated vertebrae, another group where phalanges and foot bones predominated and a pile of small and broken bones that appears to be the result of someone sweeping together a lot of small bone fragments.

Although the radiocarbon dates indicate that the Parknabinnia chambered tomb and the Poulnabrone portal tomb were in contemporary use, the stratigraphy of the bone deposits at the two tombs shows a contrasting pattern of use. The deposit at Poulnabrone appears to have been placed in the tomb as a single act, probably when the tomb was built (see *Poulnabrone portal tomb*). At Parknabinnia, there also appears to have been an initial foundation deposit of bones and stones placed in both chambers when the tomb was built, but then the clusters of bones and especially the pile of fragments that appears to have been swept into a pile, suggest that people re-entered the tomb, re-arranged its contents and probably added more bones or bodies.

There is some evidence still visible to the visitor today of this sequence of deposits in Parknabinnia. The visitor will see several slabs are blocking the back chamber from the front chamber. When the tomb was excavated it was found that the deposits in the front chamber were deeper than those in the back chamber and the front chamber deposits were piled up against these blocking stones as well. In other words, at some point in time when the deposits in both chambers were approximately level, the back chamber was sealed off and no longer entered. The front chamber, however, continued to receive deposits which built up against the blocking stones and raised the level of the 'floor' in the front chamber. During excavation, both chambers were completely emptied of their contents down to the bedrock. When we re-constructed the tomb we replaced the blocking stones in their original positions and filled both chambers with rubble to the approximate height of the top of the bone deposits. It can be seen, therefore, that the filling of the front chamber is higher than that of the rear chamber.

Both the blocking of the rear chamber and the different clusters of bones indicate a sequence of deposits at Parknabinnia rather than a single deposit, as seems to have been the case at Poulnabrone. At Parknabinnia, it's possible that bones were brought in and out of the tomb, perhaps to serve as powerful relics in the same way that bones of Christian saints are used even today. Alternatively, the bone clusters could also be the result of 'tidying' episodes when

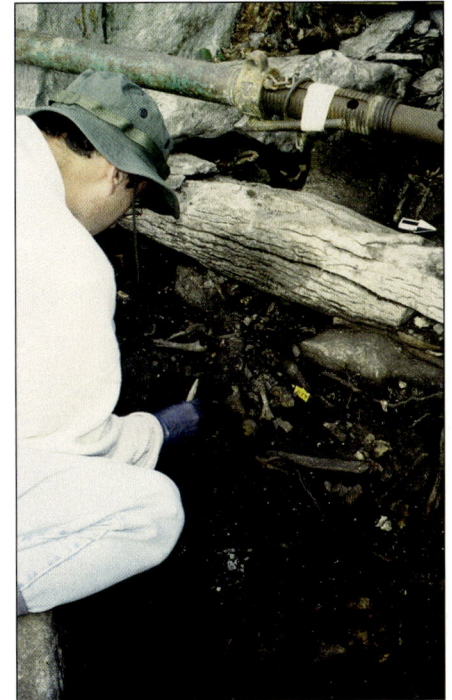

Figure 20
The Parknabinnia chambered tomb (Cl. 153) under excavation.

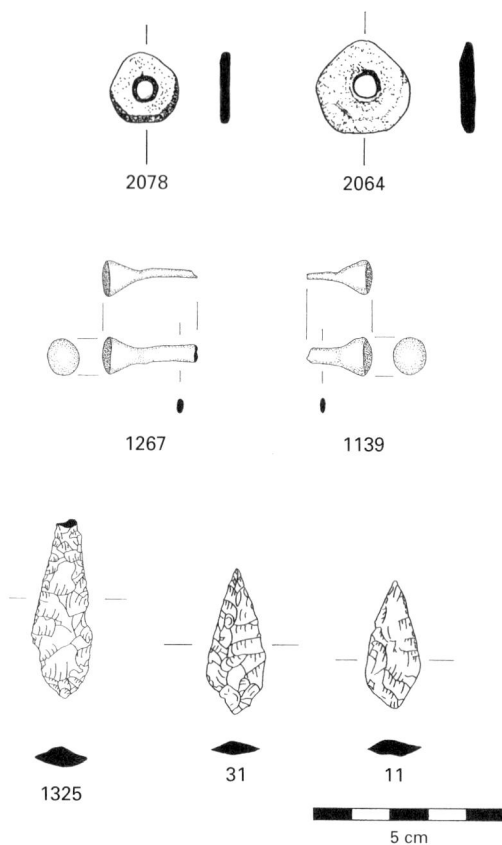

Figure 21

Selected finds from the Parknabinnia chambered tomb.

In addition to the bone recovered from the tomb, finds from the tomb included potsherds, bone and stone beads, a bone barbell-shaped toggle, leaf-shaped arrowheads, a stone knife, various stone scraping and cutting implements, some debitage (waste flakes from manufacturing stone tools), a small grinding stone, quartz crystals and a few limpet shells. Pictured here are two stone beads (No.s 2078 and 2064), the bone barbell-shaped toggle (in two pieces) (No.s 1267 and 1139), and three leaf-shaped arrowheads (No.s 1325, 31 and 11).

space was cleared to make room for the addition of another body. Either way, the excavation of the Parknabinnia tomb revealed a repetitive pattern of use which contrasts with the single act of deposition which seems to have occurred at Poulnabrone.

When we were excavating the tomb it became apparent that the side slabs lean inwards slightly and are supported ultimately by upright jamb stones, especially by the jamb stones that divide the two chambers. To prevent the whole tomb collapsing in on itself there is also a sill stone wedged between the jamb stones which divide the two chambers to keep these jamb stones upright. Even so, we found that when we removed the lower layers of rubble and bone from the chambers, the tomb was noticeably less stable. We also noticed that the tops of both the sill stone between the chambers and a sill stone in the front entrance were some distance above the bottom of the deposits and were also at approximately the same level. All of these lines of evidence point to the conclusion that the bottom layer of stones and bones in both chambers was actually an integral part of the fabric of the tomb. It would have provided necessary structural stability as well as a roughly level floor at the same height as the tops of the sill stones. This suggests that the bones in this bottom layer were part of a 'foundation deposit', built into the tomb when it was constructed. The bones above this layer, however, appear to be the result of subsequent deposits in the tomb over many centuries.

In addition to the human bones, animal bones were also present in the tomb. Some of the animals identified such as fox, hare and various rodents were undoubtedly present because they burrowed into the deposit. But other animal bones that were recovered, those of cattle, sheep/goat, pig, deer and dog appear to have been intentionally placed in the tomb. Three juvenile dog mandibles (lower jaw bones) found under a large stone near the base of the first chamber may also have been an intentional deposit. If so, it's possible that dogs had a symbolic significance for the group that built the tomb (see *Territory and Society on the Burren in the Neolithic*). Teeth from sheep/goat, deer and pig were also found throughout the deposits. It is not clear how or why these animal teeth ended up in the tomb, but their presence does indicate that these animals played a part in the economy of the tomb builders.

Another interesting point is that there seems to have been symbolic significance in the geometry of the tomb. If one squats in the first chamber today and looks out along the entrance passage it is apparent that the long axis of the tomb is aligned on the large boulder in the next field. Viewed from the tomb, the boulder intersects the horizon formed by the ridge line behind it to the east and it is very likely that this alignment marks a sunrise that was significant to the builders of the tomb, perhaps either the summer or winter solstice. Both of these events would have been highly significant indicators of seasonal change to the farmers who built the tomb. Another aspect of geometry which undoubtedly has symbolic significance is the emphasis on the south side of the entrance passage. As it appears today, the entrance passage is our reconstruction of how it would have originally appeared. What is most striking

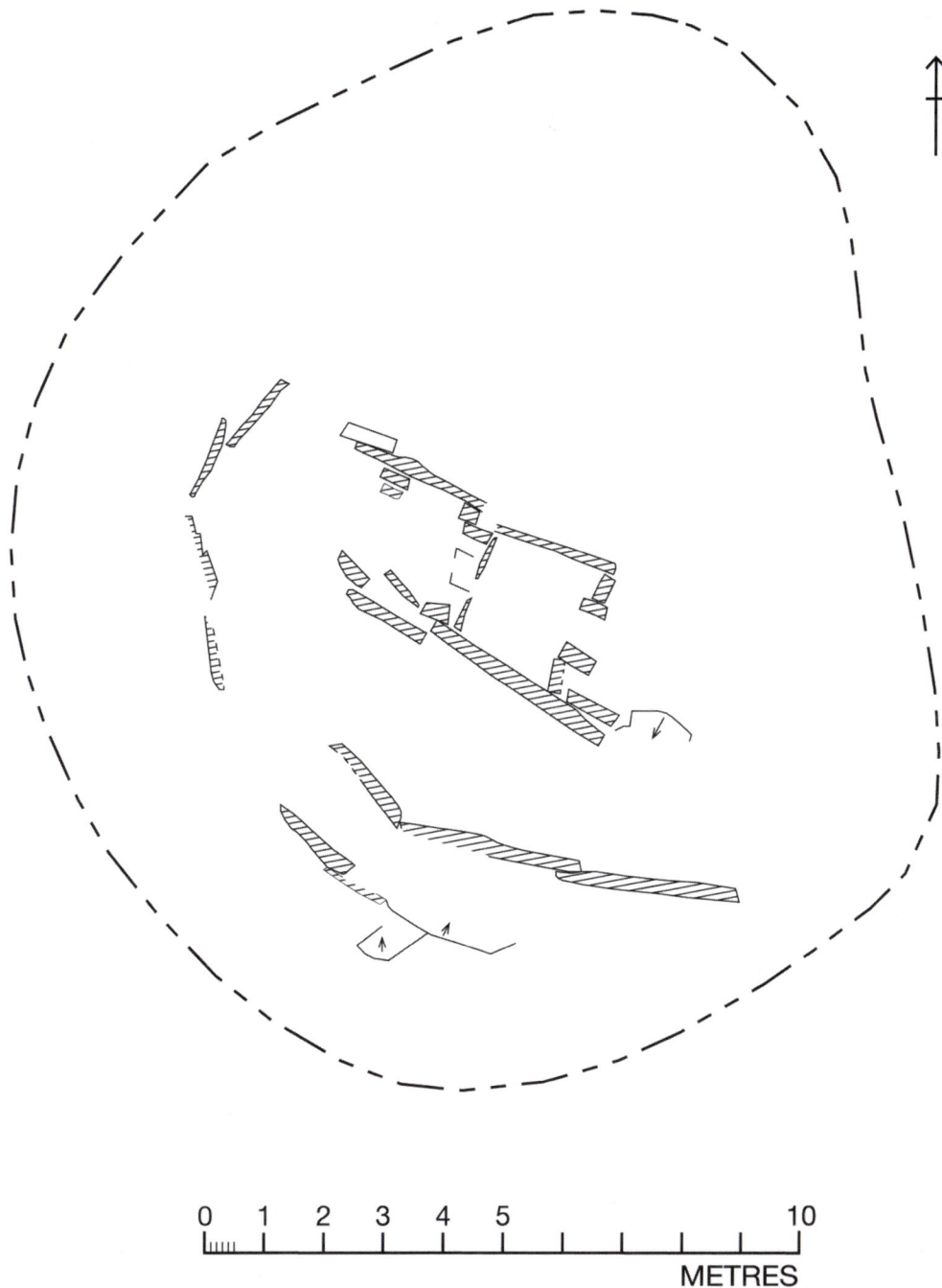

Figure 22 ▲

Planning the stones of the Parknabinnia chambered tomb during excavation.

◄ Figure 23

Plan of the Parknabinnia chambered tomb before excavation.

The Parknabinnia chambered tomb consists of a gallery of two chambers set in the centre of a U-shaped cairn and accessed by a narrow un-roofed passage leading from the east to the entrance of the first chamber. The gallery of two chambers is clearly visible on this pre-excavation plan, as is the entrance to the tomb marked by the two transversely-set jamb stones which frame the doorway at the eastern end of the first (easternmost) chamber. The narrow unroofed passage leading to the entrance was not apparent before excavation although the two stones (one upright, the other tilted) which extend from the south-east corner of the first chamber do in fact mark the southern edge of the entrance passage. The dashed line indicates the edge of the collapsed cairn but the original edge of the cairn is marked by the outermost of the two concentric lines of kerbstones.

Figure 24 ▶
The bone deposit within the Parknabinnia chambered tomb.

Although the wet and stony conditions in the tomb meant that many of the bones were waterlogged and fragmented, there was generally very good preservation. This seems to be in large part due to the low acidity of the soil in the tomb caused by the limestone from which the tomb is built.

Figure 25 (*Left*)
Vertebrae fused from osteoarthritis and additional joint disease.

Twelve bones with evidence of osteoarthritis were recovered. These included a humerus, a phalange, a metatarsal, a fibula, a sacrum and several vertebrae. The presence of osteoarthritis on these bones indicates that they belonged to individuals who probably endured a hard lifestyle where heavy lifting and carrying were common.

Figure 26 (*Right*)
Metopic suture in child's skull.

The metopic suture on the front of the skull usually closes around birth but in some cases it does not, resulting in a divided frontal bone. This does not affect the person but because the condition has a high genetic component, its presence on different individuals may indicate a familial relationship. We would expect that the individuals in the tomb were related and in fact two skulls in the tomb, the child's skull shown here and another adult skull, had a visible metopic suture.

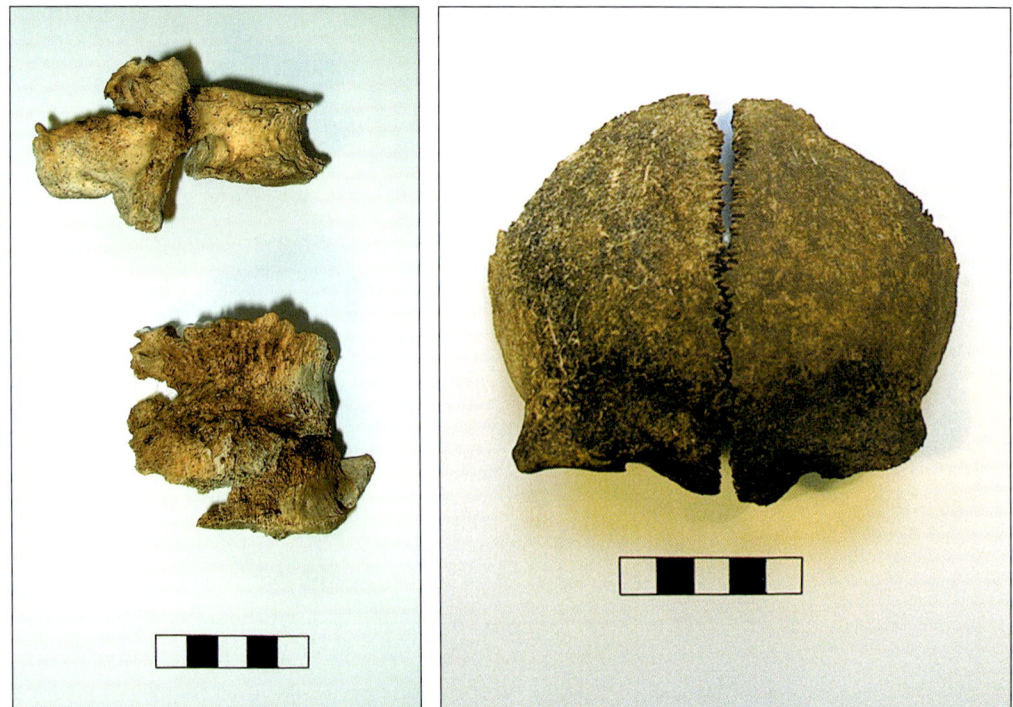

about it is the use of large stones on the south side and the lack of such stones on the north side. In addition, two of the large stones on the south side were marked by special deposits. The stone closest to the entrance had a cow skull carefully positioned at its base with the horns up against the base of the stone and its snout pointing into the passage, and the short, pillar-like stone towards the east end of the passage had a large piece of a human skull at its base, also apparently placed there intentionally. This emphasis on the south side of the entrance passage no doubt had a symbolic significance for the people, and we can start to glimpse how they may have divided their world with a sacred geometry. The special treatment of a cow skull in a ritual monument which was devoted mainly to people also highlights the importance of cattle in the lives of these early farmers. The Parknabinnia tomb was not merely a receptacle for the remains of the dead. Instead, it seems to have been a shrine for the local community who would have carried out various rituals there over many generations. Perhaps it was viewed as the 'House of the Ancestors' and therefore used as the appropriate and auspicious location for rituals spanning all of life's concerns from birth to death, much as a modern church is used.

Territory and Society on the Burren in the Neolithic

The Parknabinnia chambered tomb (Cl. 153) with its narrow entrance passage, short, U-shaped cairn and two chambers is a type of megalithic tomb which may be restricted to a group of just four tombs on the southern Burren. Two nearly identical tombs are located less than four kilometres to the west at Ballyganner North (Cl. 34) and at Leamaneh North (Cl. 135), and a very ruined tomb (Cl. 154) located less than 500 metres east of the Parknabinnia chambered tomb may be the same type as well. Although Cl. 154 is in an extremely ruinous state, the other three are all sufficiently preserved to see that they form a group.

These tombs have some interesting implications for Neolithic society on the Burren. In the first place, the fact that a local variety of megalithic tomb seems to have evolved in the south-east Burren suggests the society that built these tombs was fairly insular. This society would have had some contact with other groups but the closest groups of a similar size may have been dozens of miles away. There would have been well-known route ways between these distant groups but contact between them may have been limited to specific festivals held at different times of the year (see *Turlough Hill*).

The tombs also allow us to speculate about the structure of Neolithic society on the Burren. Figure 27 shows a possible reconstruction of Neolithic society on the Burren. Based on analogies with other societies studied by anthropologists, this Neolithic Burren society may have been structured as a set of widening kinship ties. In this society, each individual would have belonged to one of four lineages, each with its own chambered tomb. Each lineage would then be paired with another lineage to form two clans, one residing on Roughan Hill and the other a few kilometres to the west in the Ballyganner/Leamaneh area. The third, and widest level of kinship would equate to something along the lines of a tribe with the two clans joined together into a single unit. At this level, a monument such as the original Linkardstown cist with its covering cairn at Poulawack may have been erected to house the bones of a particularly revered tribal leader.

Figure 28 shows a hypothetical core territory of this Neolithic society. The circle represents in a schematic form the bounds of the core area within which most of the people of the tribe would have lived. The circle is divided into two halves to represent roughly the territories of the two clans, Roughan Hill and Ballyganner/Leamaneh. In this reconstruction, the two portal tombs on the Burren, Poulnabrone and Ballycasheen, have been used to determine the edges of the core territory. This interpretation is based on several factors: the differences in the deposits found within the Poulnabrone portal tomb and the Parknabinnia chambered tomb, differences between the architecture of portal tombs and the chambered tombs, and differences in the way the two tomb types are set within the landscape.

The evidence for multiple deposits in the Parknabinnia chambered tomb was detailed above and this was contrasted with the Poulnabrone portal tomb where the contents appear

Figure 27

A possible reconstruction of Neolithic society on the Burren.

Neolithic society on the Burren was probably structured as a widening set of kinship ties. Each group and sub-group in this society may have been identified by a totemic animal or by their place of residence. Three juvenile dog mandibles found under a large stone near the base of the first chamber of the Parknabinnia chambered tomb may indicate that dogs had a totemic significance for the lineage associated with the tomb. In other words, they may have been the 'Dog Lineage'.

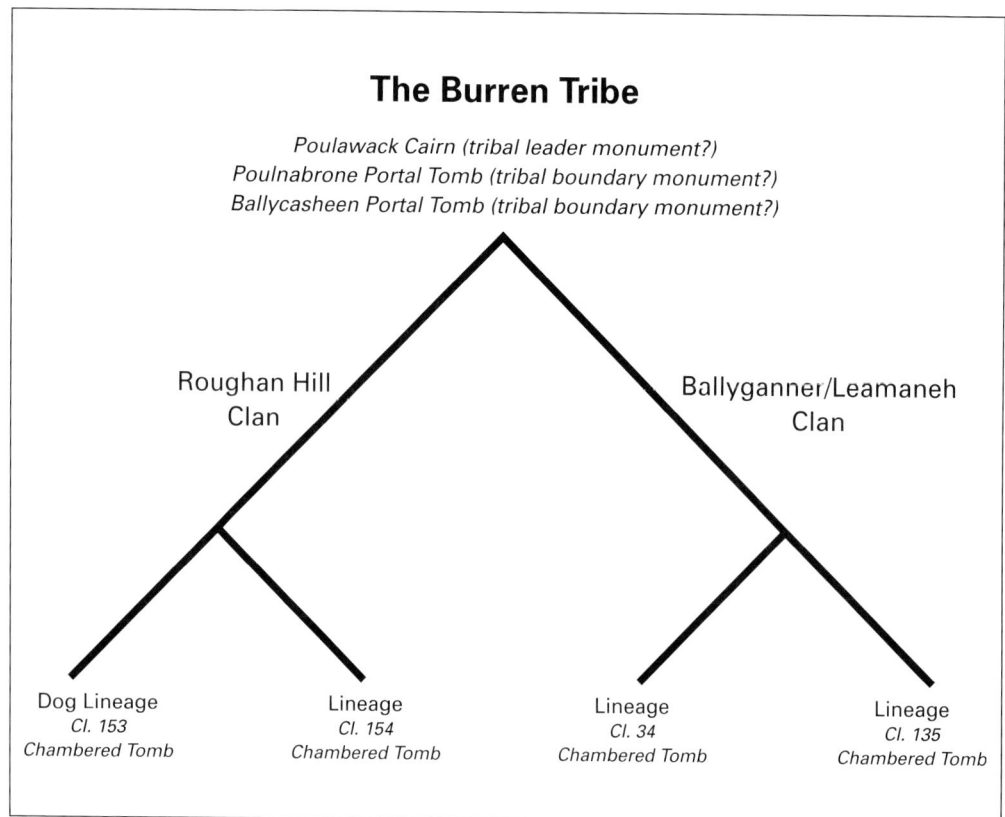

The Burren Tribe

Poulawack Cairn (tribal leader monument?)
Poulnabrone Portal Tomb (tribal boundary monument?)
Ballycasheen Portal Tomb (tribal boundary monument?)

Roughan Hill Clan

Ballyganner/Leamaneh Clan

Dog Lineage
Cl. 153
Chambered Tomb

Lineage
Cl. 154
Chambered Tomb

Lineage
Cl. 34
Chambered Tomb

Lineage
Cl. 135
Chambered Tomb

to have been placed in the tomb in a single act of deposition, possibly at the time the tomb was built. There are also contrasts in the way the different tomb types are sited in the landscape. All four chambered tombs appear to be the foci of settlement cores whereas the two portal tombs on the Burren are sited at critical points in the landscape along important route ways into the Burren. The Ballycasheen portal tomb is located at a pass between the River Fergus and the steep south-eastern edge of the Burren through which the most viable route into the Burren from the south passes (and through which the modern road passes). The Poulnabrone portal tomb is located adjacent to the major north-south route across the Burren (followed by the modern road), at the point along that route where a traveller entering

Figure 28
Hypothetical core territory of the Neolithic inhabitants of the Burren.

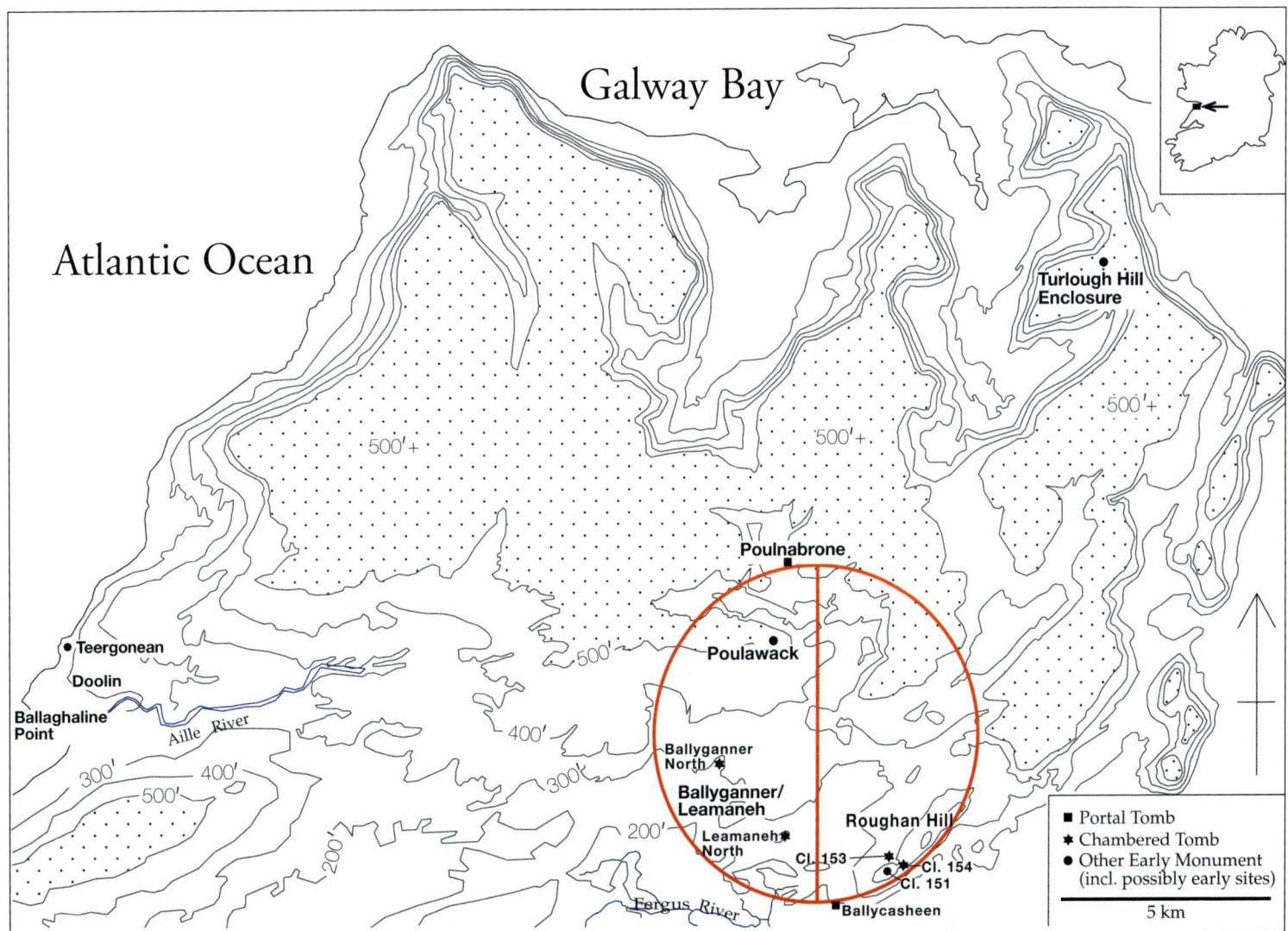

the Burren from the north would have finally crossed the crest of the Ballyvaughan valley and found themselves on the high ground of the Burren.

There are also contrasts in the architecture and the siting of the chambered tombs and the portal tombs. Portal tombs are dramatic constructions. The stratigraphy revealed in the excavation of Poulnabrone suggests that its cairn may have never been higher than the very low cairn that remains around its base today. This means that Poulnabrone would always have presented a dramatic silhouette, with its massive capstone soaring high above the ground. Additionally, portal tombs are sited so they stand out in the landscape – nobody can cross the plateau on which Poulnabrone sits without seeing the tomb. In complete contrast to this, the chambered tombs have low profiles and are not sited with an eye to making them visible in the landscape. For example, the Parknabinnia chambered tomb appears to have been positioned so that it sat partially within a small natural hollow and the Leamaneh North chambered tomb (Figure 29) is sited in a low spot in the landscape.

All these contrasts between the portal tombs and the chambered tombs indicate that although they are contemporary, their functions were radically different. The chambered tombs appear to have been entered repeatedly over several generations, they are sited in the core of the settled area, and they are neither designed nor sited to attract the attention of those who were not familiar with them. The portal tombs, however, may have only received a single deposit at the time they were built, they are sited along major route ways where those route ways enter the core settled area, and both their architecture and their siting in the landscape strive to attract the attention of people passing near to them. So while the chambered tombs may have served as foci for inter-community rituals, the portal tombs appear to have been used to broadcast the group's identity and territorial boundaries to outsiders.

Figure 29
Leamaneh North chambered tomb.
Grid Reference R 234 939

From Neolithic to Bronze Age

IN THE PERIODS KNOWN AS THE FINAL NEOLITHIC/EARLY BRONZE AGE (*c.* 2400 – 2000 BC) and the Early Bronze Age (*c.* 2000 – 1500 BC) dramatic changes were taking place in Irish society. The small-scale clan-based groups of the Neolithic were changing into Bronze Age chiefdoms where authority, power, and wealth were concentrated in the hands of a warrior elite. On the Burren we see a society that loses its insularity and develops contacts which ultimately lead beyond Ireland. Up and down the entire west of Ireland a network of closely connected groups is evidenced by the widespread construction of a new, and final, type of megalithic tomb – the wedge tomb. A new type of pottery known as Beaker pottery appears on the Burren at this time, as does metallurgy. Both of these innovations indicate that the Burren was integrated into a network of contacts that spanned the length of the Atlantic seaboard of Europe.

Wedge tombs and Beaker pottery were relatively short-lived phenomena. By *c.* 2000 BC megalithic tombs were no longer built and people tended to be buried in individual graves. Beaker pottery was also out of fashion by this time but it was just the first in a succession of new pottery types which indicate various continuing overseas contacts. Of course, some of the most important technological advances made at this time were in metallurgy, first with copper and gold working and later with bronze. All of these changes are related to the sweeping changes transforming societies at this time.

Competition and Social Upheaval on Roughan Hill

Grid Reference R 261 933

From 1994 to 2001, with the help of countless volunteers, students and others, and mainly under the auspices of Burren Archaeology Research, I directed a programme of survey and excavation on Roughan Hill that recorded a remarkably complete prehistoric landscape. The overall picture that has emerged from this research is of a vibrant farming community on Roughan Hill in the Final Neolithic/Early Bronze Age. At this time there appears to have been a hamlet of at least four farmsteads on the hill set in a landscape divided into numerous small fields and dotted with closely spaced wedge tombs. This community had its beginnings farther back in the Neolithic (see *Territory and Society on the Burren in the Neolithic*) and by the Final Neolithic/Early Bronze Age it seems to have been a community experiencing dramatic changes.

One of the first things that strikes anyone who glances at a map of Roughan Hill is the sheer number of wedge tombs packed into a small area. In fact, the wedge tombs on Roughan Hill form the densest concentration of wedge tombs in the country. These wedge tombs, however, are not all equal in size. On Roughan Hill, there are wedge tombs ranging in length from 1.8 metres up to 4.9 metres. One possible explanation of this proliferation of wedge tombs and their range of sizes is that we are looking at a society where competition between individuals, or perhaps between families, is increasing and is being expressed in megalithic tomb architecture. Earlier in the Neolithic, the community living on Roughan Hill seemed to be focused on just the two chambered tombs, both of which were similar in scale. This Neolithic society may have been held in balance by the mechanism of opposed clans which would check any attempts at self-aggrandisement by one individual, family or clan over any other segment of society. But in the Final Neolithic/Early Bronze Age the balance of this society seems to have been broken and the wedge tombs may be the products of much smaller social groups, such as families trying to assert themselves. If this was the case, the proliferation of wedge tombs and their range of sizes may reflect the varied abilities of families to pool labour for their construction.

Although it is conceivable that people were competing for the right to build their wedge tomb on a particularly sacred piece of ground, the pattern of the ancient field walls suggests that the competition was primarily focused on control of land for economic reasons. Looking at the fields in Figure 31, one is struck by how small and irregular most of the fields are on Roughan Hill. These small, irregular fields contrast markedly with other areas of prehistoric fields such as the Céide fields in County Mayo which have a more orderly layout. Orderly layouts such as the long rectangular fields of Céide, which march over the topography, indicate the planned intake of previously unenclosed areas with an efficient system of dividing the land. In contrast to this,

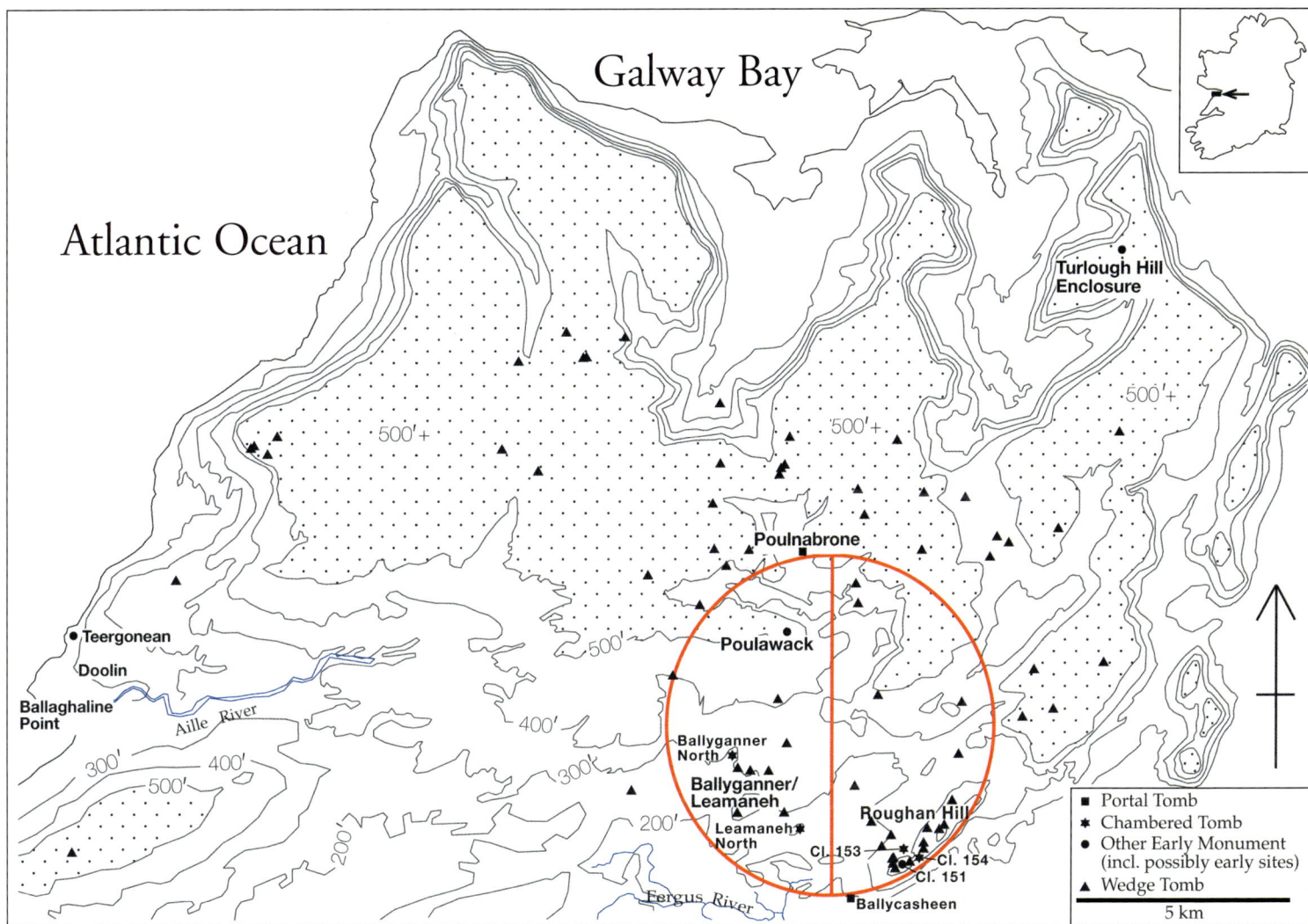

Figure 30
**Final Neolithic/Early Bronze Age
population expansion.**

Wedge tombs are found clustered around the
earlier chambered tombs of Roughan Hill and
Ballyganner/Leamaneh, but they are spread
farther afield as well. This suggests a spread
of farms beyond the old core area in the Final
Neolithic/Early Bronze Age.

the Roughan Hill pattern suggests continual sub-division and competition over fields in an
area which had been cleared and farmed for a very long time.

We can see further evidence for increasing competitiveness in society in the clustering of
wedge tombs around the earlier Neolithic monuments. This seems to suggest that the traditional home ground was the most fiercely contested. On Roughan Hill there are wedge
tombs which are only a little more than 30 metres apart and within a 500-metre radius of
the Parknabinnia chambered tomb there are nine wedge tombs. This close spacing could be
the result of different families competing on a limited patch of ground or perhaps it is the
result of one family continually reasserting itself on the same spot.

If competition for land was growing too fierce in the old core area, one option for families

Figure 31
Map of Roughan Hill.

In many landscapes only the ritual monuments are visible while for many prehistoric settlement sites, we know little about the surrounding landscape. On Roughan Hill, both secular and ritual features are present together. The surveyed area covers approximately 650 acres. The terms 'farmstead' and 'settlement' are used interchangeably here (i.e., Farmstead 1 = Settlement 1). The gaps in the numbering of the farmsteads are due to the fact that the farmsteads were numbered in the order in which they were discovered and several historic period farmsteads were also discovered which are not shown here.

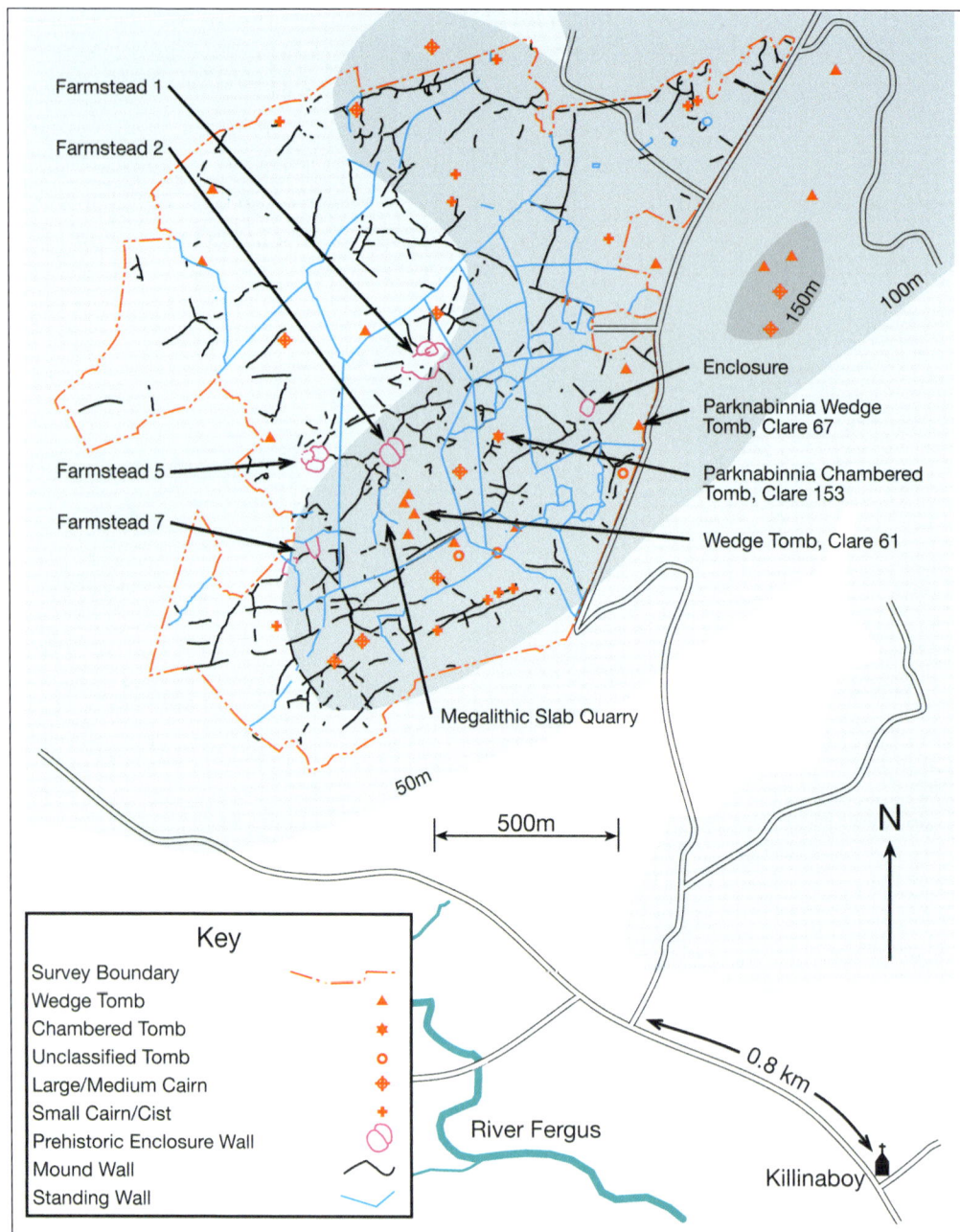

Farmstead 1
Farmstead 2
Farmstead 5
Farmstead 7

Enclosure
Parknabinnia Wedge Tomb, Clare 67
Parknabinnia Chambered Tomb, Clare 153
Wedge Tomb, Clare 61

Megalithic Slab Quarry

150m
100m
50m

500m

0.8 km

River Fergus
Killinaboy

N

Key

Survey Boundary	
Wedge Tomb	
Chambered Tomb	
Unclassified Tomb	
Large/Medium Cairn	
Small Cairn/Cist	
Prehistoric Enclosure Wall	
Mound Wall	
Standing Wall	

would be to move away from the core and in fact, although the wedge tombs are concentrated around the earlier monuments, they are spread farther afield on the Burren as well. This suggests that people were moving out of the more contested areas and into more peripheral locations. It is clear however, that this population expansion did not spread evenly across the land. The steep, bare mountains of the north and east Burren were avoided, the northern valleys, with their deep deposits of poorly drained glacial clays, were avoided, and the west Burren, which is capped by a geological strata of shale which makes it very poorly drained and boggy, was avoided as well. So although the farmers were spreading out into new areas, they were very selective about where they moved. This selectivity highlights why the south-east Burren was so attractive to the earliest farmers. The south-east Burren attracted the early farmers because it is an area of gentle topography where the soil may be thin, but more importantly, it is well-drained.

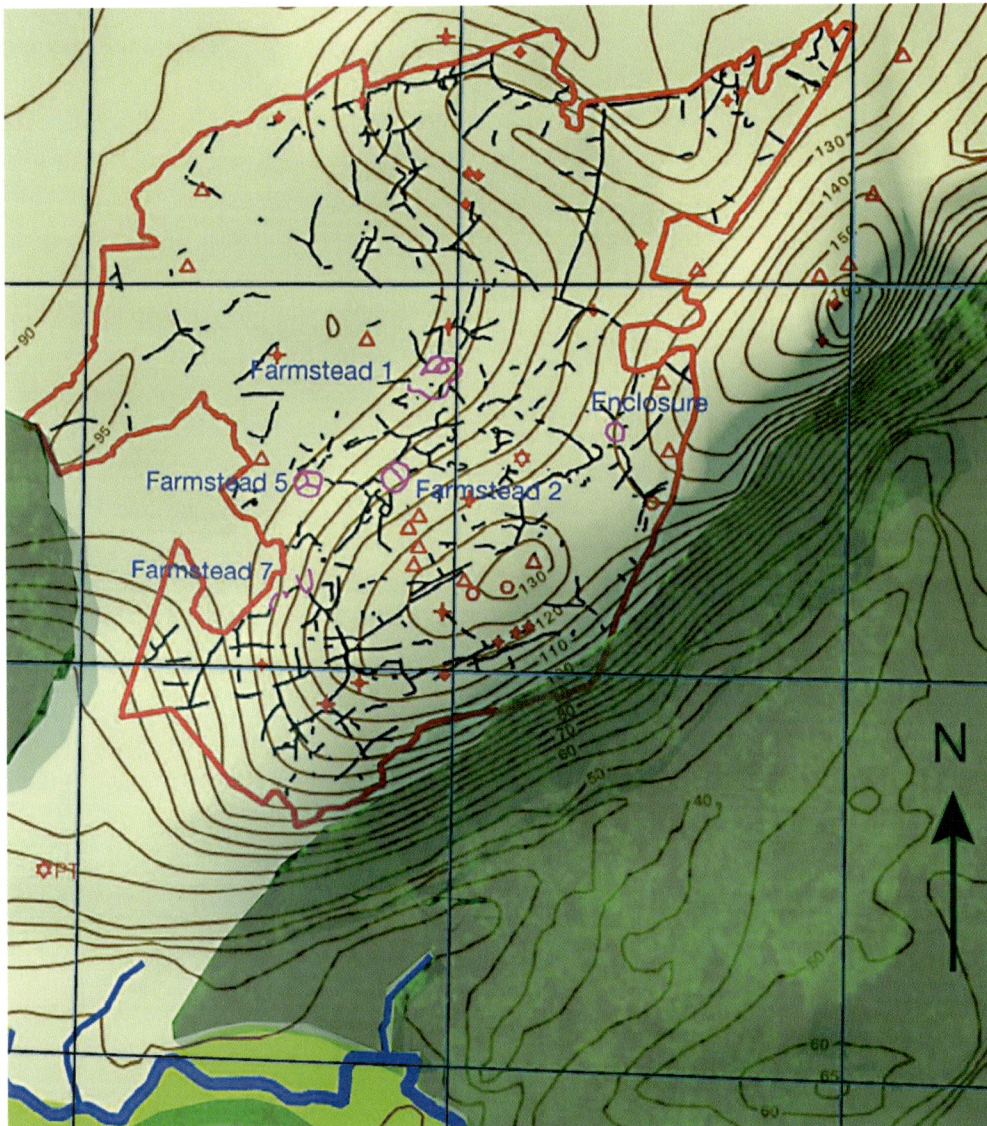

Figure 32
Three-dimensional model of Roughan Hill.

In this computer-generated model of Roughan Hill, areas with heavier, poorly-drained soils as well as the precipitously steep south-east side of Roughan Hill have been interpreted as still cloaked in forest in the Final Neolithic/Early Bronze Age. Each grid square on the model is one square kilometre.

Excavating a Farmstead on Roughan Hill

Grid Reference R 260 938

In our first summer of survey on Roughan Hill we found two prehistoric farmsteads embedded in the network of ancient walls that we were mapping. We chose one of these farmsteads, Settlement 1, for excavation the following summer. Our goal in excavating this farmstead was to learn its age and therefore anchor the 'floating' chronology of the surrounding ancient walls that we were building up at the same time (see *Dating the Ancient Field Walls on Roughan Hill*). Before excavation, Settlement 1 appeared as a kidney-shaped stone enclosure wall with the remains of several ruined stone structures at its centre. Beyond the inner, kidney-shaped enclosure wall there was an outer enclosure wall extending to the south, and radiating off both enclosure walls were further mound walls which ran out across the hill demarcating the boundaries of contemporary fields.

Our excavations concentrated on the roughly circular ruin at the centre of the site which we suspected was the remains of a prehistoric house. Excavation revealed that this was, in fact, the case although the extreme shallowness of the stratigraphy and the reoccupation of the site thousands of years after its initial occupation obscured the exact plan of the prehistoric house. Nevertheless, it seems most likely that it was a circular house, six or seven metres across on the inside, with stone walls and a thatched roof supported by some arrangement of central poles. We did not find a hearth but a large irregular pit at the centre of the structure was filled with black clayey silt flecked with charcoal and fragments of charred hazelnuts.

The excavation also produced animal bones which show that cattle, sheep/goat and pig were all raised, while the numerous quern fragments and the one complete quern stone recovered indicate that plant foods were also being used. The charred hazelnut fragments show this plentiful source of wild food was being used but the people probably also grew domesticated cereals such as wheat and barley. If crops were grown in the area, the most likely sites for growing crops would be in the small natural depressions that contain deeper soil and are sheltered. These are ideal spots for garden plots and many, including one within Settlement 1, were used as potato plots in recent times.

The most significant items in terms of dating the site were the hundreds of potsherds and smaller fragments of pottery which were recovered. All but one of the potsherds were Beaker sherds which date to between *c.* 2500 – 2300 BC. The single non-Beaker sherd was a Food Vessel sherd which is either contemporary or slightly later than the Beaker sherds. The Beaker sherds were a fantastic find because they gave us the date we needed to fix the occupation of the farmstead and thereby its associated field walls, while at the same time showing us the farmstead was contemporary with the surrounding wedge tombs.

Other finds from Settlement 1 consisted of a range of stone tools and two bone awl tips.

The stone tools included arrowheads, convex scrapers, utilised flakes, blades, punch/drills, hammer stones, polishing stones, grinder/pounders and quern stones. Debitage (debris from manufacturing chipped stone tools) and flakes from polished stone axes (possibly from re-sharpening the axes) were also recovered. Almost all the chipped stone tools from the site were made from chert which was probably quarried from local bands of chert which occur in the limestone of the Burren. The quern stone fragments were all sandstone which can be found as isolated cobbles scattered across the surface of the Burren and the grinder/pounders were shale cobbles which probably came from the west Burren. One particularly intriguing tool appears to be made from a fine-grained and very dense stone of non-local origin. It is roughly 'chisel' shaped with two tapering, blunted ends and it may be a very early metal-working hammer.

Figure 33 ▲
Settlement 1, Roughan Hill under excavation.

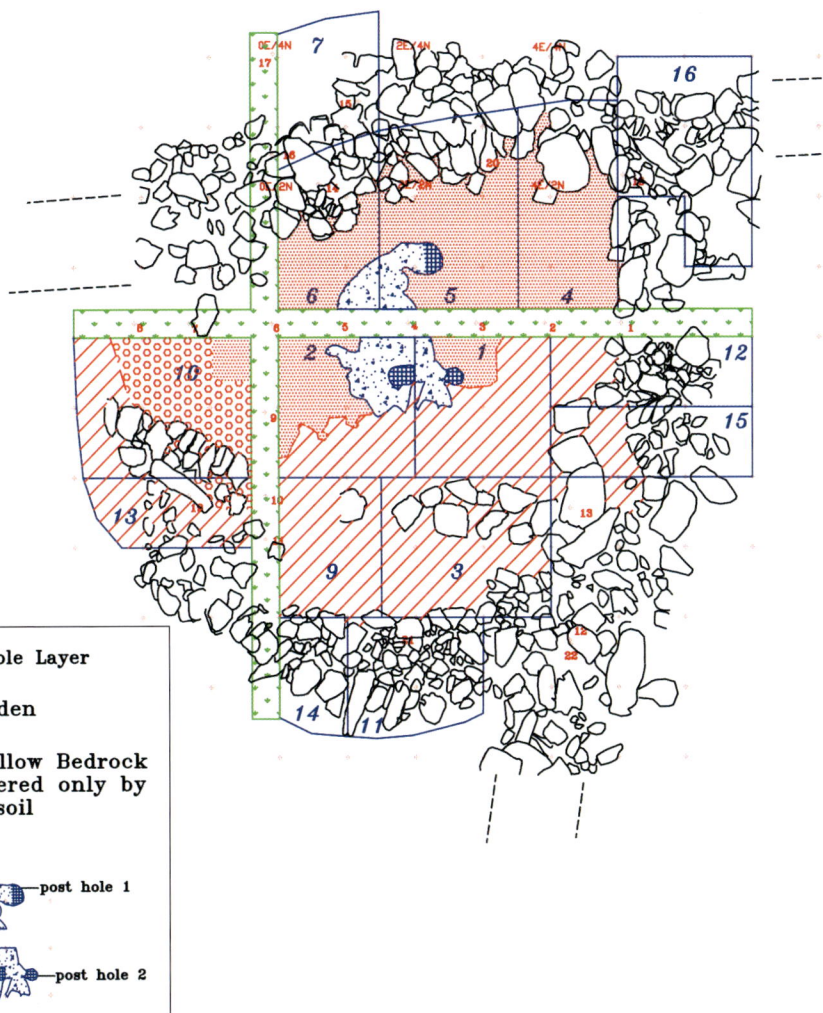

◀ Figure 34
Plan of the Settlement 1 excavation.

A grid of one metre squares was imposed on the site and then the excavation was carried out within sixteen separately numbered areas, with a cross-shaped baulk left unexcavated. Within the structure, the best preserved stratigraphy occurred in the north, probably because of the slight downhill slope in this direction and the large amount of wall tumble capping the deposits in this area. The most significant aspect of the stratigraphy, however, was its extreme shallowness. The deepest deposits encountered were only 50 cm deep.

Cobble Layer

Midden

Shallow Bedrock covered only by topsoil

1 m

post hole 1
pit 1
pit 2
post hole 2

Figure 35
Selected finds from the Settlement 1 excavation.

Top row: Concave-based arrowheads.
Row 2: Convex scrapers. **Rows 3-5:** Beaker pottery sherds and Bowl Tradition sherd (no. 12).

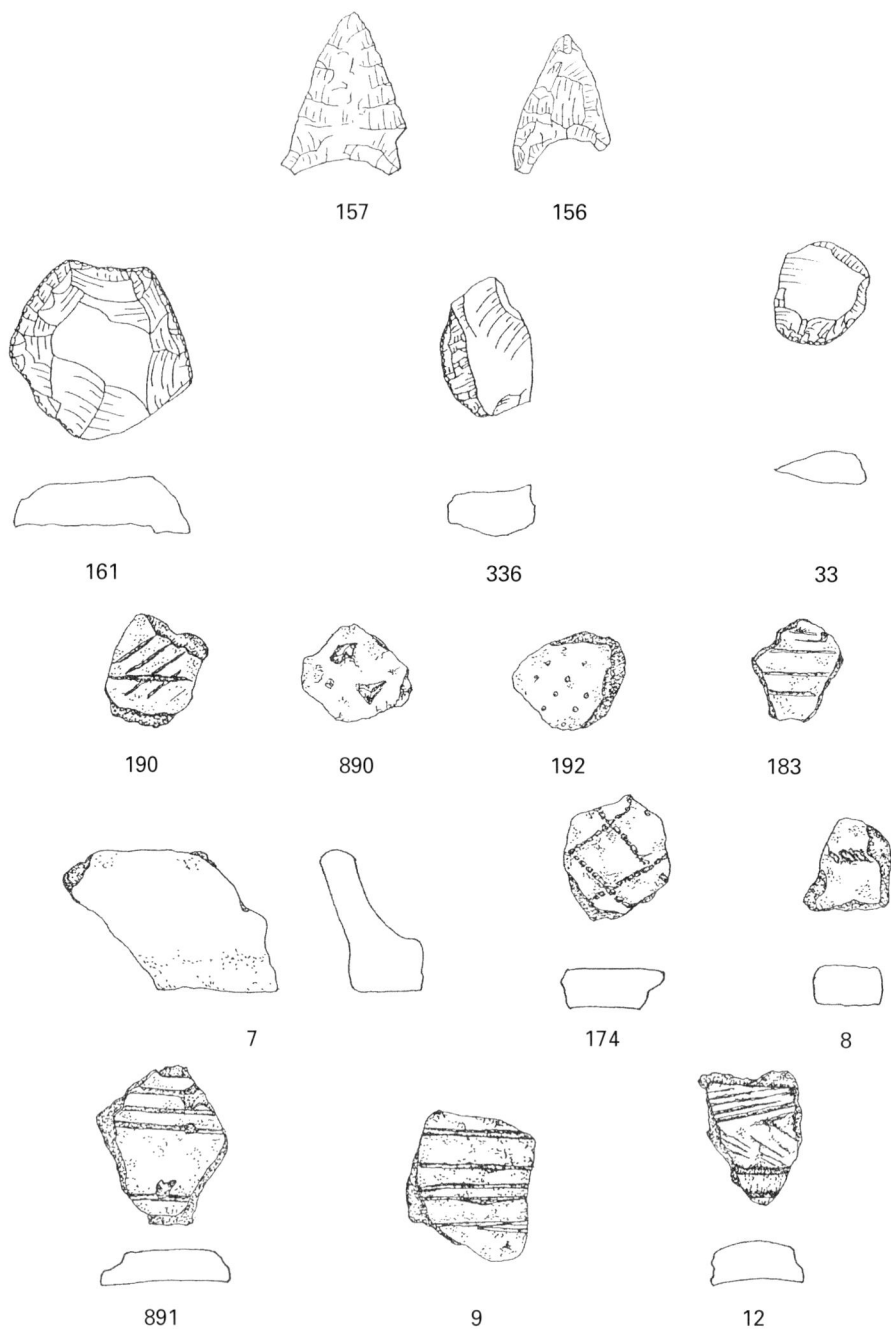

157   156

161   336   33

190   890   192   183

7   174   8

891   9   12

5cm

Dating the Ancient Field Walls on Roughan Hill

One of the primary aims of the Roughan Hill project was to discover how old the ancient field walls on the hill were. There are several types of field wall on Roughan Hill and it was apparent from the way these different walls overlapped that the oldest walls on the hill were what we termed 'mound walls'. Mound walls are just a faint trace of an ancient wall rather than a still-standing wall. Today they appear as low grass-covered mounds no more than 80cm high and generally 80–150cm wide. They are difficult to see with an untrained eye but once you get a feel for them they can be seen snaking all over Roughan Hill and other parts of the Burren as well.

Although it was clear when we began the Roughan Hill project that the mound walls were the oldest walls on the hill, we did not know how old they were. To discover the date of the walls we developed a method which relies on the fact that because the Burren is composed of soft limestone, its surface is lowered a little every year by erosion. Over the millennia, this very gradual process has resulted in a noticeable reduction in the height of the bedrock. The ancient walls, however, shelter the bedrock underneath from the erosion and the result is a 'pedestal' of bedrock under ancient walls that is higher than the surrounding bedrock. Although other factors – such as the changing acidity of the soil cover and the robbing of wall stones for later constructions – complicate the picture, in general the higher the preserved bedrock pedestal under a wall, the older the wall.

We therefore set about excavating trenches across a range of ancient walls on Roughan Hill and measuring the bedrock pedestals preserved under them. In the end, we excavated 43 trenches across ancient walls on the hill. This provided us with a range of pedestal heights which we then ordered from smallest to largest. Those with the smallest pedestals were the youngest and those with the highest pedestals were the oldest. We now knew the chronological position of each wall relative to the other walls, but we did not know the 'absolute' or calendar date of any of the walls. To get this we needed to anchor our floating chronology, which we did by excavating Settlement 1. The Beaker pottery from the excavation gave us a date of *c.* 2500 – 2300 BC for the occupation of Settlement 1 and, by association, the same date for the field walls related to the farmstead. Comparing the pedestal heights of the walls associated with Settlement 1 with other walls across the hill not directly associated with Settlement 1 showed that the majority of mound walls on Roughan Hill were contemporary, that is, they dated to the Final Neolithic/Early Bronze Age. There are, however, some mound walls that have higher pedestals and these are probably older walls, perhaps as old as the Parknabinnia chambered tomb and the first farmers on Roughan Hill.

Although the Roughan Hill project was focused on the prehistoric landscape, in the course of our investigations we discerned later patterns of land use on the hill as well. It seems as if Roughan Hill, and probably other parts of the Burren, have seen three major phases of field wall building over the six millennia that people have been farming the Burren. The first phase was in the prehistoric period. This began as initial tree clearances and field wall building in the Neolithic and culminated in the repeated sub-division of these fields in the Final Neolithic/Early Bronze Age. After this, the next two and a half millennia do not appear to have seen any significant field wall building and the old walls eventually collapsed and formed the mound walls that we see today. The next phase of field wall building dates to early in the historic period, probably in the Early Medieval period. On Roughan Hill, the walls of this phase are termed slab walls (which resemble lines of tipped dominoes) and slab/standing walls and these walls divide the hill into a system of long and narrow rectangular fields with a north-south orientation. On Roughan Hill and elsewhere on the Burren, the farmsteads associated with these fields have various forms, but the most common form of farmstead of this period is the cashel. This system of fields appears to have been used until some time in the late Medieval or even possibly some time in the post-Medieval period when the fields were completely reorganised into the much larger fields divided by the standing walls that are still in use today. On Roughan Hill there are no obvious farmsteads for this late period but there are goat *crós*, tiny huts for goat kids with associated yards, and it seems likely that Roughan Hill was incorporated into a larger estate at this time, perhaps the estate of the O'Briens residing in nearby Leamaneh castle (see *Leamaneh Castle*).

Figure 36
Measuring the bedrock pedestal under a mound wall.

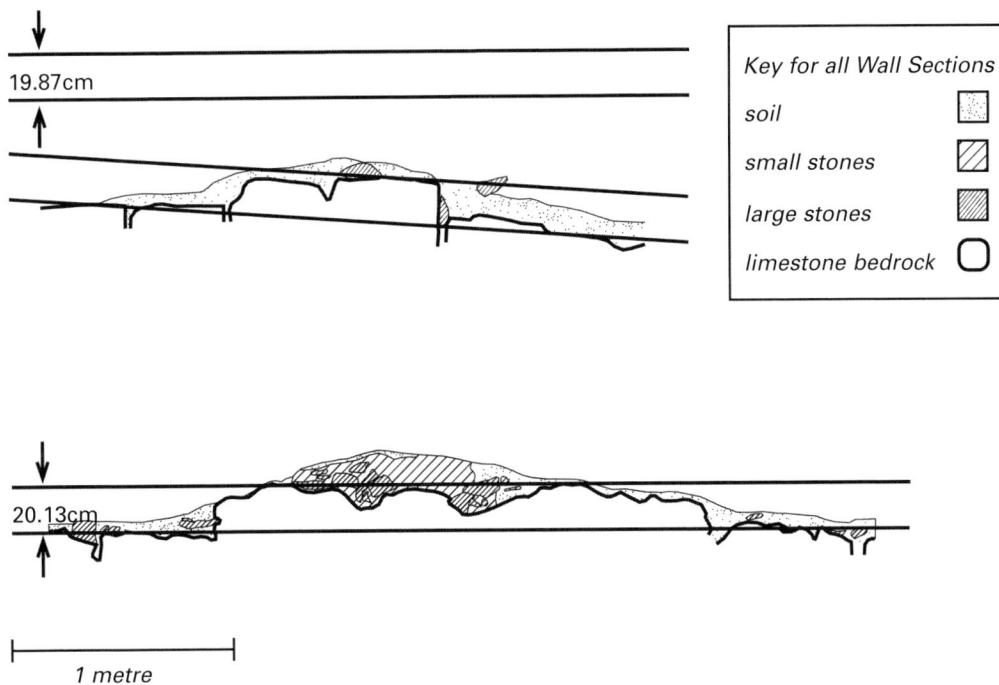

19.87cm

Key for all Wall Sections

soil	▦
small stones	▨
large stones	▨
limestone bedrock	◯

20.13cm

1 metre

Figure 37

Sections across mound walls showing the underlying bedrock pedestals.

Sections through the ancient walls were produced by excavating trenches across the walls. The revealed section was then drawn to scale and parallel 'best-fit' lines were drawn across the section to measure the height of the pedestal. The bottom line was positioned so that it came as near as possible to resting on the bedrock at a standard distance of 1.5 metres from the centre of the wall on both sides of the wall while still touching as many points of bedrock as possible. The top line was positioned parallel to the bottom line and resting on the highest point of bedrock under the wall. The pedestal height was then measured as the perpendicular distance between the two lines. In the two sections through mound walls shown here, the pedestal in the upper section measures 19.87 cm and the pedestal in the lower section measures 20.13 cm. In the upper section, the wall is on sloping ground and this has been taken into account when measuring the pedestal.

The Wedge Tombs of the Burren

Of all the various types of megalithic tombs built in Ireland, the wedge tombs are the last in the sequence. Radiocarbon dates suggest that most wedge tombs were constructed between *c.* 2300 – 2000 BC and that many continued to be the sites of ritual activity for many centuries after. On the Burren, wedge tombs are the most numerous type of megalithic tomb. Compared with the eight or nine earlier megalithic tombs that have been identified on the Burren, around 80 wedge tombs are recorded. Not only are wedge tombs the most common type of megalithic tomb on the Burren, but the densest concentration of wedge tombs in the country is located in the south-east Burren on Roughan Hill. Despite this abundance, no wedge tomb on the Burren has been excavated and so what we know of the deposits made in and around them is based on analogy with wedge tombs in other parts of Ireland.

Many of these excavated wedge tombs in other areas have produced very little, but some human remains have been found in wedge tombs, both inhumations and cremations. Animal bone is also sometimes found in wedge tombs and in one case a complete ox was buried adjacent to a wedge tomb. Finds from wedge tombs consist of pottery, stone tools and debitage, and occasionally metal finds and finds related to metal working including moulds, a crucible fragment and lumps of unworked copper.

It appears that most wedge tombs were probably used repeatedly over a long span of time

Figure 38
Wedge tomb at Ballyganner South.
Grid Reference R220 944

Wedge tombs are characterised by a chamber that lowers and narrows towards the rear of the tomb. On the Burren, they are constructed with massive slabs of limestone and therefore have a very characteristic box-like appearance. Off the Burren, however, in areas with different rock types, wedge tombs look different if they are constructed with smaller and less slab-like stones. Some wedge tombs have traces of cairns surrounding the chamber but many wedge tombs may never have had a substantial cairn.

and that the finds in them are the result of successive deposits. The bones and finds from wedge tombs occur in many different contexts. They are found on the floor of the chambers, within deposits of earth in the chambers, within pits, cists and compartments in the chambers, within pits and cists adjacent to the tombs, and at least one wedge tomb had a matrix of earth, potsherds, animal bone and human bone used as a wall-filling. Many of the human remains may have been 'token' deposits of just a portion of the remains while many of the other deposits may represent offerings of food.

The alignment of wedge tombs is very consistent – the front, or wide end, almost always faces to the south-west or west. This orientation towards the setting sun, combined with their characteristic funnel shape, has led to the suggestion that wedge tombs served as openings into the 'Otherworld'. It's possible that the specific orientation of each wedge tomb preserves the position of the setting sun on a significant day for the community that built it, perhaps the occasion of a death.

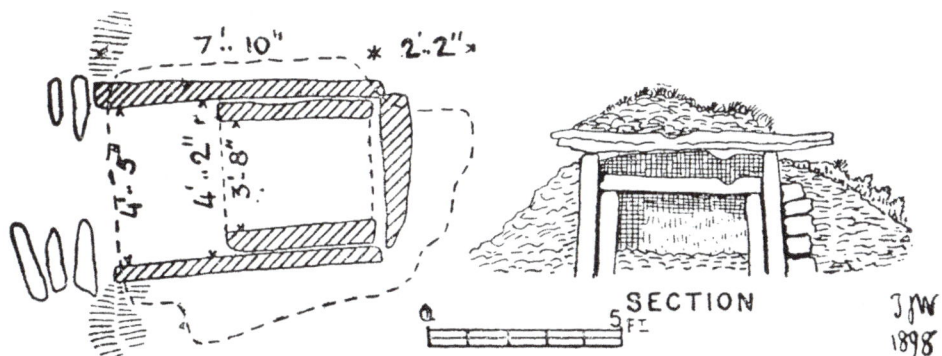

Figure 39
Wedge tomb on Roughan Hill (Cl. 61).
Grid Reference R 258 933

On Roughan Hill and the adjacent high ground in Leana townland there are at least fifteen wedge tombs within an area approximately 2.5km by 1.75km. This is the densest concentration of wedge tombs in Ireland. The tombs are particularly concentrated on Roughan Hill, just upslope from the cluster of contemporary farmsteads.

Figure 40
The 'double' wedge tomb at Baur South.
Grid Reference M 218 001

The wedge tomb at Baur South is an interesting monument that may be the result of 'upgrading' a monument over time. It's possible that it is a two-phase construction, starting as a small wedge tomb that was later enclosed in a larger wedge tomb. Of course without excavation it is impossible to know whether Baur South is a two-phase construction or even if it is, what the sequence of construction was. If it is a smaller wedge tomb subsequently enclosed in a larger wedge tomb though, it may be the result of ongoing competition between families leading to the upgrading of a previously unimpressive monument.

Figure 41

Creevagh wedge tomb.

Grid Reference R 273 957

The Creevagh wedge tomb is located within a much later, Early Medieval cashel.

Building a Wedge Tomb

One might expect that building a wedge tomb was a purely pragmatic affair, carried out by the prehistoric forerunners of today's engineers and architects. In fact, what we find at wedge tombs is evidence for the intertwining of ritual and pragmatic activities during their construction.

Figure 42

Megalithic slab quarry on Roughan Hill.

Grid Reference R 257 933

The first step would have been the quarrying of suitable slabs. This megalithic slab quarry is located very close to a cluster of wedge tombs on Roughan Hill. In the quarry, slabs have been prised up from the bedrock, fracturing along their natural bedding planes. Small boulders were then wedged under the slabs to hold them up. It is unclear why these slabs were left only partially quarried but the negative spaces where other slabs were completely removed can also be seen in this quarry. The slabs were probably prised up with long wooden levers and then dragged the short distance to the construction site by oxen or people. Wooden sleds or rollers may have been used.

Figure 43
Shifting a large stone with a rope and timbers. ▲

During the excavation of the Parknabinnia chambered tomb we had to shift several large stones and as the tomb is far from the road, bringing in any machinery to aid in the task was out of the question. Instead, we found that just a length of rope and a sturdy timber A-frame which transferred our pulling energy into lifting energy was an efficient and versatile way to move the large stones. Shifting many of the stones was a very delicate task because we had to avoid crushing the archaeological deposits which were still in place but we found that with this system we could gently lift the stones and shift them just a few centimetres at a time when that was what was required. It's quite possible that a similar system was used by the builders of the megalithic tombs. Some of their muscle power could have been provided by oxen but the instances of osteoarthritis which have been identified on several bones from the Parknabinnia chambered tomb show that the ancient inhabitants of Roughan Hill were well used to heavy lifting and carrying (see Figure 25).

Figure 44
Manufacturing scars on wedge tomb Cl. 61 on Roughan Hill.
Grid Reference R 258 933

After the slabs had been quarried, they were shaped by battering their edges with a hammerstone. This leaves distinctive crescent-shaped scars along the edge of the slab identical to the flake scars on small chipped stone tools such as arrowheads. The position of the scars on the side slab pictured here suggest this shaping took place after the slab had been erected at the tomb site. This shows us that the slabs were at least partially shaped at the construction site rather than at the quarry. This could be attributed to the purely practical concerns of 'fine-tuning' the stones to ensure a good fit in the same way that a modern mason will shape the stones of a wall as he builds the wall. But with the wedge tombs, there seems to have been something more to it as well. At two excavated wedge tombs in County Cork, pits were found in front of the tombs on both sides of the entrance that contained the flaking debris from shaping the slabs. In other words, the prehistoric masons did not merely fling their debris into the bushes or let it lie where it fell. They carefully collected all the flaking debris, dug pits at specific locations in front of the tomb and buried the flakes. So even the debris from building the wedge tomb was ◄ imbued with a ritual significance.

Figure 45
Small wedging stone beneath capstone of Cl. 61.

This small stone is wedged between the capstone and the top of the northern side slab. It raises the capstone on this side of the tomb by just a few centimetres and demonstrates the level of precision sought by the wedge tomb builders. Most of the capstones on Burren wedge tombs weigh several tonnes and were probably dragged into place on earthen ramps, possibly from the rear of the tomb.

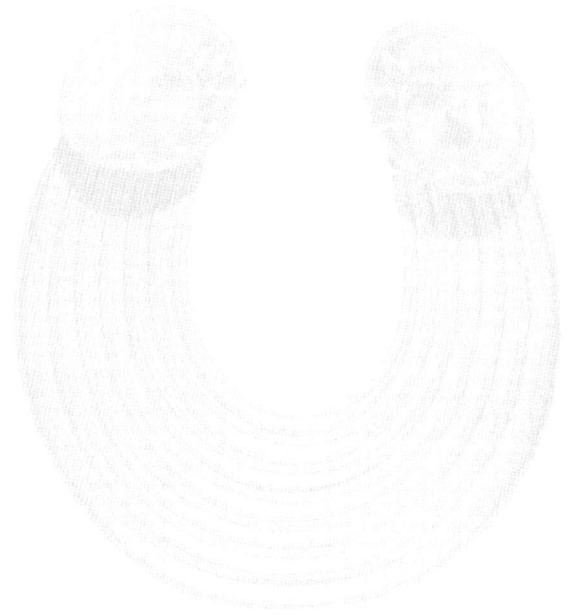

Gold, Power and War

WARFARE WAS ONE OF THE HALLMARKS of Bronze Age Europe and in Middle and Late Bronze Age Ireland (*c.* 1500 – 600 BC), many regions appear to have been dominated by an upper stratum of warrior elites. Alliances, competition and the ostentatious display of wealth and power were all important. Large hillforts were built and these appear to have functioned as both defensible sites and symbols of a group's solidarity and power. Bronze was used in increasing amounts to produce weapons which were continually evolving and gold was used to fashion personal ornaments of increasing sophistication. In Ireland, warriors were equipped with swords, spears and shields, and the large numbers of these items that have been found in Ireland show that combat was an important part of life. Some of the weapons and shields appear to have been more for show than for battle, but many show clear signs of use. Sometimes these metal items were purposefully deposited in watery places and many of these acts of deposition were probably staged as public displays of wealth and power. The metal objects were also traded over long distances and were probably used as gifts to establish and maintain relationships between the elite groups of neighbouring areas.

In the preceding Neolithic, the population in Clare appears to have been concentrated in the southern Burren, by the Final Neolithic/Early Bronze Age the population had become more widespread on the Burren and had expanded into south-east Clare as well. By the Late Bronze Age, the earlier small-scale societies of the region had transformed into larger political units and the Burren appears to have become a peripheral area, incorporated into a larger territory that had its centre elsewhere. The most likely scenario is that the Burren became incorporated into a chiefdom which was centred on the hillfort of Mooghaun, south east of

Figure 46

Bronze dagger from a sandpit near Carron.

Throughout the Neolithic archery was used for both hunting and fighting and the prominence of the bow and arrow as the preferred weapon of the warrior continued into the Early Bronze Age. As the Bronze Age progressed, however, daggers and then spears and swords replaced bows and arrows as preferred weapons and as potent symbols of the warrior.

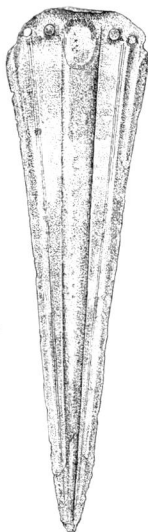

Ennis. In the Late Bronze Age, Mooghaun appears to have been the capital of a powerful chiefdom which dominated the lower reaches of the Shannon. The chiefs of Mooghaun were probably hereditary and they probably collected food and craft goods from the population as a type of tax. They would have bestowed and withheld favours as they saw fit and they would have skimmed off a profit to support themselves, their warriors and other hangers on. Mooghaun and its neighbouring chiefdoms probably expanded and contracted according to their fortunes in war but the population of the chiefdom was probably always at least several thousand and may have reached as high as around 10,000. The chiefdom of Mooghaun probably rose to prominence by controlling the very important prehistoric crossroads at Killaloe where a major east-west land route seems to have crossed the river Shannon. The power of this chiefdom is demonstrated by the fact the largest Bronze Age gold hoard in western Europe was found at Mooghaun. It consisted of at least 150 gold bracelets, neck rings and collars.

There is, of course, another impressive Late Bronze Age hillfort on the other side of the Burren at Dún Aonghasa on Inishmore (see *The Late Bronze Age Chiefdom of Dún Aonghasa*) and it is possible that the Burren was under the sway of a chiefdom centred on the Aran Islands. Like Mooghaun, the chiefdom of Dún Aonghasa probably rose to prominence by controlling trade routes, in this case, sea routes. In any case, there are no sites on the Burren which rival the scale of either Mooghaun or Dún Aonghasa and so it does seem likely that the Burren was a peripheral area at this time.

The only possible candidates for comparable sites on the Burren are Turlough Hill in the north-east Burren and Caherballykinvarga near Kilfenora. However, Turlough Hill is possibly a Neolithic ritual site (see *Turlough Hill*) and Caherballykinvarga is more likely the residence of an Early Medieval chief rather than a Bronze Age chief (see *The Chiefdom of Corcu Modruad*). Neither has been the focus of any intensive investigations and so their dates and functions are still a matter for speculation.

Figure 47 ▼

Leaf-shaped sword found near Lough Inchiquin.

Daggers gradually evolved into longer rapiers which were essentially straight-sided thrusting swords (see Figure 50) and these in turn evolved into leaf-shaped swords which were used as slashing weapons. These leaf-shaped swords have blades which are weighted towards the tip so they can be swung with the ease of a pendulum and they represent a real advance. Other weapons available to Bronze Age warriors had many limitations. A fighter thrusting with a spear or a rapier needs to take his time and be accurate but as soon as he makes a thrust his sides are undefended. Axes and clubs were another option but they are heavy and therefore tiring to use in a prolonged battle. In contrast, slashing swords are light and easy to wield, the user can deliver debilitating blows without aiming at any particular part of the body and a sword fighter can move quickly between offensive and defensive postures.

Gifts to the Gods

In the Bronze Age, hoards of metal objects and sometimes single metal objects were deliberately deposited in rivers, bogs and lakes. It seems likely that the social hierarchies of the Bronze Age were maintained in part by controlling the exchange of prestige items including metalwork and although depositing metal objects in watery places seems to have generally been carried out in a ritual context (possibly coinciding with another event such as a birth or a death), the deposits would also have had political and economic benefits for those who made them. Ritually depositing metal in a watery place would be a public display of the destruction of wealth and could be used to build personal status. At the same time, the metal would be taken out of circulation, thereby controlling the supply and preventing the devaluing of the metal that would invariably occur if supplies were always increasing. Finds of Bronze Age metal objects are not common on the Burren but there have been a few, particularly in the bogs that occur in the shale lands of the western Burren and just off of the Burren in the vicinity of Lough Inchiquin.

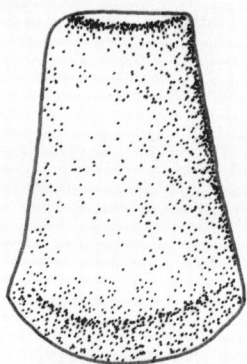

◀ Figure 48
Early copper axehead from near Lough Inchiquin.

Copper axes cast in one-piece moulds were the most common metal artefacts in the earliest stages of metal use in Ireland. These very early metal axes are simple flat shapes which were hafted in the same manner as stone axes, by slotting the axe head into a perforated club-shaped handle. Bronze axes followed, and throughout the Bronze Age axe types were developed which required increasingly sophisticated metal-working skills and which show increasingly effective hafting techniques.

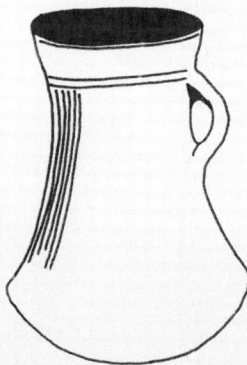

◀ Figure 49
Boultiaghdine hoard.

The exact findspot of this Late Bronze Age hoard of bronze implements is not known but the townland it came from is a very boggy area just west of Lough Inchiquin. The hoard consists of a socketed axe, a chisel and a razor. The socketed axe is a Late Bronze Age development which provides a much sturdier hafting than the early flat axes (see Figure 48).

Figure 50 ▼
Bronze rapier found in a bog near Lisdoonvarna.

So many weapons of high quality have been recovered from watery places in Ireland, particularly from rivers, that accidental loss seems unlikely. Indeed, these weapons were deposited at a time when the practice of burying the dead with grave goods went out of favour. It has been suggested that these weapons found in rivers and other watery places are 'grave goods without a grave'. In other words, on the occasion of a funeral the weapons may have been cast into the water while the body was disposed of elsewhere or, in the case of rivers, the weapons may have accompanied a body that subsequently drifted away.

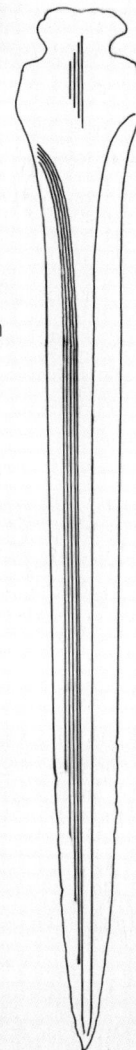

Figure 51
Gleninsheen gorget.

Gorgets are broad crescent-shaped collars of hammered sheet gold. The edges are sometimes reinforced by wrapping them around a wire and the terminals are gold discs which are usually stitched to the crescent with gold wire. They are generally decorated with raised, concentric, semi-circular ribs. This decoration may, in fact, be an imitation in gold of the stiff folds of a leather collar. Gorgets like this have been found mainly around the lower reaches of the river Shannon and are one element of a Late Bronze Age cluster of high quality gold and bronze objects in this area. Gorgets were probably worn by chiefs on ceremonial occasions as symbols of their rank and power. The Gleninsheen gorget seems to have been hidden in a rock fissure on the Burren for safe-keeping where it remained until it was found by a local farmer hunting rabbits in 1932.

Figure 52 ▼

Excavated *fulacht fiadh* at Fahee South near Carron.

Grid Reference R 292 988

Some evidence for settlement on the Burren in the Bronze Age is provided by *fulachta fiadh*. These are low U-shaped mounds of burnt stones surrounding a water-filled trough. These sites are found in low boggy areas or next to a stream or lake and thousands are known throughout the country. *Fulachta fiadh* are usually interpreted as cooking places but other viable interpretations include their use as saunas or as places where hides were processed. A recent series of radiocarbon dates has shown that most date to the middle of the Bronze Age.

Fulachta fiadh have been found on the Burren in appropriately watery locations and one was excavated in the early 1980s at the edge of the Carron turlough. Like many *fulacht fiadh* excavations, however, this one produced little except a few fragments of animal bone, a few animal teeth, charcoal, burnt stones and the waterlogged remains of an oak trough.

◀ Figure 53

Knockstoolery standing stone in Doolin.

Grid Reference R 077 968

Although the Burren lies north of the main concentration of stone circles, stone alignments and single standing stones in south Munster, a few standing stones and stone alignments do occur on the Burren. These are enigmatic monuments and excavation often sheds little light on their function but small deposits of unburnt human bone and cremated bone, sometimes with a pottery vessel, have been found near the bases of some standing stones which have been excavated in other areas. Most probably date to the second millennium BC (i.e., between 2000 BC and 1000 BC). Many stone alignments have a south-west to north-east axis and some have been found to point towards prominent peaks or high passes where either the sun or moon rises or sets. Lunar alignments are the most common and were probably important to Bronze Age people because they signalled the changing seasons.

The standing stone of Knockstoolery is on top of a prominent hill in the village of Doolin. There was a lot of prehistoric activity in the Doolin area and so there is a good chance that the Knockstoolery standing stone is prehistoric and is in its original location, but without excavation this is not certain. Some standing stones may not be prehistoric, but instead may be landscape features erected in the past few centuries by landlords, and some genuinely prehistoric standing stones seem to have been moved to more aesthetically pleasing locations by landlords as well. The fact that there is a particularly good view of the Knockstoolery standing stone from the site across the river where Doolin House, the old MacNamara residence, used to stand does raise doubts about its antiquity.

Figure 54

Excavated and reconstructed cairn at Coolnatullagh.

After this cairn was damaged during the construction of a wall, Dúchas (The Heritage Service) provided funds for a partial excavation, directed by James Eogan of ADS Ltd in 1997.

The Cairns of the Burren

All across the Burren one comes across stones heaped together into cairns. These cairns range from small cairns just a few metres across to large cairns, such as the cairns on top of Turlough Hill and the summit of Slieve Carran (which translates as 'the mountain of the cairn'). Most are probably prehistoric burial cairns but only a few have been excavated and so we do not know a lot about them. The excavation of the large cairn of Poulawack near the centre of the Burren showed it began as a Neolithic burial monument which was subsequently enlarged and used for more burials in the Bronze Age (see *Poulawack Cairn*). Excavation of a much smaller cairn at Coolnatullagh in the eastern Burren has shown it was constructed in the Final Neolithic/Early Bronze Age and then used for more burials and other deposits later in the Bronze Age, and perhaps even after the Bronze Age as well.

Coolnatullagh Cairn

Grid Reference M 309 025

The cairn at Coolnatullagh is a modest structure, a little over seven metres in diameter and less than a metre high, adjacent to the road but hidden from view by the high wall that borders the road. It is a circular heap of stones bounded by a kerb of upright slabs which are held in place by a low drystone revetment which encircles the monument. The cairn was partially excavated in 1997 and several burials were uncovered. At the centre of the cairn is a cist which contained at least one and possibly two inhumations along with a cremation. Another inhumation was found within the cairn east of the central cist, and other deposits of both cremated and unburnt human bone were found throughout the cairn as well.

Because the monument was only partially excavated it is not certain that the burials in the central cist were the primary burials in the monument, but it's very likely that they were. The burials in the central cist consisted of the partial remains of an adult inhumation, a single bone from an infant and a deposit of cremated adult bones. A radiocarbon sample from the adult inhumation gave a Final Neolithic/Early Bronze Age date of 2460–2140 BC which probably marks the construction of the cairn. Several hundred years later, a pit was dug into the cairn and the body of a 13–14 year old teenager was placed in it and covered over with stones. A radiocarbon date from this burial gave an Early Bronze Age date of 1880–1610 BC. In addition to these burials, five other deposits of cremated bone and seven deposits of unburnt bone were found within the cairn. These deposits of bone may be token deposits that were incorporated into the cairn as it was being built, they may be token deposits that were placed on the surface of the cairn which have since percolated down through the stones, or they may be scattered remains from the disturbed central cist or other disturbed burials which were not identified during the excavations. At least two adults and one child (9–10 years old) are represented by the deposits in the cairn.

There were a few finds in the cairn but none were associated with any of the human remains. The finds consisted of a chert scraper, a flint blade, three pieces of debitage, what is possibly a sandstone pin sharpener, a dog's tooth which was partially perforated so that it could be suspended on a string (but which appears to have been abandoned because it cracked while the hole was being bored), a glass bead and potsherds. The lithic finds are similar to finds from the Final Neolithic/Early Bronze Age farmstead which was excavated on Roughan Hill (see *Excavating a Farmstead on Roughan Hill*), the potsherds appear to be from a single Late Bronze Age vessel which was placed upside down at the foot of the revetment and the glass bead is probably either Iron Age or Early Medieval in date. A small amount of animal bone (cattle, pig, sheep/goat and dog) was also recovered in the excavations, including a concentration of pig and cattle teeth associated with the Early Bronze Age burial of the teenager in the cairn.

Figure 55

Large cairn on the western summit of Turlough Hill.

Grid Reference M 303 068

Although most cairns appear to have been built with sloping sides, the original vertical sides of the cairn on Turlough Hill can still be seen around a good portion of its circumference. This cairn is probably related to the large enclosure and other features on the summit of Turlough Hill (see *Turlough Hill*).

Celts?

THE IRON AGE IN IRELAND (*c.* 600 BC – *c.* 400 AD) is very obscure archaeologically. Metalwork deposits are few, burials often consist of token deposits of cremated bones and small trinkets, and few settlement sites are known that date to this period. Despite this lack of evidence, the Iron Age has traditionally been equated with the large-scale movement of a new ethnic group into Ireland, the Celts. The traditional explanation is that the iron-using and Celtic-speaking population expanded from their central European homeland and invaded Ireland at this time, either killing or assimilating the native Irish. This traditional explanation is based mainly on the fact that Ireland has a native Celtic language and also on the fact that a small number of Iron Age artefacts with either western European affinities or origins have been found in Ireland. Today, however, this explanation appears to be flawed.

The Celts or Keltoi are first named by the Greeks and subsequently described by various Roman authors. It is in these early descriptions where we find the beginnings of stereotypes that persist to this day. Early accounts characterise the Celts as warlike, high spirited, terrifying in appearance, and people who use few words and speak in riddles. These descriptions should not, however, be taken at face value. They are made by urbanites who found themselves far from their sophisticated home cities around the Mediterranean, encountering strangers in the wilds of western Europe. In fact, the descriptions are very similar to those made by the descendants of those same wild western Europeans when they first encountered native Americans many centuries later. Similarly, just as early Europeans in the Americas lumped vast and diverse populations together with the generic term 'Indians', the Greeks and Romans seem to have used the label 'Celts' for a variety of groups who would not necessarily have considered themselves to be a single ethnic group. Indeed, when we consider that even with the effects of modern transportation, multi-national corporations and all the other factors that help to homogenise the world today there is no ethnic group in Europe as widespread as what is claimed for the Celts, it is hard to believe there was such a widespread ethnic group in prehistory.

This, of course, leads us to the problem of what we mean when we talk about an ethnic group and the related question of how we might identify ethnic groups in the archaeological record. Traditionally, the Celts have been identified with the material culture (i.e., pots, metalwork, houses, burials, etc.) associated with a group of chiefdoms which occupied an area north of the Alps stretching roughly from Paris to Prague which were named after a site in Switzerland called La Tène. Although there are a few La Tène-type artefacts in Ireland, all the things that we would expect to find if there was a folk movement into Ireland, namely – normal La Tène domestic material, burials and settlements – are missing. Instead, what we find in Ireland is a scattering of La Tène-style artefacts, most of which are pieces of ornate metalwork. Additionally, many La Tène objects in Ireland are decorated in what is known as the 'insular' style. The forms and decoration of these Irish objects are within the broad La Tène tradition but they also have more subtle local variations. These variations in style show that most pieces found in Ireland were made by local craftsmen who were copying and modifying an exotic art style. There are almost no items which might be direct imports brought in by a group of foreigners recently arrived from the continent.

Further confusion has been added to the issue by the use of what now appears to be a flawed model of linguistic diffusion and development. What modern scholars term Celtic languages are a group of related languages which occur along the western seaboard of Europe including Ireland, Wales and Brittany. There is no denying that the native language of Ireland belongs to this group of related languages grouped under the term 'Celtic' by modern scholars but there is vigorous debate as to how the diverse peoples of the western seaboard came to speak similar languages. The traditional model was developed in the nineteenth century by linguists who were heavily influenced by the theories of biological evolution and diffusion which were being developed at that time. The linguists based their model on the 'genetic tree model' that had at its 'trunk' an ancestral language which then 'branched' out into the various related descendant languages. The linguists then joined their model of linguistic diffusion with archaeological models that were current at the time, which explained all cultural changes as the result of population movements. The result was a model which explained the occurrence of the related Celtic languages along the western seaboard as the end result of a vast migration and dispersion of people from an ancestral homeland to the east where their ancestors all originally spoke a common language.

Since these theories were first formulated, however, archaeologists have moved away from using population movements as an explanation for all cultural change, but the linguists have been slow to follow. A model which fits the archaeological data much better than the traditional genetic tree model is one which sees the natives of Ireland speaking a Celtic language because Ireland was part of a social and trade network stretching along the Atlantic seaboard. Instead of a Celtic homeland in central Europe with an expanding population spreading its language through migration, it now seems more likely that western areas, including Ireland, developed similar languages because they were united in an Atlantic seaboard zone of social and economic ties over several millennia.

The idea that the Irish are ethnically Celts, however, is deeply embedded in modern concepts of 'Irishness'. This is due in large part to the nineteenth century Celtic Revival movement which was embraced by Irish nationalists because it provided a non-English golden age to rally around. Then, after Ireland gained its independence, the notion of a distinct Celtic identity was reinforced by school curricula and the media. Archaeologists, like everyone else, are influenced by the social and political context they find themselves in and for the most part Irish archaeology has been carried out within this 'Celtic paradigm' without any real questioning of the social and political circumstances that formed the paradigm. Some archaeologists are now challenging this paradigm but emotions run high and millions of euros are at stake in both the tourism and publishing industries. One prominent archaeologist who has spent considerable time researching these issues was accused of being an 'intellectual terrorist' because he was denying modern people their Celtic heritage.

As with the rest of Ireland, archaeological evidence dating to the Iron Age on the Burren is slight and what there is we should attribute to the native Irish rather than to invading Celts. Some burial mounds such as the ring barrows around Doolin probably date to this period and there are a few stray finds of this date as well. Of particular interest are the two bridle bits found near Corrofin and the bridle pendant found in a bog near Lisdoonvarna. Bridle bits are the most numerous Iron Age find in Ireland and this suggests a significant development in transport and possibly also in warfare at this time.

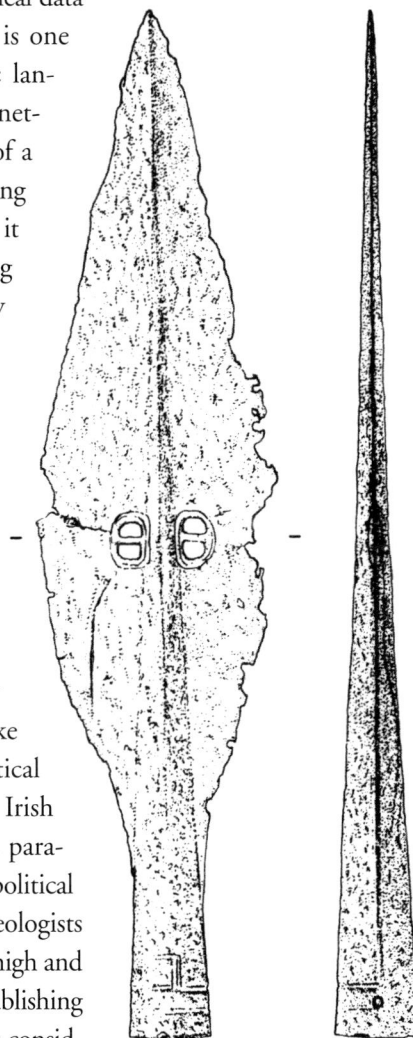

Figure 56
Iron spearhead found near Lough Inchiquin.

This iron spearhead was found in the river Fergus near where it flows into Lough Inchiquin when the river was drained in the nineteenth century. It is decorated with an incised fret pattern around the base of its socket and also with two openings on the blade which have bronze insets. The spearhead is a fairly showy piece and it was probably valued as much for display as for function. In addition to spears, which were used as both thrusting and throwing weapons, warriors would have been equipped with shields and swords.

Figure 57
Ring barrows near Doolin.
Grid Reference R 067 959

Ring barrows are low mounds of earth encompassed by a ditch with an external bank. Excavations of ring barrows in other parts of the country have revealed that they generally cover only a small token deposit of cremated bone sometimes accompanied by small objects such as glass beads, bone pins or bronze rings. Although some are earlier, many appear to date to the Iron Age.

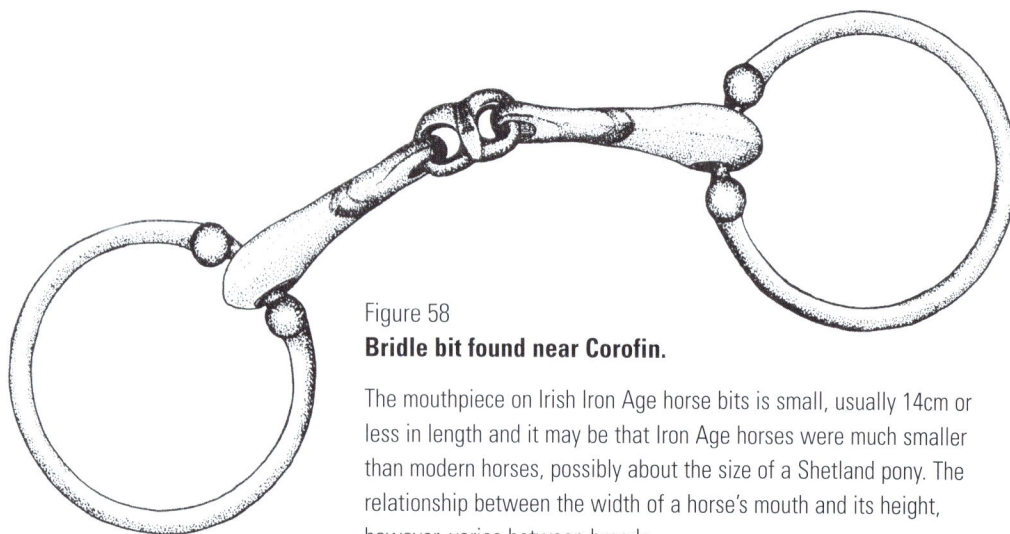

Figure 58
Bridle bit found near Corofin.

The mouthpiece on Irish Iron Age horse bits is small, usually 14cm or less in length and it may be that Iron Age horses were much smaller than modern horses, possibly about the size of a Shetland pony. The relationship between the width of a horse's mouth and its height, however, varies between breeds.

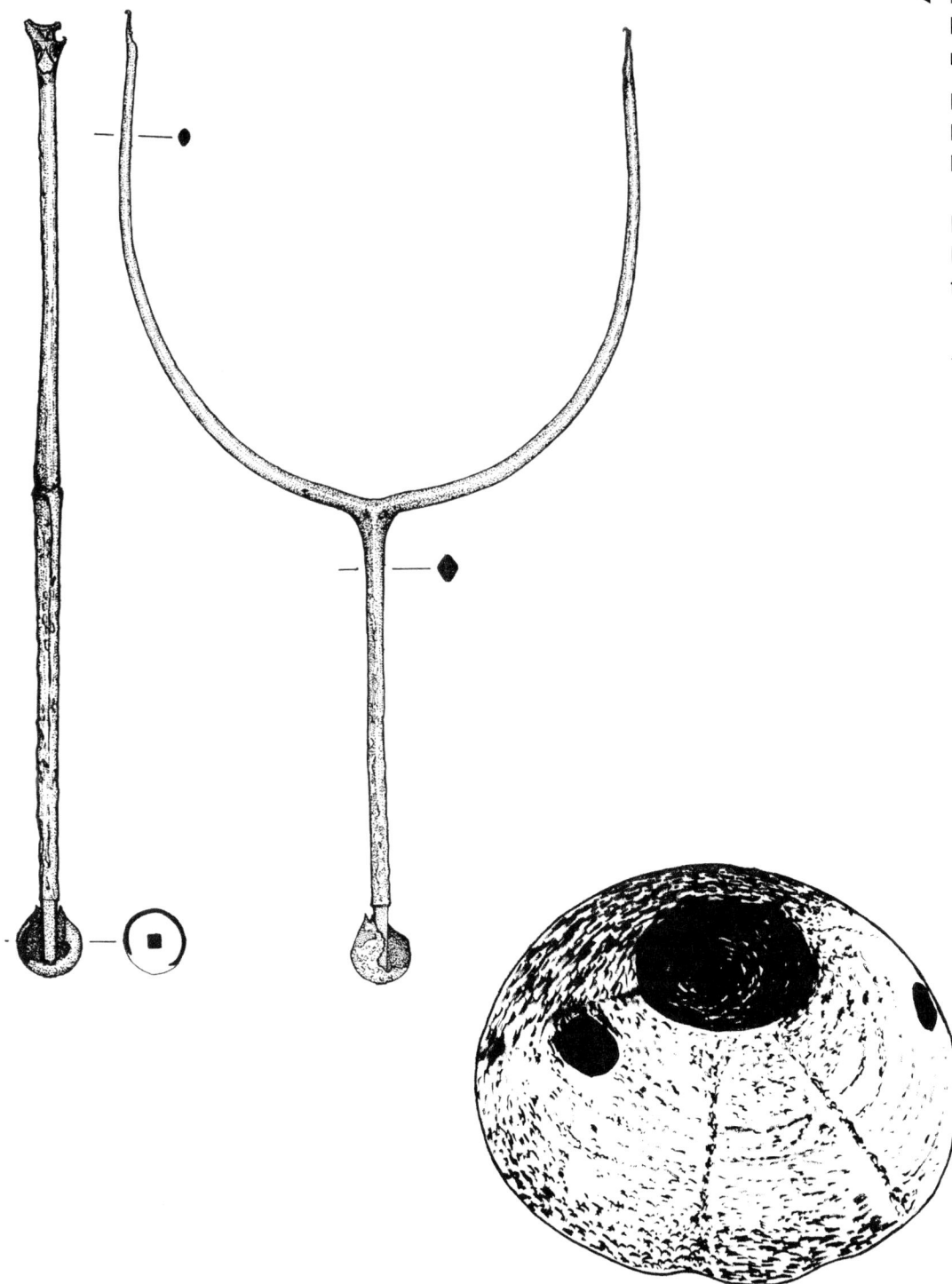

◀ Figure 59
**Bridle pendant found in a bog
near Lisdoonvarna.**

Bridle pendants appear to have been suspended
below the horse's mouth and used to lead the
horse during processions.

Figure 60 ▼
**Beehive-shaped quernstone
from Cohy, near Carron.**

Beehive-shaped quernstones were an important labour-saving innovation in the Iron Age.
Before the introduction of the beehive quern,
grain was ground by hand in saddle-shaped
querns. Beehive querns consist of a heavy,
beehive-shaped upper stone which was
rotated on a lower disc-shaped stone with a
wooden handle that protruded from a hole in
the upper stone.

Two beehive querns have been found on the
Burren, the one pictured from Cohy and another
from Glencolumbkille. Around 200 beehive
querns have now been found in the country but
the two on the Burren are the most southerly
examples known. The concentration of these
artefacts in the north may indicate some sort
of a cultural zone which the Burren was at the
southern edge of during the Iron Age.

The Coming of Christianity

Prior to the fourth century ad Christianity was primarily a Mediterranean religion but with the conversion of the Roman emperor Constantine in the early fourth century AD, Christianity spread more widely across north-west Europe. It was during this expansion of the religion that Christianity first appeared in Ireland. The first Christians in Ireland were probably a diverse group. Some may have been slaves brought back to Ireland from raids on Britain, some may have been Irish mercenaries returning home after serving abroad in the Roman army and some may have been traders from Roman Britain. What we do know is that by 431 AD there were enough Christians in Ireland for the Pope to send Palladius to be bishop for 'the Irish believing in Christ'. Palladius was soon followed by Patrick, who appears to have begun converting Irish people to Christianity some time later in the fifth century.

Irish society at this time was composed of small-scale tribal groups with no centralised government. The fragmented nature of Irish society meant that as Christianity spread through Ireland in the fifth and sixth centuries, the early Christian Church developed differently in Ireland than elsewhere in Europe. In Ireland, many churches were semi-independent monasteries where monks lived in a community and obeyed a set of rules whereby holiness was achieved through austerity and strict discipline. Some monasteries were large compounds and others small hermitages, but in general the monastic nature of early Irish Christianity contrasted with the centrally-administered, diocese-based European system.

Early monastic sites are generally set within a circular or oval enclosure that may have provided some defence but which was primarily a spiritual boundary where sanctuary was provided within the enclosure. Sometimes the sites are enclosed by two or three concentric walls and on these sites the churches are generally within the central enclosure, with most of the associated settlement contained within the outer enclosure. The earliest churches were constructed of wood and it is unclear when stone churches became the norm. Although the first stone churches probably date to the eighth century, there was probably a period of overlap and wooden churches may have been common up to the eleventh or twelfth centuries. Another feature of the monasteries were the crosses placed around the monastery, sometimes in the centre of the enclosure, sometimes at the four cardinal points and sometimes at the entrances to the monastery. Often these crosses marked the *tearmann* or boundary of the area of sanctuary. As with the churches, the first crosses were probably fashioned from wood, with stone crosses first appearing in the eighth century.

There may be as many as nineteen early ecclesiastical sites on the Burren. These range in scale from small and simple hermitages to larger monastic complexes. Traditionally, archaeologists have identified early ecclesiastical sites in the field by the presence of characteristic features such as a roughly circular enclosure around the site, special graves (see Figure 217 and Figure 218), *leachtanna* (see Figure 67), a round tower, bullaun stones (see Figure 61), cross-inscribed slabs, a holy well, sometimes a souterrain, and sometimes an association with an early saint. Particular architectural features which occur on some churches are also traditionally taken to be indicators of an early date. These architectural features are trabeate doorways (see Figure 221 and Figure 227), *antae* (see Figure 198 and Figure 226), projecting corbels (see Figure 68) and cyclopean masonry (see Figure 69, Figure 198 and Figure 226).

This 'list of early features' approach is the one commonly in use by archaeologists today and although it is the best approach, given the current state of knowledge, archaeologists are beginning to realise its shortcomings. In particular, there is a continuing accumulation of evidence which suggests that many of the supposed 'early' features may not be all that early. The cyclopean masonry, for instance, may be no earlier than the eleventh century and at St Mac Duagh's hermitage there is a *leacht* (an open-air, rectangular stone 'altar') built on top of the ruins of the church which indicates a late date for that particular *leacht* at least (see *St Mac Duagh's Hermitage at Keelhilla* and also *Radiocarbon Dating the Churches of the Aran Islands*). A traditional association with an early saint may not be a reliable indicator of an early date either, as it seems that most sites are associated with early saints and many of these associations may have been drawn centuries after the saints had died and therefore give no real evidence for the site's date.

The placename elements *kil* and *disert* are also sometimes taken as clues that an ecclesiastical site may have early origins. *Disert* is derived from the Latin *desertum* and means 'hermitage'. *Kil* is derived from the Latin *cella* meaning 'a room within a building', sometimes 'a shrine within a temple' and when used in placenames, translates as 'church, monastic settlement, churchyard or graveyard'. Placenames on the Burren that incorporate the *kil* element include Kilfenora 'the church of the white ridge/meadow', Killeany 'the church of St Éinne/Enda',

Killonaghan 'the church of St Onchu', Kilmoon 'the church of St Mogua' and numerous others. The element *disert* is not included in any Burren placenames but does occur in the nearby Dysert O'Dea.

All in all, the question of which ecclesiastical sites may have had early origins is a very difficult one and one which in most cases can probably only be answered with excavation. The four sites discussed here – Rathborney, Oughtmama, St Mac Duagh's and Glencolumbkille – all have hints of early beginnings but most of the visible archaeology on these sites is Medieval.

Rathborney

Grid Reference M 208 047

Rathborney is an interesting site located on the steep northern bank of the Rathborney River, one of the rare rivers that flows for a short distance on the surface of the Burren rather than in an underground channel. Although the church at Rathborney is late Medieval, probably built in the late fifteenth or early sixteenth centuries, several features suggest that the Medieval church is located on a much earlier ecclesiastical site. These indicators of an early Christian site at Rathborney are a souterrain in the graveyard west of the church, the curving south wall of the graveyard which may follow the line of an early enclosure and a bullaun stone.

Figure 61
Bullaun stone at Rathborney.

Bullaun stones or basin stones are often found on early ecclesiastical sites. Their use is not clear but they may have been used to pound grain or herbs, or perhaps as receptacles for holy water. The one pictured here is in the graveyard at Rathborney and can be found seventeen metres south west of the south-west corner of the church.

◄ Figure 62
Carved stone head at Rathborney.

This carved stone head protrudes from the south wall near the south-west corner of the late Medieval church at Rathborney. It is difficult to determine the date of this head but somewhat similar examples have been found in other late Medieval churches. The longer and narrower face on the Rathborney head seems to distinguish it from the Glencolumbkille head which is probably earlier (see *Glencolumbkille*).

Figure 63 ▼
Late Medieval church at Rathborney.

In the Medieval period Rathborney was in the territory of the O'Lochlain clan. The capital of the Burren O'Lochlain's was at Gragan's castle, just over a kilometre to the south and the Medieval church at Rathborney was probably the clan's primary church.

Oughtmama

Grid Reference M 305 079

The name Oughtmama means 'breast of the pass' and the site is utterly lonely and deserted, though once occupied by a considerable village – Thomas Westropp 1900.

One of the most impressive monastic sites on the Burren is the site of Oughtmama located in a high valley just below Turlough Hill. Visible on the site today are the remains of a double enclosure wall, three churches, a *leacht*, a holy well, a horizontal mill race, terraced fields and settlement remains. There is no history of Oughtmama other than a few very brief mentions in ecclesiastical texts, taxation lists and census records but there does seem to be an association with three different St Colmáns. One of them, St Colmán Mac Duagh, had a hermitage in the remote cave at Keelhilla, five kilometres to the south east (see *St Mac Duagh's Hermitage at Keelhilla*) and on the steep north-eastern slope of the Oughtmama valley there is a holy well dedicated to St Colmán which is reputed to be a cure for eye ailments.

The enclosure walls, the *leacht*, the associations with early saints and several architectural features on the original portion of the western church (see below) all suggest that the monastery at Oughtmama may have been an early foundation but much of the visible archaeology on the site today is Medieval and some may even be post-Medieval. The earliest portion of the western church seems to pre-date the Medieval period (i.e., some time before the late twelfth century) but for the most part the churches at Oughtmama are twelfth/thirteenth century with later alterations. On the present evidence it looks like Oughtmama may have been founded at the very end of the Early Medieval period (some time post-tenth century), risen to prominence in the eleventh–twelfth centuries and then continued as a monastic site perhaps into the post-Medieval period (i.e., post-fifteenth century).

There are three churches at Oughtmama arranged in an east-west layout which is quite rare in Ireland. The layout is common in England but similar monastic churches in Ireland are typically arranged in a north-south pattern. The western church at Oughtmama is the largest and probably witnessed several phases of construction. The original church was a single-celled building with several indications of an early date including a lintelled west doorway, projecting corbels on the gables and cyclopean stone work. In the late twelfth century additional windows were inserted and in the early thirteenth century a chancel was added to the eastern end of the church, thus converting the original building into a nave to accommodate more worshippers. A large arched window stone lies on the ground to the west of the church which may be the top of the original east window that was removed when the chancel was added. In its present position it is reputed to be a cure for headaches.

The two other churches on the site are both small, single-cell buildings which may have been used as small oratories, private chapels or possibly, in the case of the eastern church, a lady chapel (i.e., a chapel for women) as lady chapels were often located away from the centre of monastic sites. Both of the smaller churches were probably built at about the time when the chancel was added to the western church and they may have taken over some of the functions that belonged to the western church before it was expanded. The eastern church is distinguished from the other two in several ways. Whereas the western church and the middle church share the same east-west orientation, the eastern church deviates from their axis and is oriented north-east to south-west. The eastern church is also the only church of the three to have a southern door rather than a western door. Also very significant is the fact that while the western and middle churches were contained within the inner enclosure, the most sacred part of the monastery, the eastern church, seems to be outside the inner enclosure.

The two enclosures seem to have been roughly concentric circles with the diameter of the inner enclosure a little over 100 metres and the diameter of the outer enclosure around 200 metres. The enclosures are not always easy to discern in the field today but standing in the valley the southern semi-circle of the outer enclosure is marked by a wall that runs along the divide between the completely bare crag outside the enclosure and the area within the enclosure which has a thin soil cover. The northern half of the outer enclosure can be clearly seen when one looks down on the site from Turlough Hill. The inner enclosure is even harder to see because its southern half is completely cloaked in hazel and its northern half seems to have been removed.

Interestingly, the enclosures straddle an ecological divide, with the northern half of the enclosed area consisting of deep, glacially deposited soil and the southern half consisting of limestone crag with only a very thin soil cover. The half with deep soil has been terraced and divided into long strip fields, suggesting that crops were grown here. Long narrow fields were often preferred when the fields had to be ploughed because the cumbersome teams of oxen pulling the plough didn't have to be turned as often. Cereals would have been the main crop but vegetables, peas, beans and herbs for cooking and medicine were probably grown as well. In contrast, the craggy half of the enclosure was probably used exclusively for grazing and it has few features within it, other than some flimsy enclosures that were probably used for managing animals.

In the fields just east of the eastern church, the foundations of several rectangular buildings are visible. There has been no excavation at Oughtmama and so the date of these buildings is unknown but its likely that they are either Medieval or post-Medieval. Because the buildings are located outside the inner enclosure, they are most likely the remains of the domestic buildings of the monastery. These buildings may have been the dormitory, kitchen, dining hall, workshops and classrooms of the monastery. We can get some idea of the variety of the monk's diet in the third field east of the eastern church. This field has been terraced and was probably used as a garden plot. The terrace is flecked with fragments of shells and animal bones suggesting that rubbish was tipped here, probably to fertilise the garden. The shells show the monk's diet included limpets, periwinkles, oysters and clams. The presence of limpets is particularly interesting as limpets in shell middens on the coast have sometimes been explained by archaeologists as evidence for their use as bait, the assumption being that limpets are too unpalatable to be used as food. The presence of limpet shells at Oughtmama, 2.5 kilometres from the shore, clearly shows they weren't being collected just for bait.

The Horizontal Water Mill at Oughtmama

(see Figure 66 for location)

Because of the porous nature of the limestone, there are very few above-ground streams on the Burren. Rather than running on the surface, streams tend to follow underground paths. Oughtmama is one of the rare places on the Burren where water emerges from springs and then runs on the surface for a short distance before disappearing underground again. The streambed at Oughtmama runs down the middle of the enclosed area and the very faint remains of a millrace for diverting the stream into a chute to power a mill wheel can just be made out here. Horizontal watermills were introduced into Ireland in the seventh century, and they were a major labour-saving improvement on the earlier hand-powered rotary querns. As there is no trace of the wheelhouse at Oughtmama it was probably a wooden two-storeyed building with the horizontal mill wheel in the lower storey and the millstones

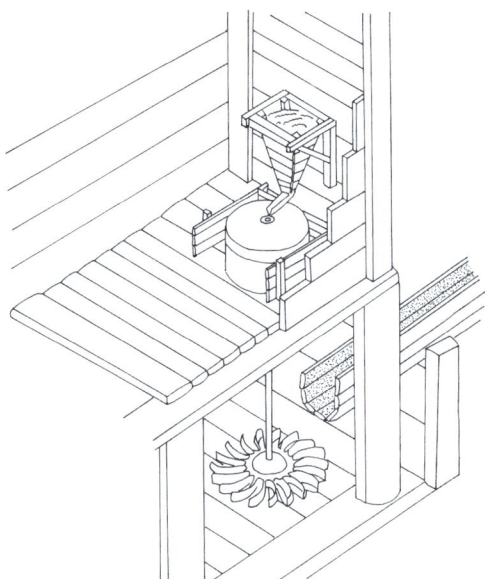

Figure 64 ▲
Conjectural reconstruction of the horizontal mill at Oughtmama.

Figure 65 ▶
View of Oughtmama looking north from Turlough Hill.

The two western churches of the monastery are visible as well as the narrow strip fields which run north from the churches and terminate at the northern wall of the outer enclosure which is visible here as a slightly curving wall lined in places with bushes. Beyond the outer enclosure the remainder of the valley floor is divided into much larger fields.

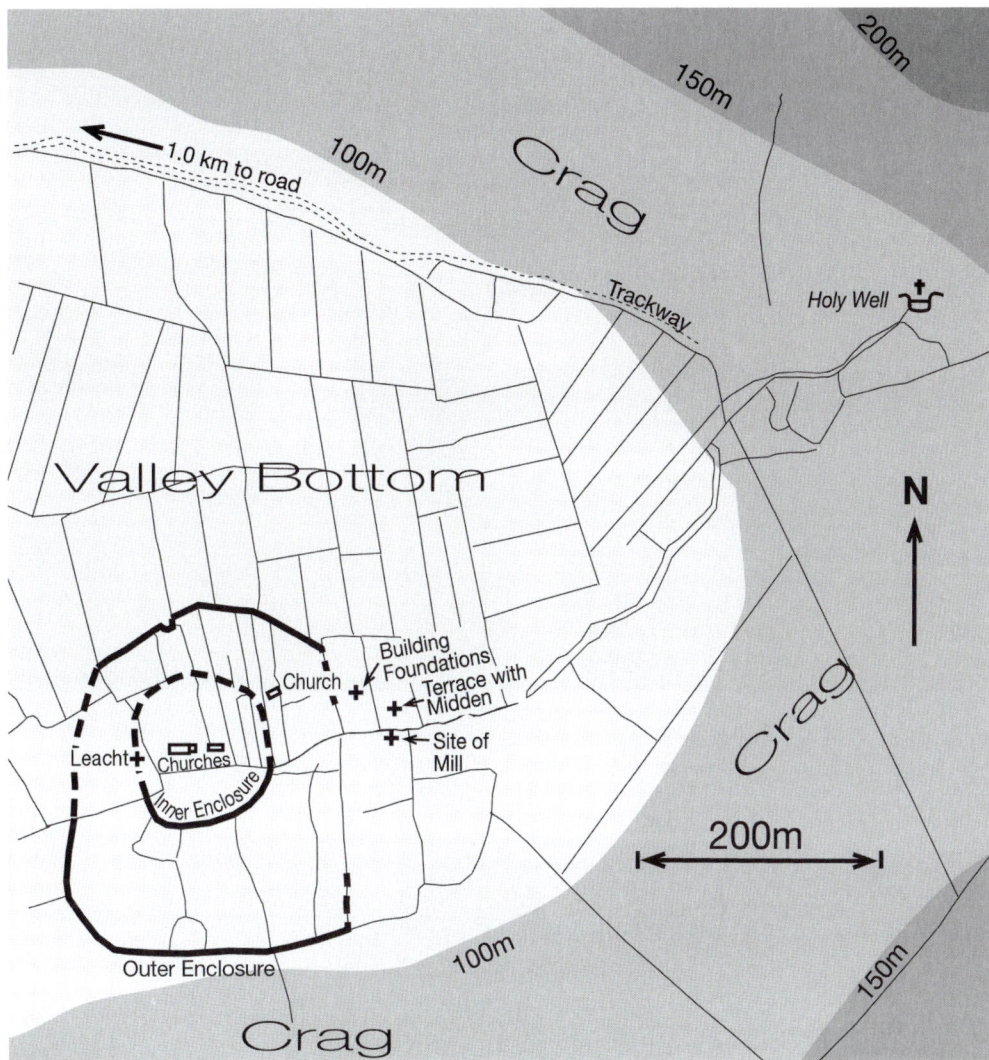

The map of Oughtmama showing Valley Bottom, Crag, Trackway, Holy Well, Church, Building Foundations, Terrace with Midden, Site of Mill, Leacht, Churches, Inner Enclosure, Outer Enclosure. Scale 200m. Contour lines at 100m, 150m, 200m. 1.0 km to road.

Figure 67
Leacht at Oughtmama. ▲

Leachtanna (the plural of *leacht*) are small rectangular stone mounds found on many early ecclesiastical sites. Some may have been used as open-air altars and some were certainly incorporated into pilgrimage rounds. Although by no means certain, it's possible that some *leachtanna* may mark the graves of important people such as early saints, while others may have been dedicated to people buried elsewhere. The word *leacht* translates as a 'grave', a 'grave mound' or a 'memorial cairn'. The example shown here is located in the field just west of the western church.

◀ Figure 66
Map of Oughtmama.

in the upper storey. Water would have entered the lower storey via a chute or sluice that directed its flow against the paddles of the mill wheel. This would turn the wheel which had a central shaft that projected through the ceiling into the upper storey and was attached directly to the upper millstone. The lower millstone remained stationary while the upper stone turned, thereby grinding the grain. This is a simpler mechanism than a vertical watermill which requires a gear mechanism to convert the vertical rotation of the mill wheel into the horizontal rotation of the millstone. A water-powered mill would have been important not only to the monks of Oughtmama but probably also to the economy of the surrounding area as well.

Figure 68 ▶
The western church and the middle church at Oughtmama.

The west gable of the western church has a lintelled trabeate doorway and projecting corbels on the gables, both of which are early features. The chancel on the western church can be seen clearly here as a later addition extending the church to the east beyond the original eastern gable of the church.

Figure 69
South wall of the western church at Oughtmama showing cyclopean masonry.

The term 'cyclopean' refers to the massive size of some of the stones used in this early style of masonry. The effect was usually achieved by placing large, relatively thin slabs on edge as inner and outer courses of the wall and then filling the core of the wall with smaller stones. ▶

Figure 70 ▼
East window of the eastern church at Oughtmama.

St Mac Duagh's Hermitage at Keelhilla

Grid Reference M 329 042

Part of the early monastic tradition in Ireland was the practice of retiring from the world to a hermitage. Favoured locations for hermitages included offshore islands such as Skellig Michael off the Kerry coast and islands in lakes. Other remote locations, however, were also used and St Mac Duagh's hermitage at the base of the cliffs of Kinallia, on the remote and barren eastern edge of the Burren, is a good example of an inland hermitage.

Tradition tells us that here, in a small cave at the base of the cliff, St Colmán Mac Duagh meditated, prayed and fasted for seven years. One day his servant complained that he was hungry and St Mac Duagh replied that God would provide. There was a banquet at the time in King Guaire's castle in Kinvarra and at that moment the dishes of food suddenly rose and floated out the window. The surprised king and his men followed the dishes and were led to St Mac Duagh and his servant. But when the king's party arrived at the hermitage their feet became rooted to the stone and they couldn't move. Luckily for the king and his men, St Mac Duagh was able to perform a miracle and free them, whereupon the king was so impressed with St Mac Duagh he asked him to found the monastery of Kilmacduagh on the lowlands near Gort. While this was taking place St Mac Duagh's servant was eating King Guaire's food with gusto but unfortunately had grown so accustomed to the meagre diet he received in the service of St Mac Duagh that the rich banquet food killed him. These traditions are preserved to this day in the name of the track that leads to the hermitage, *Bóthar na méisel,* or 'way of the dishes', and in the nearby 'Grave of the Saint's Servant'.

St Mac Duagh's cave can still be seen and there are several other interesting features on the site as well, including a small oratory, two *leachtanna*, a bullaun stone and a holy well. About 400 metres to the south east is the 'Grave of the Saint's Servant', which consists of a semi-circular stone enclosure and two more *leachtanna*, each with an undecorated upright slab on top. The features at Keelhilla, its remote location and the traditions associated with it all suggest the site was an early hermitage site, possibly dating to the seventh century, when St Mac Duagh is supposed to have lived. The site had certainly become a place of pilgrimage by the nineteenth century and it is likely that pilgrims began visiting the site much earlier, in Medieval times.

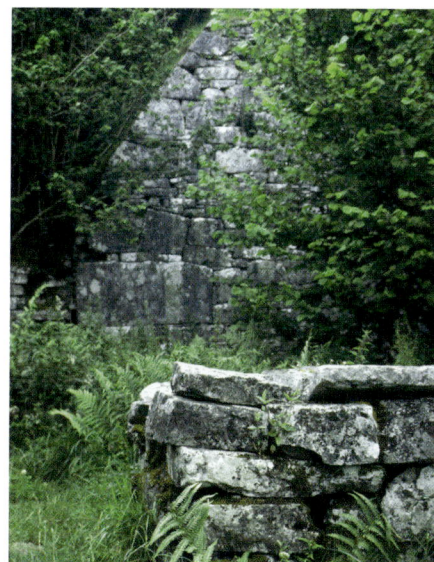

◄ Figure 71
The cliffs of Kinallia.

St Mac Duagh found this remote location at the base of the cliffs of Kinallia a suitable retreat from the world.

Figure 72 ▲
Leacht **and gable of the oratory at St Mac Duagh's hermitage.**

Figure 73 ▲
St Mac Duagh's cave.

Figure 75 ▶
Holy well at St Mac Duagh's hermitage.

Figure 74 ▶
Stones formerly on top of a *leacht* at St Mac Duagh's hermitage.

In the late nineteenth century, Thomas Westropp reported . . . *several round stones, and a flat stone with two long round-ended depressions* . . . on top of one of the *leachtanna*. The round stones may have been used in a manner similar to rosary beads to keep count of the prayers and 'rounds' performed at each station. Similar stones on other sites were moved, one for each round, as the pilgrim progressed. They are also sometimes referred to as 'cursing stones'. The flat stone with the two depressions was probably an Early Medieval mould for metal ingots. It's likely that it was found elsewhere and placed on the *leacht* because its finder thought its curious shape had some significance.

Glencolumbkille

Grid Reference R 319 992

Glencolumbkille is another ecclesiastical site located on the eastern Burren that may have begun as an early monastic foundation. At Glencolumbkille the presence of a circular enclosure and some possibly early finds from the site (Figure 77) suggest it may have had an early foundation date. Although its location might seem fairly remote today, we know from Medieval historical accounts that the pass above Glencolumbkille was used as an entryway into the Burren. Today, the visible remains on the site consist of the ruins of a Medieval church, traces of a large oval enclosure around the church, the shaft of a stone cross, a nearby holy well and penitential stations on the pass high above that may be associated with the site. There is also a stone bearing 'the mark of the saint's fingers' concealed in the bushes alongside the road near the church but only a local will be able to point it out to you.

Figure 76
The church at Glencolumbkille.

Figure 77 ▼

Carved stone head from Glencolumbkille.

This very interesting carved stone head was found during an archaeological survey of Glencolumbkille in 1989 directed by Dr. Sinéad Ní Ghabláin. The shape of the face and flattened profile of the face are similar to some pre-Christian stone carvings but the simple closed mouth contrasts with the pre-Christian examples which generally have large, open mouths. The date of the carving is, therefore, not clear but stylistic similarities with other carvings would seem to place it in the eighth or ninth century AD. Also interesting in light of the possibly early date of the stone head is an antiquarian account of an Iron Age beehive quernstone being found on this site in the nineteenth century. It may be that Glencolumbkille is a site that spans the pre-Christian / Christian divide. The Glencolumbkille head is now on display in the Clare County Museum.

Much of the enclosure has been destroyed in the recent past but in the early twentieth century Thomas Westropp described it as being ten to twelve feet thick, six feet high in some places and faced with stone. Today, only a short section of the enclosure survives. It consists of a low earthen bank topped with shrubs south-east of the church. Originally, the enclosure was a large oval measuring approximately 75 by 100 metres across with the church at its centre. The church is also in a more ruinous state then when Westropp visited the site but the east gable is still standing with its tall lancet window and this part of the church probably dates to the twelfth century. Westropp recorded a later fifteenth century doorway in the church but this has since collapsed. The fifteenth century door on the church indicates that the site was still in use late in the Medieval period, but its exact function at this time is unclear. It may have functioned as a parish church or it may have been a private chapel for the local O'Loughlins who lived in Glencolumbkille Castle, just a kilometre to the north.

◄ Figure 78

Base and shaft of a cross at Glencolumbkille.

It's likely that this cross marked the entrance to the enclosure which surrounded the site. It is located just east of the church where a gate leads on to the road. Although an earlier cross may have stood at this location, the form of the present shaft indicates that it is probably late Medieval.

Figure 79
Penitential stations at the summit of the pass above Glencolumbkille.
Grid Reference R 310 996

These penitential stations at the summit of the pass above Glencolumbkille were presumably approached from the direction of the church (ascending from the east being the only difficult approach and, therefore, the only approach worthy of penance). They may, therefore, be associated with a penitential pattern that included the church site in the valley below.

Cahercommaun and the
Early Medieval Chiefdoms of the Burren

Grid Reference R 282 965

Cahercommaun is a spectacularly sited cliff fort in the eastern Burren near the village of Carron. It is an impressive triple-walled construction with an inner wall up to 8.5 metres thick and an outer wall that encompasses an area 116 metres across. Altogether, around 16,500 cubic metres of stone were used in its construction. The imposing nature of Cahercommaun and its spectacular location did not come about by chance. Cahercommaun was the residence of a wealthy and powerful Early Medieval chief and the impressive dimensions and location of his residence emphasised his high status.

In the Early Medieval period Ireland was divided into small chiefdoms or kingdoms called *túatha*. Each *túath* had a chief or king, several lesser lords of various ranks, free farmers who held land, free farmers with no land and at the bottom of the hierarchy, slaves. The number of chiefdoms in Ireland would have varied according to the course of politics but at any one time there were probably around 150 chiefdoms, each composed of around 3,000 people. Each *túath* was organised in a strict hierarchy where the amount of land held, the number of clients an individual had and an individual's honour price (the amount that was paid to rectify an offence against the individual) all increased with rank. Power was based on a system of 'clientship' where the lord advanced a grant of livestock to the client and received food rents, labour services and military services in return. In this society, where cattle were of paramount importance, a man's status was based on the number of cattle he owned, and land was valued in terms of cattle as well.

Figure 80 ▶
Silver brooch from Cahercommaun.

This spectacular silver brooch was found in one of the souterrains of Cahercommaun. The expanded terminals of the hoop are richly decorated with settings of amber and gold, as well as representations of birds and a four-legged animal. The head of the pin also has a setting with traces of gold plate and two elongated animals facing each other. The pin stem is actually a replacement and, whereas the original pin head and the hoop are silver, the replacement pin stem is a tinned copper alloy.

As there were no banks at the time, elaborate brooches such as this could be held as assets and wealthy people accumulated stocks of jewellery, precious metals and coins. Ring brooches and other jewellery were often given by a king to his lords in return for loyalty and service, and wearing these gifts could indicate one's loyalties, as well as proclaiming one's rank and wealth.

◀ Figure 81
Cahercommaun from the air.

The three concentric walls of Cahercommaun enclose a total of just under two acres. The inner wall is a complete circuit, although it is much thinner along the edge of the cliff. The outer walls probably originally terminated at the cliff but today they stop a bit short, probably because they have been robbed out to provide stones for the more recent field wall that runs along the cliff top. The walls are of drystone construction. Each is constructed with a relatively carefully laid inner and outer course and a rubble core.

Figure 82 ▶

Inner wall of Cahercommaun.

The inner wall is by far the most massive. It has a maximum width of 8.5 metres and today rises to a maximum height of 4.3 metres. It is terraced on the interior with the lowest terrace surviving around most of the wall and a second, higher terrace surviving along the south-west portion.

Figure 83 ▶

The entrance way of Cahercommaun.

The entrance to the fort is a paved path flanked by walls. It passes through all three walls and opens to the east. Where it passed through the inner wall, the entrance way was probably a covered passage but today there is no roof. Immediately inside the entrance to the inner enclosure, there are buildings on both sides of the entrance which have the effect of extending the entrance passageway several metres into the fort.

◀ Figure 84

Wall joint in the masonry of Cahercommaun.

Throughout the fort there are vertical joints in the masonry. It's quite possible that these joints are the result of one work gang finishing and another beginning. The chief's power was based on a system of 'clientship', where those under the chief were obligated to provide labour and these joints appear to be physical evidence of the power relationships between the chief and several different sub-groups in the *túath*. Interestingly, the joints do not extend through the basal courses of the walls, demonstrating that the outline of the fort was initially laid out with courses of stones just a few centimetres high.

The Excavation of Cahercommaun

Cahercommaun has a long history of research. It was excavated in 1934 by Hugh O'Neill Hencken as part of the Harvard Archaeological Expedition to Ireland, it was the focus of a survey in the 1980s by Blair Gibson of UCLA who was investigating the chiefdom centred on Cahercommaun, and in the 1990s Hencken's excavation was reassessed as part of the Discovery Programme's 'Western Stone Forts Project'.

The cliff fort as we see it today was probably built some time in the ninth century AD but there is also evidence for occupation of the site dating back to the fifth and sixth centuries AD. The majority of the artefacts recovered from the excavation are ordinary, functional artefacts that cannot be precisely dated. A few, however, are chronologically diagnostic and these finds cover the period from the fifth to the tenth centuries AD. This date range for the occupation of the site has also been supported by recent radiocarbon dates obtained from some of the cattle bone that Hencken excavated back in the 1930s. The radiocarbon dates give a range from the late seventh to the late tenth century AD.

The focus of habitation at the fort appears to have been the inner enclosure as hardly any trace of occupation was found in the outer two enclosures. Most of the flimsy walls visible today in the outer enclosures are probably much later constructions, built amongst the ruins of the fort long after it went out of use. There are, however, two radial walls dividing the area between the middle wall and the outer wall that are original. These walls indicate these areas were segregated during the occupation of the fort – perhaps animals were housed here.

In the inner enclosure Hencken identified eleven stone structures and two occupation layers. The occupation layers consisted of ash-rich layers with hearths separated by a 're-flooring' layer of stones and earth. Unfortunately, the structures and the occupation layers could not be related as the structures occurred for the most part in the northern portion of the interior and the occupation layers were in the south. Because all the structures were resting directly on the bedrock, Hencken concluded they were all built at the same time. He also thought the structures had remained in use throughout the two phases of occupation evidenced by the separate ashy layers.

In the 1990s the Discovery Programme reassessed Hencken's excavation and replaced his interpretation of a two-phase occupation with a three-phase occupation scheme. In this new scheme, the main phase of occupation at Cahercommaun is represented by two sets of conjoined circular buildings and the two souterrains that lead off of them in the north of the interior enclosure (Structures 5&6 and 7&8 on Hencken's plan, see Figure 86). These buildings appear to have been substantial round houses and they have features such as under-floor drains and central hearths lined with slabs. Prior to this main occupation, there appears to have been an initial phase represented by some back-filled buildings and a rotary quern fragment built into Structure 6.

The houses of the main occupation are arranged along the north side of the interior. The remainder of the interior at this time may have been clear or it may have been occupied by less substantial timber buildings, possibly work sheds. The final occupation phase is represented by the structure in the centre of the inner enclosure, Structure 4 on Hencken's plan (see Figure 86). The walls of this structure survived to a height of almost a metre in places and were the most visible remains in the inner enclosure before excavation, suggesting Structure 4 was later than the other buildings. Also, the floor plan of Structure 4 appears to be rectilinear, and therefore contrasts with the circular buildings of the main occupation. It is generally thought that throughout Early Medieval Ireland, rectangular houses are later than round houses.

Figure 85
Hencken's overall plan of Cahercommaun made during his 1934 excavation.

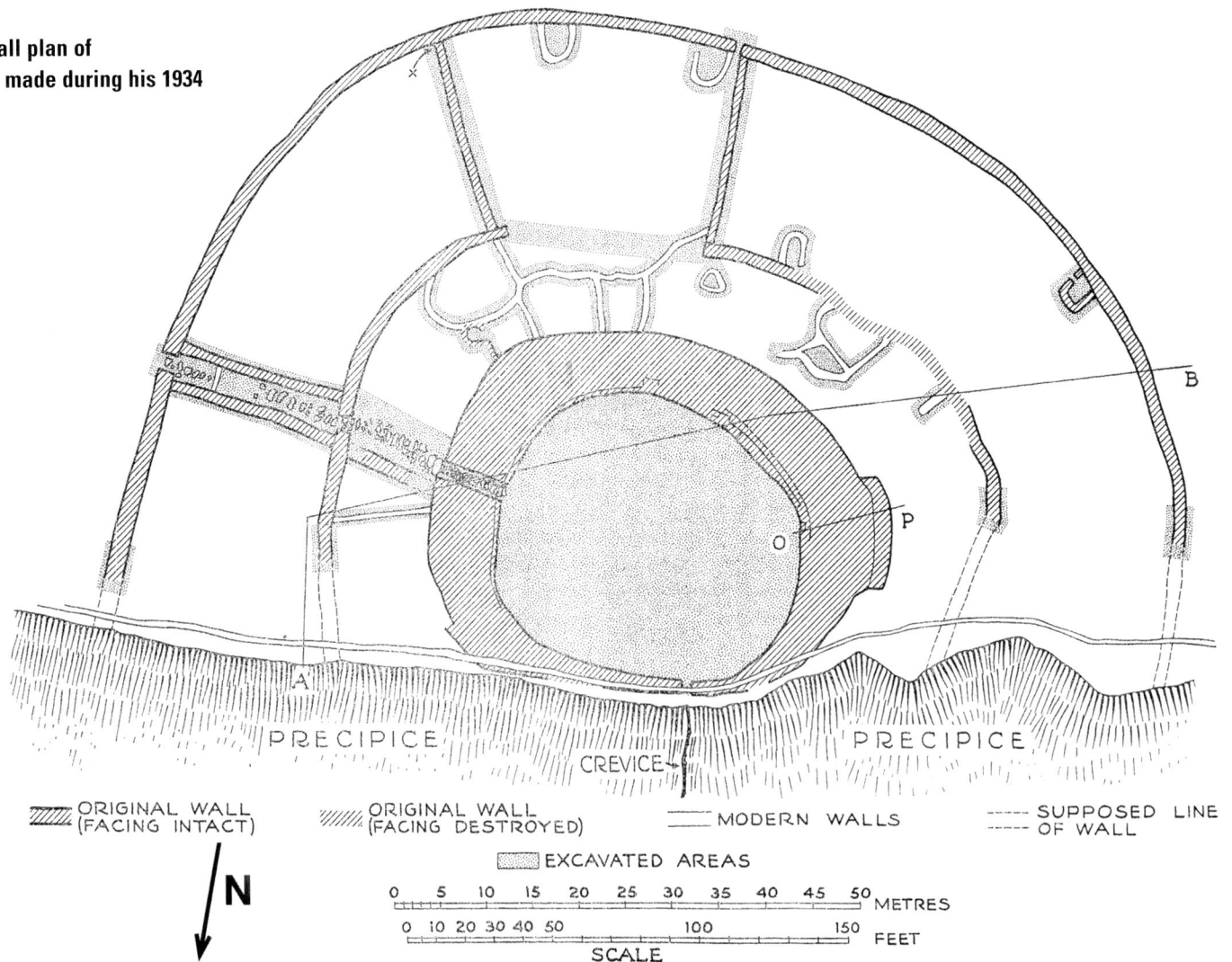

PRECIPICE   CREVICE   PRECIPICE

ORIGINAL WALL (FACING INTACT)   ORIGINAL WALL (FACING DESTROYED)   MODERN WALLS   SUPPOSED LINE OF WALL

EXCAVATED AREAS

N

0 5 10 15 20 25 30 35 40 45 50 METRES

0 10 20 30 40 50   100   150 FEET

SCALE

Figure 86

Hencken's plan of the inner enclosure and one of his sections through the stratigraphy.

Hencken's excavation of Cahercommaun was part of the Harvard Archaeological Expedition to Ireland. The Expedition excavated fifteen sites in Ireland between 1932 and 1936 with the goal of investigating sites from early prehistory to the eleventh century AD. This work marked the beginning of scientific archaeological excavation in Ireland. The Harvard team had a research design, used modern excavating techniques, investigated large and complex sites and published detailed excavation reports. An integral part of the excavation was the production of plans (views from above) and sections (views of vertical sections through the stratigraphy). These drawings were used to establish the relationships between different layers on the site and between the artefacts contained in those layers.

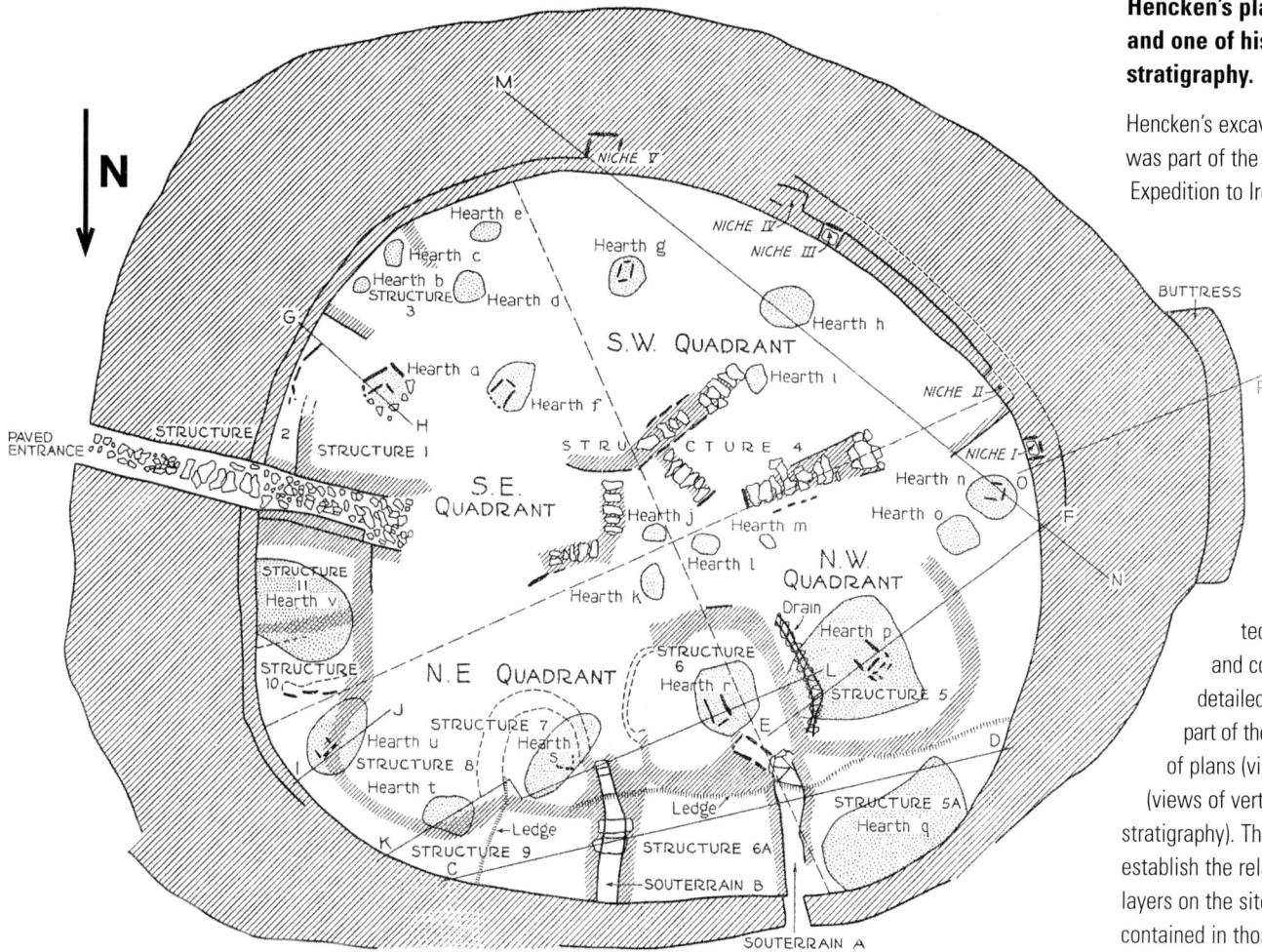

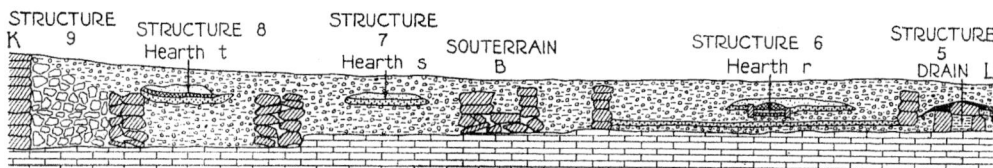

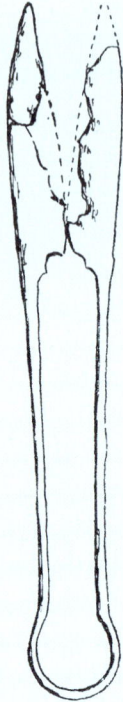

Figure 87 ▲
Shears from Cahercommaun.

Shears were used to cut the wool from the sheep.

Wool Production at Cahercommaun

Fifty-five spindle whorls, twenty possible pin beaters and five shears were recovered from the Cahercommaun excavations. The large number of these artefacts suggests that wool processing was a significant activity on the site.

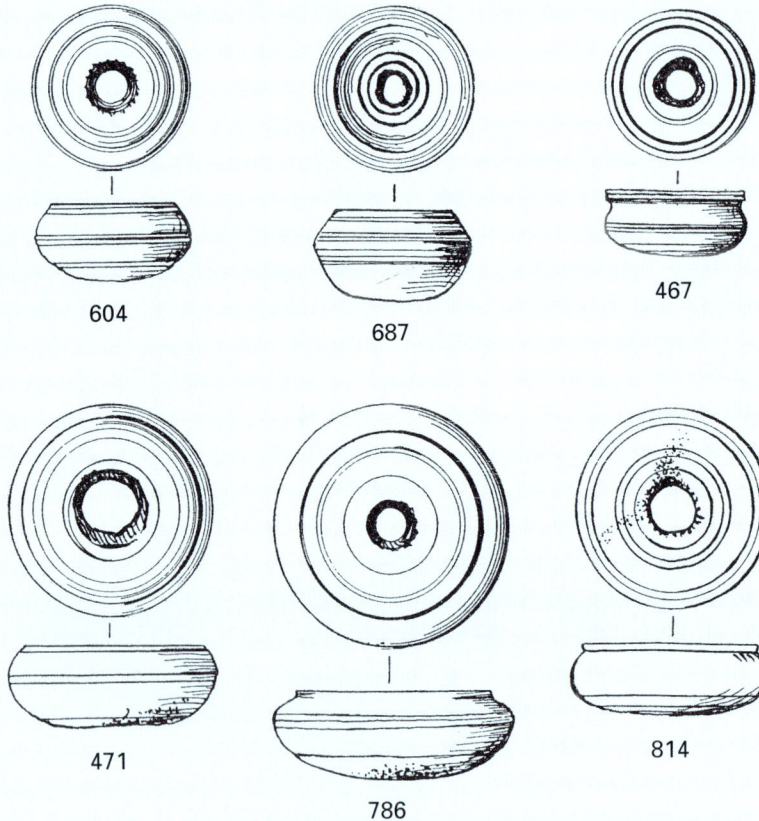

604

687

467

471

786

814

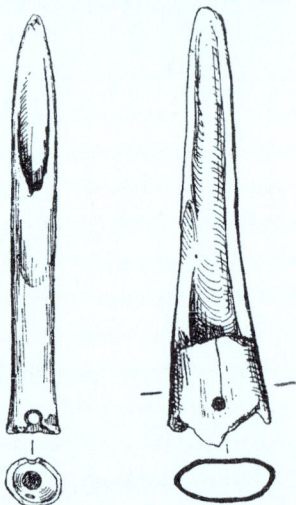

◀ Figure 88
Bone tools from Cahercommaun.

After the thread had been spun it was woven into cloth on a loom. It's possible that these bone tools were used as pin beaters to beat down the weft during weaving. (This is only one possible interpretation of these tools. Other similar tools have been interpreted as bone spear heads.)

Figure 89 ▲
Spindle whorls from Cahercommaun.

These whorls were mounted on wooden pins, or spindles, which were used to draw the raw wool into thread.

Ironworking at Cahercommaun

Ironworking was a widespread and common activity in Early Medieval Ireland. There appears to have been a large degree of self-sufficiency in ironworking and iron slag has turned up on nearly all excavations of Early Medieval settlement sites. At Cahercommaun, many small pieces of slag were found scattered about the site as well as three large circular cakes of slag that had come from the bottom of a smelting furnace. There were also over 500 whetstones and scored sharpening stones, most of which appear to have been used to sharpen pins and pointed implements made of metal or bone. Iron objects were very common finds in the excavations at Cahercommaun and some of these were probably manufactured or repaired on the site. These iron objects included over 60 knives, a bell, a padlock, nails, a belt buckle, a bucket handle, a pot handle, bill hooks, an axe-hammer and many other pieces.

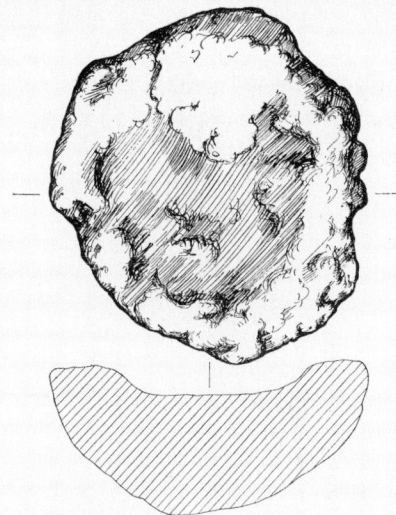

Figure 91
Cake of iron slag from the bottom of a furnace.

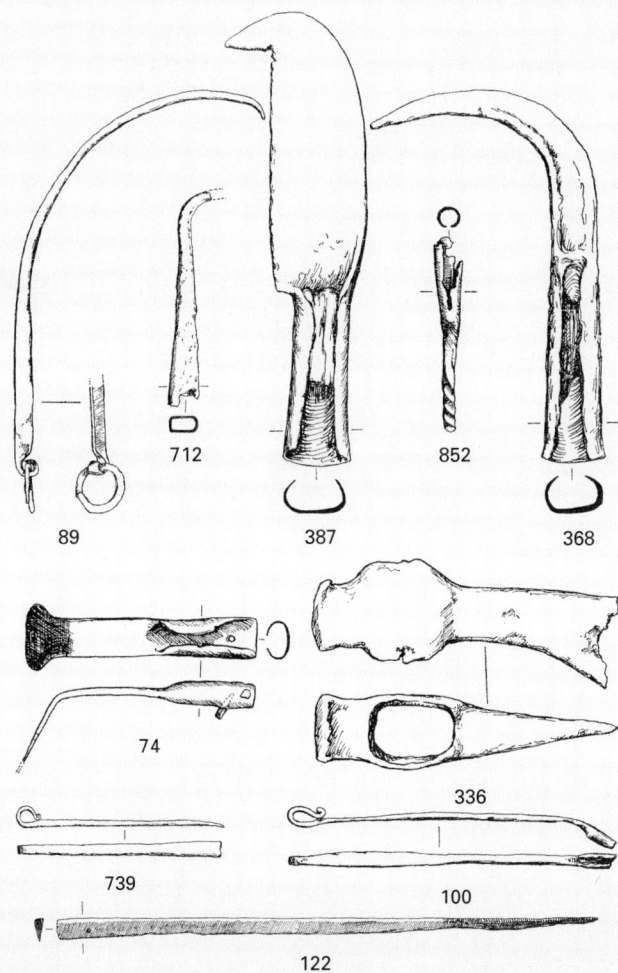

◀ Figure 90
Iron objects from Cahercommaun.

89 & 712 – hooks,
387 & 368 – bill hooks,
852 – socket with twisted end, 74 – pot handle,
336 – axe-hammer, 739 & 100 – possible keys,
122 – spike/skewer.

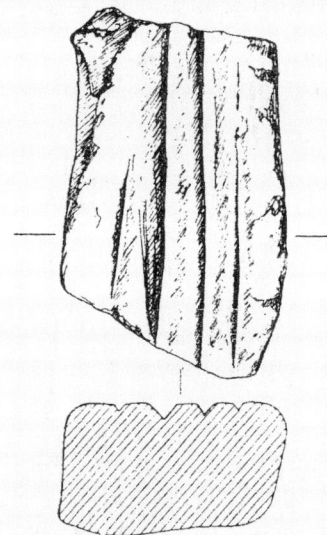

Figure 92
Scored sharpening stone.

Figure 93
Souterrain A at Cahercommaun.

Souterrain A leads from inside Structure 6 to the top of a vertical crevice that runs down the cliff face. The crevice could be scaled, especially with the help of a rope, and it is possible that the souterrain provided a secret escape route down the cliff.

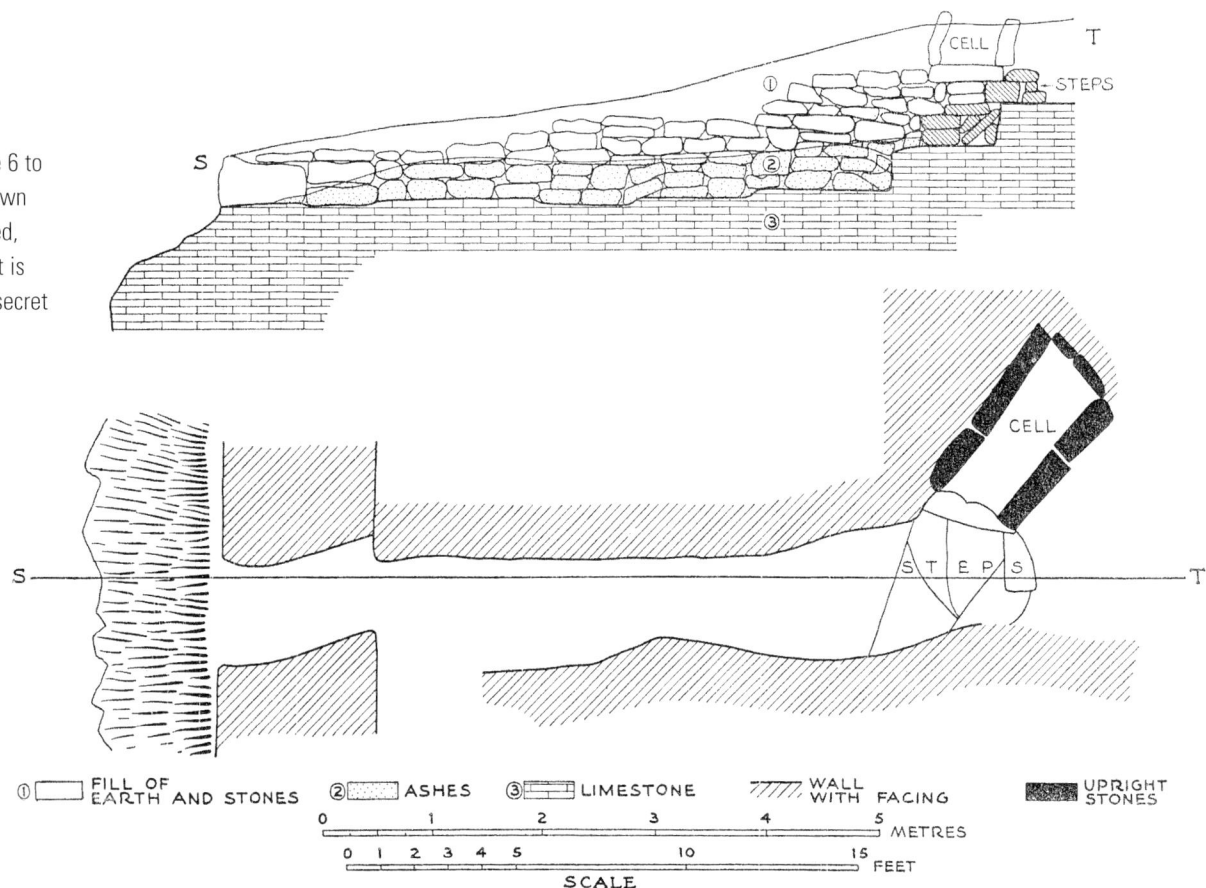

Figure 94
Stone axes from Cahercommaun.

Hencken found some artefacts in his excavations, such as these stone axes, that indicate a prehistoric occupation of the site. These prehistoric finds, however, cannot be linked to any structures on the site. Additionally, some were found in stratigraphic layers that were late in the sequence and so it appears they were reworked into the Early Medieval strata. This is not surprising given the thin soil cover on the Burren and the abundant evidence for prehistoric settlement in the vicinity of Cahercommaun.

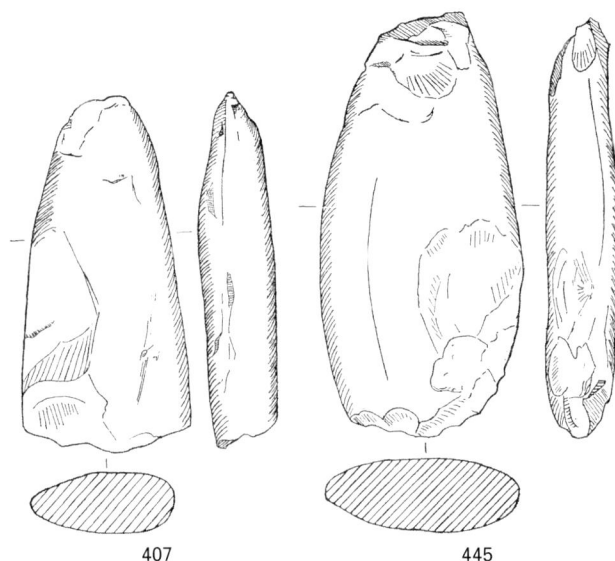

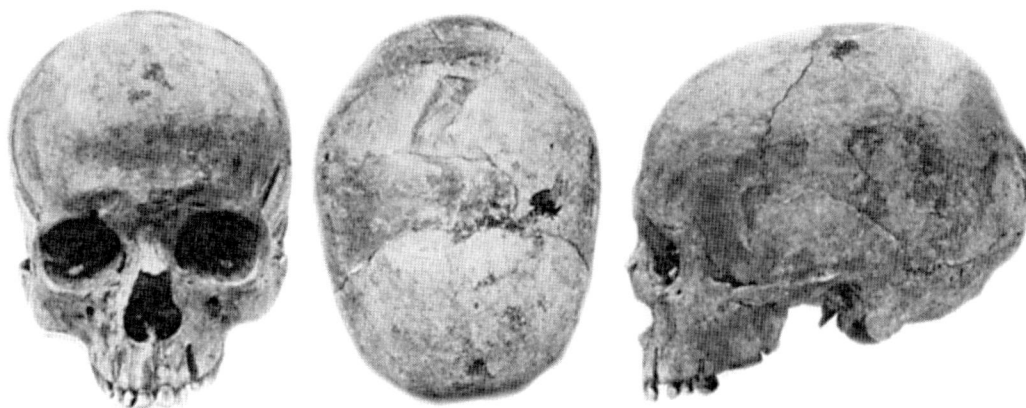

◀ Figure 95
Skull burial from Cahercommaun.

This skull was found placed on a small slab and surrounded by other carefully laid slabs in one of the souterrains. Directly beneath the skull was a large iron hook that may have been used to display the head before it was buried. No other bones of the skeleton were found but directly below the slab on which the skull rested were a complete iron knife and a portion of another.

◀ Figure 96
Animal-headed brooch.

Expensive jewellery was often imitated in less expensive materials. Precious stones were imitated with glass and gold was imitated with gold-coloured copper alloys as is the case with this copper alloy animal-headed brooch.

Figure 97
Enamelled brooch. ▼

This head of a copper alloy brooch is decorated with red and yellow enamelling. Ring brooches are versatile clothes-fastening accessories that were used by men, women and children across Europe. They were used to close the neck of garments, to fasten cloaks and aprons, and, because clothes did not generally have pockets, ring brooches were also used to hang purses, keys, knives and other items from clothing.

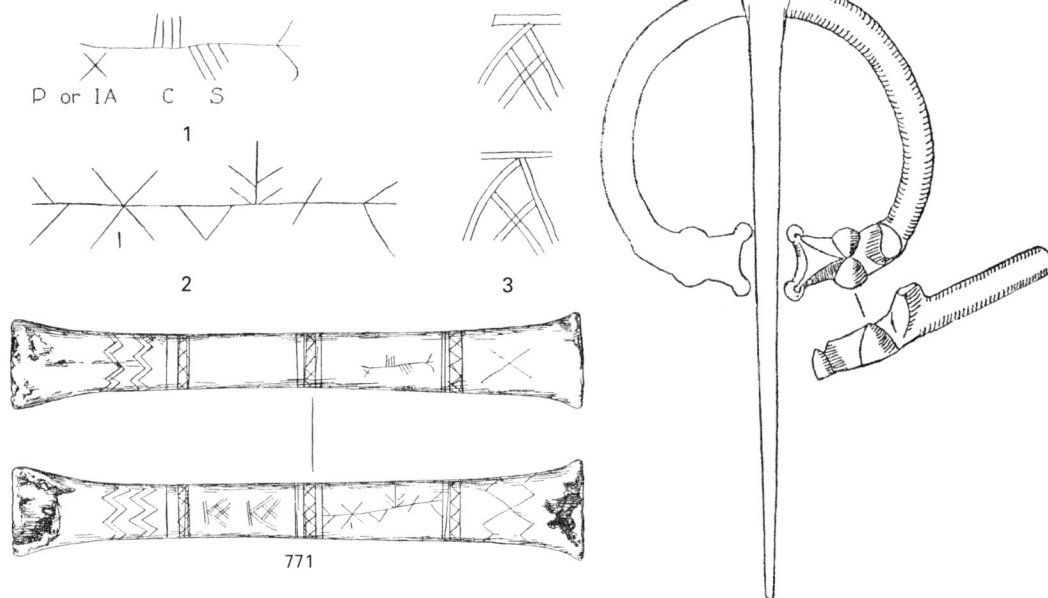

Figure 98 ▲
Sheep bone decorated with incised lines and an *ogham* inscription.

Ogham is an alphabet made up of twenty letters based on the Roman Latin alphabet and it was the first script to be used to write the Irish language. *Ogham* letters are made up of groups of stroke marks set at different angles against a vertical base line. Most *ogham* is carved on pillar stones and the inscriptions are usually commemorative such as 'the stone of X son of Y' or 'the stone of X son of the tribe of Y'. Most *ogham* inscriptions probably date to the fifth and sixth century AD although some may be as early as the fourth century or as late as the eighth century. Inscription number 1 on the bone is shown along with its translation while inscriptions 2 and 3 may be a type of 'cryptic *ogham*'. This 'cryptic *ogham*' may have been used to convey a secret word, possibly one which had magical powers.

The Chiefdom of Corcu Modruad

In the centuries immediately preceding the eighth century AD a chiefdom referred to as the *Corcu Modruad* occupied much of north county Clare. The capital of this chiefdom may have been the impressive stone fort of Caherballykinvarga on the southern edge of the Burren near Kilfenora. At the height of its power, the chiefdom of Corcu Modruad may have stretched from Galway Bay in the north to as far south as the present-day town of Ennis, and from the Atlantic coast on the west to the modern Clare-Galway border on the east.

During the Early Medieval period there was a prolonged struggle for political control of this area and at some point, possibly in the eighth or ninth centuries AD, the *Corcu Modruad* lost the southern portion of their territory to encroaching groups. The principal groups responsible for this encroachment on the *Corcu Modruad* were the *Uí Fidgeinti* from south of the river Shannon and the *Déis Tuaisceart* from south-east Clare. In view of these events, the location and date of the cliff fort at Cahercommaun are very interesting. Cahercommaun is located in what probably became the new border zone between the *Corcu Modruad* and the encroaching groups, and its main occupation coincides with the probable date of the incursion as well. Given these concordances, it has been suggested that Cahercommaun may have been occupied, and possibly even built, by a king of one of the encroaching groups. If this was the case, it is also possible that Cahercommaun was used as a collecting point for tribute from the diminished *Corcu Modruad*.

Figure 99
Caherballykinvarga from the air.
Grid Reference R 201 946

Caherballykinvarga is the possible capital of the Corcu Modruad. The thick band of upright stones around the fort is called a *chevaux de frise* and is intended as an obstacle to attackers.

The Vikings

In the late eighth century AD the Vikings began raiding Ireland and by the ninth century their raids were becoming more and more frequent. They started by raiding monasteries on offshore islands but soon began sailing up rivers in search of new targets. The initial raids were followed by the establishment of 'longphorts' (defended ship ports) and finally by the establishment of the five important coastal trading towns of Dublin, Wexford, Waterford, Cork and Limerick. The Vikings of Limerick controlled a hinterland surrounding their town but probably stretching no further north than the present-day town of Quinn, just outside Ennis. The Burren, therefore, appears to have remained outside the area of prolonged contact with the Vikings. The excavation of Cahercommaun, however, did produce one small piece of evidence of contact, a Scandinavian iron arrowhead.

Figure 100
Scandinavian tanged leaf-shaped arrowhead from Cahercommaun.

The Ringforts of the Burren

All across the Burren are ringforts that are smaller and less impressive than Cahercommaun and Caherballykinvarga. There may be as many as 450 ringforts on the Burren and most of these are enclosed by a single wall or bank rather than multiple walls. These simpler ringforts were the homes of people below the chief in the social hierarchy. Although these sites are termed 'forts' they are really farmsteads with minor defences, built on a scale to deter cattle raiding but not to resist a sustained attack. Ringforts are often referred to as 'cashels' or 'cahers' if they are built of stone or as a 'lios' or a 'rath' if built of earth. There is no functional difference between earthen ringforts and stone-built ringforts – it is merely a reflection of the materials available on a site. Because the Burren is rocky, the majority of its ringforts are built of stone rather than earth and this is reflected in the prevalence of the word 'caher' in their names.

There has been some debate among archaeologists recently as to whether all ringforts were constructed in the Early Medieval period or whether they continued to be built throughout the Medieval period as well. On the one hand, radiocarbon and dendrochronological dates from ringfort excavations in Ireland have fallen consistently between the fifth and the tenth century AD which has led some to suggest that all ringforts date to within this time bracket (i.e., all are Early Medieval). Other researchers, however, have pointed out that most of these dates come from eastern Ireland, the part of Ireland that came under Anglo-Norman control in the late twelfth century and that by contrast, there have been very few ringforts excavated in the west of the country, and therefore few dates from regions that remained under the strongest Gaelic control up to the seventeenth century. These archaeologists argue that although ringforts are the characteristic settlement type of the Early Medieval period in Ireland, in some areas which remained under Gaelic control such as the Burren, this traditional form of Irish farmstead may have continued to be used throughout the Medieval period as well.

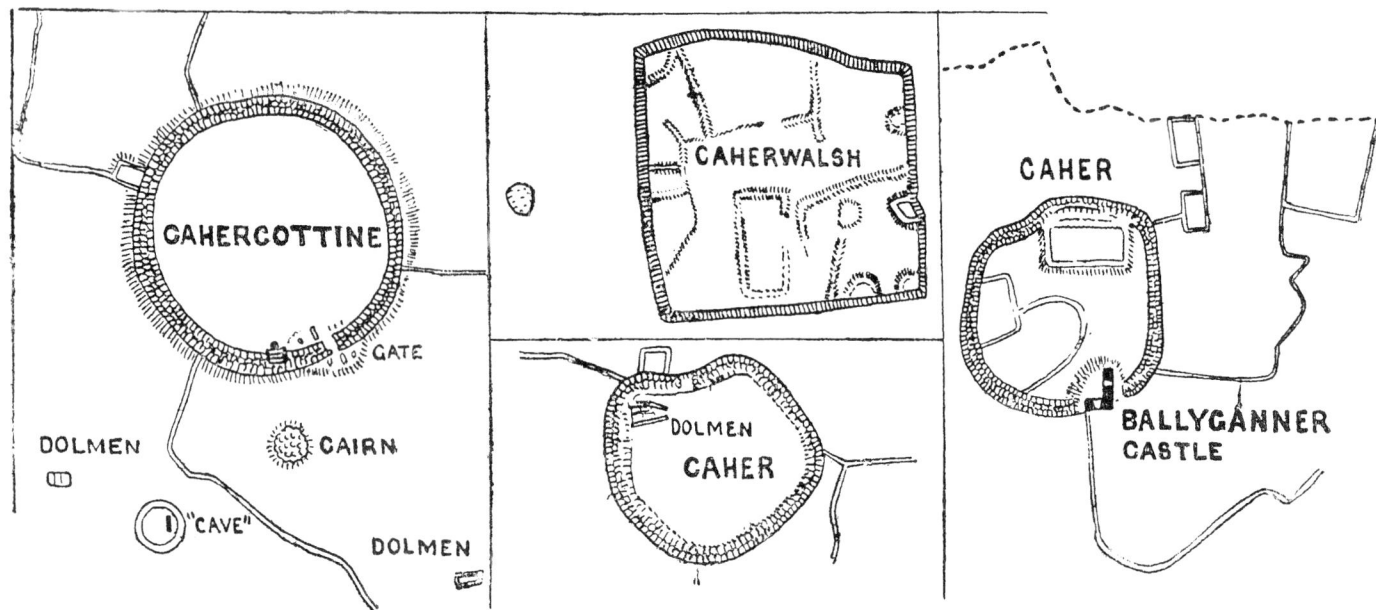

Figure 101
Cashels near Noughaval.
Grid References: Cahercottine R 213 966, Caherwalsh R 213 964, Ballyganner R 220 947,
Cathair na mBithiúnach R 224 953

Cashels are widely spread on the Burren but they are not distributed evenly. One remarkable concentration occurs in the triangle between Kilfenora, Noughaval and Leamaneh and includes the massive fort of Caherballykinvarga. Caherballykinvarga may well have been the capital of the *Corcu Modruad* chiefdom (see *The Chiefdom of Corcu Modruad*) and if so, the concentration of cashels in this area probably represents the densely populated *Corcu Modruad* tribal heartland. This illustration shows four of the cashels in this area and illustrates some of the variations found. Some are quite circular, others are more irregular, some have visible foundations of buildings in their interiors, others do not. Some are even square rather than round but are similar to the circular cashels in the style of their masonry and in their possession of features such as souterrains. At least two cashels on the Burren have tower houses built within them (the black 'L' shape marked at Ballyganner in this figure indicates the collapsed remains of the tower house there) which suggests that these cashels may have been continuously occupied up to the time when tower houses came into vogue some time in the fifteenth or sixteenth century (see *The Tower Houses of the Burren*).

Figure 102
Souterrain in a rectilinear cashel at Caherfadda.
Grid Reference R 259 942

Underground structures called souterrains are often found in ringforts and cashels. We know from documentary sources that they were used as refuges in times of danger and many have defensive features such as sharp directional changes, drop creeps in the floor, sloping passages to prevent the accumulation of smoke and low roofs to constrict movement. When they were used as refuges, they were probably used during short cattle raids where one only had to remain concealed for a brief time. They could have also been used as cool storage cellars, perhaps for dairy products. Because the soil is so shallow on the Burren, the souterrains here tend to be quite simple constructions, often just a straight section of passage that was quarried out along the natural bedding lines of the limestone bedrock and then covered with long lintels.

Figure 103
Caherminnaun and adjacent cashels.
Grid Reference R 197 945

These cashels are clustered around the large chiefly residence of Caherballykinvarga (see Figure 99) and were probably the homes of lower status families. There are some indications in the historical records that people of very low rank might be housed close to the chief while trustworthy relations might occupy more distant cashels located at strategic points in the territory. Some excavated ringforts, however, have yielded no trace of structures or occupation and so it is also possible that some were used as animal enclosures.

◀ Figure 104

Cashel and associated fields at Castletown.

Grid Reference R 280 978

Figure 105 ▶

Caherconnell.

Grid Reference R 236 995

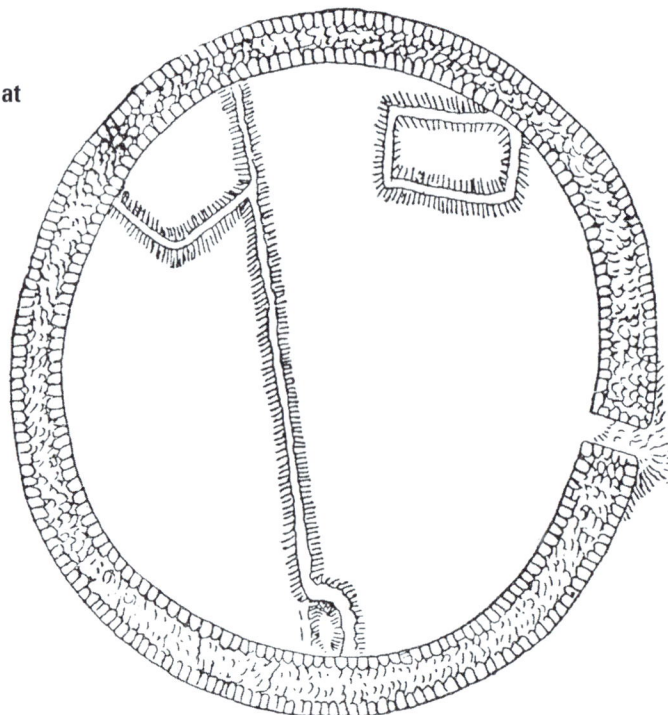

Figure 106 ▶

Cahermore gateway.

Grid Reference M 220 045

Several cashels on the Burren have dressed stones indicative of a Medieval date and at least two of the Burren's cashels, Cahermore and Cahermacnaghten, have Medieval gateways. A limited excavation of just the gateway at Cahermore was undertaken recently and this showed that the gateway was a later addition to the cashel. It consisted of a passageway built with mortared stone which was roofed with stone and probably timber, and flanked by two chambers or small towers. The gateway dates to the fifteenth or sixteenth century, showing that Cahermore was occupied very late in the Medieval period.

The O'Davoren Law School at Cahermacnaghten

In the Early Medieval and Medieval periods legal scholars were trained in special schools such as the O'Davoren school at Cahermacnaghten. The early Irish laws did not operate like our system of modern criminal law, that is, with a view towards punishment or reform. Instead early Irish law prescribed damage liability when someone was wronged. For instance, if one person was injured by another, the law prescribed the fee to be paid to the injured party based on that person's rank and the nature of the injury.

The law tracks tend to be incredibly detailed and include things such as a list of children's games where injured players have no right to compensation and those where they do. Laws also detailed grounds for divorce, stipulating that a man could divorce his wife if she tainted his honour by any of a number of actions including infidelity, constant thieving, obtaining an abortion, or 'making a mess of everything'. A woman might divorce her husband on grounds of his sterility or impotence, or if her husband had a habit of discussing the intimate details of their marriage with others. Laws also detailed the level of violence allowed in a marriage. A husband was allowed to strike his wife to correct her, but if his blow left a lasting mark, she could divorce him.

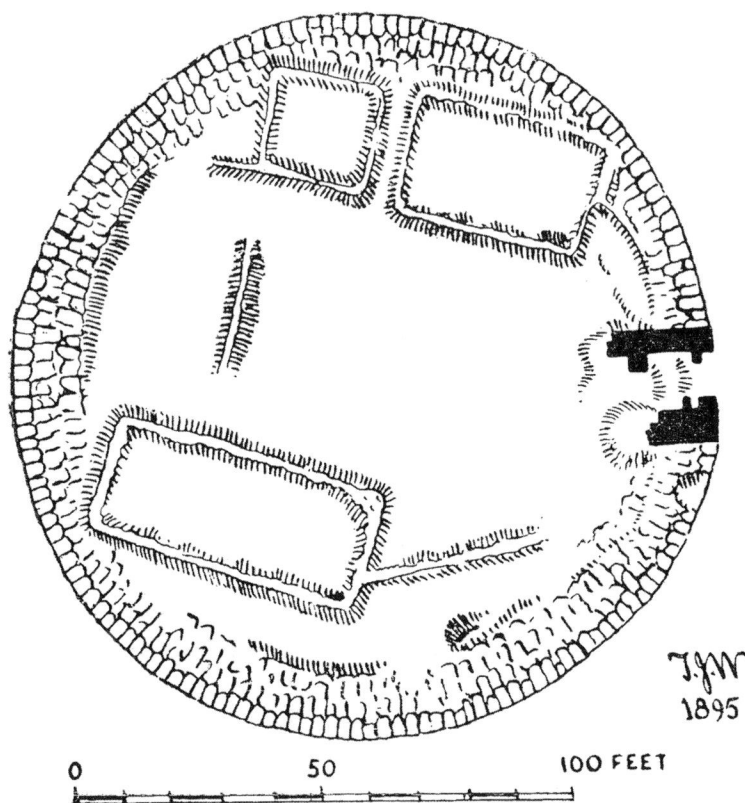

Figure 107
The O'Davoren Law School at Cahermacnaghten.
Grid Reference M 197 001

The outlines of the buildings within the cashel that are visible may be a large house and a kitchen which were described in a 1675 will of one of the O'Davorens.

Figure 108
Cabhail Ti Breac.

Grid Reference R 189 997

Less than a kilometre west of Cahermacnaghten is the site of Cabhail Ti Breac. It is a rectangular building divided into two rooms and it has corbels on the inside indicating that there was once an upper storey. The style of the windows suggest that the building is seventeenth century and it is likely it was a residence or possibly a schoolhouse associated with the law school.

Figure 109
O'Davoren mortuary chapel at Noughaval.

The small eighteenth century chapel and crypt adjacent to the medieval parish church of Noughaval is a mortuary chapel of the O'Davorens (see *Noughaval Church and Settlement*).

Medieval Churches and Society on the Burren

BY THE EIGHTH AND NINTH CENTURY AD some ecclesiastical sites in Ireland had grown into large monastic centres that were focal points for merchants, craftspeople, scholars and artists. Some of these large monasteries had equally large incomes derived from farming their estates, fees for burial and patronage (support) from the rich and powerful members of society. By the tenth century the abbots of many of these important monasteries were members of the ruling families with the result that secular and ecclesiastical power became intricately entwined. As the political power and wealth of the monasteries increased, the largest monasteries became centres of federations of monasteries and some monasteries even went to war to protect their interests.

This period came to an end with a series of synods (ecclesiastical councils) in the twelfth century designed to reform the Irish church and bring it more in line with continental practices. As part of the reforms, the European religious orders of Cistercians, Augustinians, Dominicans and Franciscans were introduced into Ireland. There are two monasteries on the Burren of these continental orders, the Cistercian monastery of Corcomroe and the Augustinian monastery of Kilshanny. Another area of church reform was the division of Ireland into dioceses headed by bishops and the establishment of the four archdioceses headed by archbishops at Armagh, Dublin, Cashel and Tuam. With this reform, all the Irish churches were incorporated into a centralised government for the first time. Tithes (a church tax based on a tenth of the produce of the land and animals) were now paid by all churches to the clergy and bishops of their dioceses and a portion of the tithes eventually made its way to Rome.

One interesting outcome of the establishment of dioceses was that the boundaries established were based on secular territorial divisions that already existed. In Gaelic areas such as the Burren, the twelfth century ecclesiastical land divisions appear to follow tribal and sub-tribal land divisions and so we are given a glimpse of the tribal organisation of the Burren in the Medieval period. The largest territorial division is the territory of the chiefdom and in the case of the Burren, the territory of the *Corcu Modruad* chiefdom became the diocese of Kilfenora. The diocese was then divided into two baronies under the two leading families. In the east were the O'Loughlins in the Barony of Burren and in the west were the O'Connors in the Barony of Corcomroe. Parishes were composed of several *baile* or *ballybetaghs* which usually all belonged to the same sept (a sept is a clan or a family who are all descended from a common ancestor). The word *baile/ballybetaghs* is preserved today in the prefix 'Bally' or 'Balli' in many Irish placenames. The *baile/ballybetaghs* were then subdivided into quarters and most of the townlands in the diocese of Kilfenora were originally quarters. Townlands were the smallest territorial divisions, averaging around 1.3 km^2, and they may have been held by individual families.

Kilfenora

Grid Reference R 184 940

Kilfenora became the principle church of the diocese of Kilfenora in the twelfth century but prior to that there was probably an early monastery on the site. The founding of Kilfenora is attributed to St Fachtnan, a sixth-century saint, and a holy well dedicated to St Fachtnan is located down a laneway north of the cathedral. Another possible remnant of its early monastic beginnings is the outline of its roughly oval enclosure which can be seen today in the curve of the main road as it passes through the village to the south of the cathedral and less clearly in the curve of field walls to the north of the cathedral. In the 1980s the exterior rendering was removed from the nave of the cathedral (the portion which is today roofed) and large blocks typical of the 'cyclopean' architecture that characterises early stone churches were visible. It is possible, therefore, that the north wall of the nave preserves a section of a much earlier church.

Kilfenora was transformed in 1152 AD when it became the see of the diocese of Kilfenora (seat of the bishop) which was created that year at the reforming synod of Kells. The see of a diocese, and therefore its cathedral, was generally located in the most important town in the territory and in view of this it is interesting that Kilfenora cathedral is located less than two kilometres from Caherballykinvarga, the likely capital of the *Corcu Modruad* chiefdom (see *The Chiefdom of Corcu Modruad*). Most of the visible archaeology on the site today dates to the Medieval period around the time of the formation of the diocese and in the centuries that followed.

The main structure of the cathedral consists of a late twelfth or early thirteenth century chancel and north wing with a thirteenth or fourteenth century Gothic-style nave (the portion west of the chancel which is today roofed). The chancel also has a south door, two windows in the south wall and a late Gothic tomb niche in the north wall which were added in the fifteenth century. The carved stone head of the bishop above the tomb niche is earlier than the niche and dates to the early fourteenth century and a similar bishop's head is located above the south door of the nave. There are three carved figures in the chancel, two fourteenth-century bishops and an early fifteenth-century cleric. Also of interest in the chancel are several seventeenth-century grave slabs on the floor and on the south wall.

Figure 110
Holy well at Kilfenora.
Grid Reference R 183 941

The holy wells of the Burren are a modern expression of a tradition of sacred water that goes back at least to early Christian times and possibly further. Today, as in times past, many of these wells are associated with cures for particular ailments. There are wells for toothaches, eye problems, headaches, warts, rheumatism, swollen limbs, backaches, and more. Holy wells are often found on early ecclesiastical sites and this one at Kilfenora is located just a few hundred metres north of the cathedral at the end of the small lane that leads north from near the north-east corner of the graveyard wall. The well is dedicated to St Fachtnan, the sixth-century patron saint of Kilfenora and an inscription on one of the stones states that the covering was built over the well in 1687 by Donald Mac Donogh.

Figure 111
The east window of Kilfenora.

After 1200 AD, Gothic style churches became popular in the Anglo-Norman controlled eastern part of the country but in the Gaelic west a distinctive transitional style developed which incorporated elements of both the earlier Romanesque style and the new Gothic style. This transitional 'School of the West' style is characterised by the combination of Romanesque features such as rounded arches with new Gothic features such as pointed arches, square-edged or moulded arch rings, capitals covered with foliage and windows completely framed by mouldings. Not all of these elements are always present and the eastern window of Kilfenora cathedral is a good example of this 'School of the West' style where some of these features can be seen. The three lights of the Kilfenora window are not pointed but the entire window is framed by mouldings. The ends of the hood moulding on both sides are carved into branches which terminate in bunches of grapes with birds pecking at them and the two central piers are topped with carved capitals, one a group of ecclesiastics gazing down and the other with what is probably a floral design.

Figure 112 ▲
Detail of east window capitals at Kilfenora.

Figure 113 ▶
Fifteenth-century window in the chancel of Kilfenora.

The left-hand terminal of the hood moulding on this intricately carved window is formed by a biting animal.

◀ Figure 114
Fourteenth-century carving of a bishop in the chancel of Kilfenora.

One of this bishop's hands is raised in blessing and the other holds a crozier. With the church reforms of the twelfth century, Kilfenora became the seat of the bishop of Kilfenora which explains why there are so many carvings of bishops at Kilfenora.

Figure 115 ▶
Carving of a cleric in the chancel of Kilfenora.

This early fifteenth-century carving of a cleric shows him with a tonsure (the hair style achieved by shaving just the crown of the head).

Figure 116
The 'Doorty' Cross.

This cross gets its name from the fact that the lower portion of it was used, upside-down, as a tomb stone by the Doorty family until it was recognised for what it was and re-united with its top half. The cross is decorated on both faces and along both narrow sides as well. East Face: the top is occupied by either a bishop or an abbot who is identified by the pointed mitre he wears on his head and the crozier he holds in his left hand. Either birds or angels rest on his shoulders and his right hand is held in the gesture of blessing while at the same time pointing down to the scene below. This lower scene shows two figures linking arms and holding croziers in their free hands. These figures may well be Saints Paul and Anthony and they seem to be warding off evil which is represented by a winged beast devouring people beneath their feet. West Face: the upper portion of the cross is occupied by a badly weathered figure of Christ with a bird in each of the hollows of the cross head. At the base of the cross is a shingled roof which may represent a reliquary (see *Relics and Pilgrimage on the Burren*). Above the shingled roof stand the figures of a man and a horse which may represent one of the horsemen of the apocalypse. Rising above the man's head is a complex interlaced scroll pattern.

The High Crosses of Kilfenora

Kilfenora is home to a famous group of high crosses which date to the twelfth century. While earlier high crosses often had biblical scenes, many of these later high crosses feature large-scale and prominent figures of Christ and a bishop. These crosses reflect the enhanced status of bishops after the twelfth century reforms and may also have been intended to dramatically proclaim the new authority of bishops. Originally there were at least seven high crosses at Kilfenora but one was moved to Killaloe in the nineteenth century. In addition to the three illustrated here, there are two shaft fragments with interlace decoration and a slender octagonal shaft still at Kilfenora. Up until 2003 all the crosses except the West Cross were located either in the graveyard or within the church. None of these were necessarily in their original positions and they have now all been moved into the north wing of the cathedral for their protection. The West Cross remains outside the cathedral, in what is probably its original position, 200 metres to the west.

N.   W.   S.   E.

Scale of feet

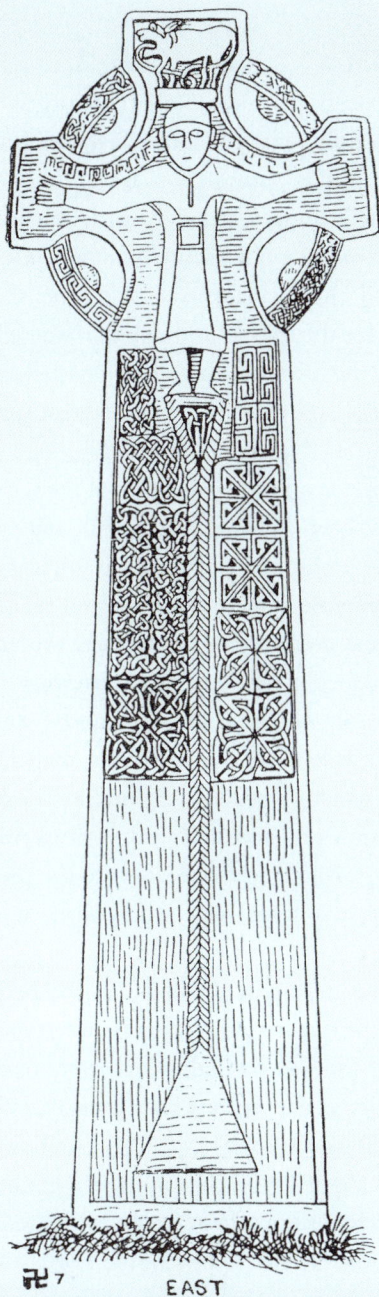

Figure 117

The North Cross. ▲

One face of this cross has a domed boss at its centre and roll mouldings along its edges which end in spirals. The other face is decorated with a pattern of interlace and knotwork.

Figure 118

◄ **The West Cross.**

This impressive cross is over 4.5 metres high and stands by itself in a field 200 metres west of the cathedral. The east face is dominated by the figure of Christ while below his feet, rope mouldings lead to a blank triangular area which may have accommodated a reliquary at one time (see *Relics and Pilgrimage on the Burren*). Above Christ is a lion-like animal which is biting its own tail. The remainder of the decoration on the east face as well as the west face consists of interlace, fretwork and various other decorative motifs.

EAST

WEST   1887.
1900.

Corcomroe Cistercian Abbey

Grid Reference M 295 090

The Cistercian Abbey at Corcomroe is the most spectacular medieval ecclesiastical building on the Burren. At the time it was built it was certainly the most impressive building in the area and even today, in its ruined state, it is a very imposing construction. It was founded in the late twelfth century and construction probably started shortly after, in the early thirteenth century. The Cistercians were a continental monastic order and their introduction into Ireland in the twelfth century was part of the widespread church reforms at this time. Cistercian doctrine called for a simple and self-sufficient life for the monks and one that was filled with prayer. Architecturally, the Cistercians introduced the idea of laying out monasteries according to orderly geometric principals rather than the somewhat haphazard layout of earlier Irish monasteries.

However, although Corcomroe loosely follows the geometric principals of the Cistercians, it is certainly not a rigid adherence. It has, in fact, been suggested that while the craftsmen who built Corcomroe were excellent masons, their architectural skills were not as good and they were out of their depth with a building as elaborate and large as Corcomroe. This contrast between their skills as masons and their skill as architects is particularly evident at the eastern end of the church where there is an abundance of finely carved stonework, but also obvious mistakes in the architecture. The most easily observed mistake can be seen if one looks at the uppermost lancet window in the east wall. Here it can be seen that the top of the window is actually cut by the line of the vault which shows that the builders didn't accurately predict the height of the vault as construction progressed. A less obvious mistake at first glance, but a much more serious one, is the crooked arch that leads into the presbytery. Here, the northern base of the arch is a full ten inches (33cm) west of its southern counterpart, skewing the entire arch.

Despite these mistakes in the eastern end of the church, it is still by far the better built half of the church. There is a striking disparity in the quality of building between the eastern and the western halves and there are also parts of the western half which were never completed. One of the more obvious shortfalls in quality in the western half of the church is that the arched arcades are not even symmetrical. The north arcade has three arches and the south arcade has two arches, neither of which are aligned with their northern counterparts. It also seems as if the north aisle, which should have been a mirror image of the south aisle, was never completed and this is probably the reason the two arches in the north arcade are blocked, because without a north aisle they would have opened directly to the outside. The masonry of the two halves of the church is also of visibly contrasting quality, with the eastern half of the church built with fine ashlar masonry consisting of large stones laid in even courses, and the western half built with smaller stones laid in much more irregular courses. The vertical break between these two different types of masonry is clearly visible on the outside of the southern wall at the west edge of the bell tower.

It seems likely that the difference in quality between the east and the west ends of the church along with the unfinished northern aisle are due to a serious shortfall in funds partway through the construction of the church. It is not clear what may have caused this shortfall but one possible contributing factor was famine and war in the neighbouring province of Connaught in 1227 and 1228. Whatever the cause of the setback, the abbey never really recovered and in 1417 it was recorded that the abbey was so poor it could not support all its monks. At some point in the fifteenth or sixteenth centuries though, more funds were obtained and there was a final period of alterations. These include the insertion of a new doorway in the west wall and the construction of the bell tower. The upper few feet of walls east of the bell tower were also rebuilt at this time and the line of gutter holes perforating the rebuilt upper portion of the walls suggests that the eastern half of the church may have been re-roofed at this time as well.

In addition to the church, many other remains of the monastery can still be seen today and, like the church itself, although they follow the general Cistercian pattern, they do not follow it precisely. Cistercian monasteries were laid out around an enclosed grassy garth which was surrounded by a cloister. One side of the cloister was formed by the church, the opposite side was formed by the kitchen and the refectory, another side was formed by the abbot's quarters and a chapter house (a meeting house for all the monks) and the final side was formed by a communal dormitory for the monks and storerooms. At Corcomroe, the grassy garth is occupied today by the modern graveyard, the west wall of the cloister is still standing, the basal courses of the south cloister wall remain and the building forming the eastern side of the cloister, although ruined, is still partially present (see Figure 120). There is an arched doorway in the western wall of the cloister that leads to the outside and another arched doorway in the northern wall of the cloister that leads into the south aisle of the church.

The exact function of the ruined building forming the eastern side of the cloister is not certain but given the unfinished nature of the church it is quite possible that the various buildings which were meant to surround the cloister were never completed either. If this was the case, the eastern building may have served the combined functions of dormitory, chapter house and storerooms. It was evidently a two-storeyed building and although the two ground-floor doorways that open onto the cloister today appear very short, this is because the level of the eastern cloister garth has been raised to accommodate the modern burials. The side of the building that faces away from the cloister has another door and three windows at the ground floor level. Inside the building, the floor level of the upper storey can be seen as a ledge that runs just above the tops of the doors and windows. Part of the gable line of the sloped roof can be seen as a line of slabs protruding from the church wall where the

Figure 119
Corcomroe Abbey.

eastern building abutted it. A round-headed door leads from the upper floor of the eastern building directly into the church and for this reason the identification on Westropp's plan of the northern portion of the eastern building as the Sacristy is probably correct (see 'h' in Figure 120). The Sacristy was where the sacred utensils and vestments of the church were kept.

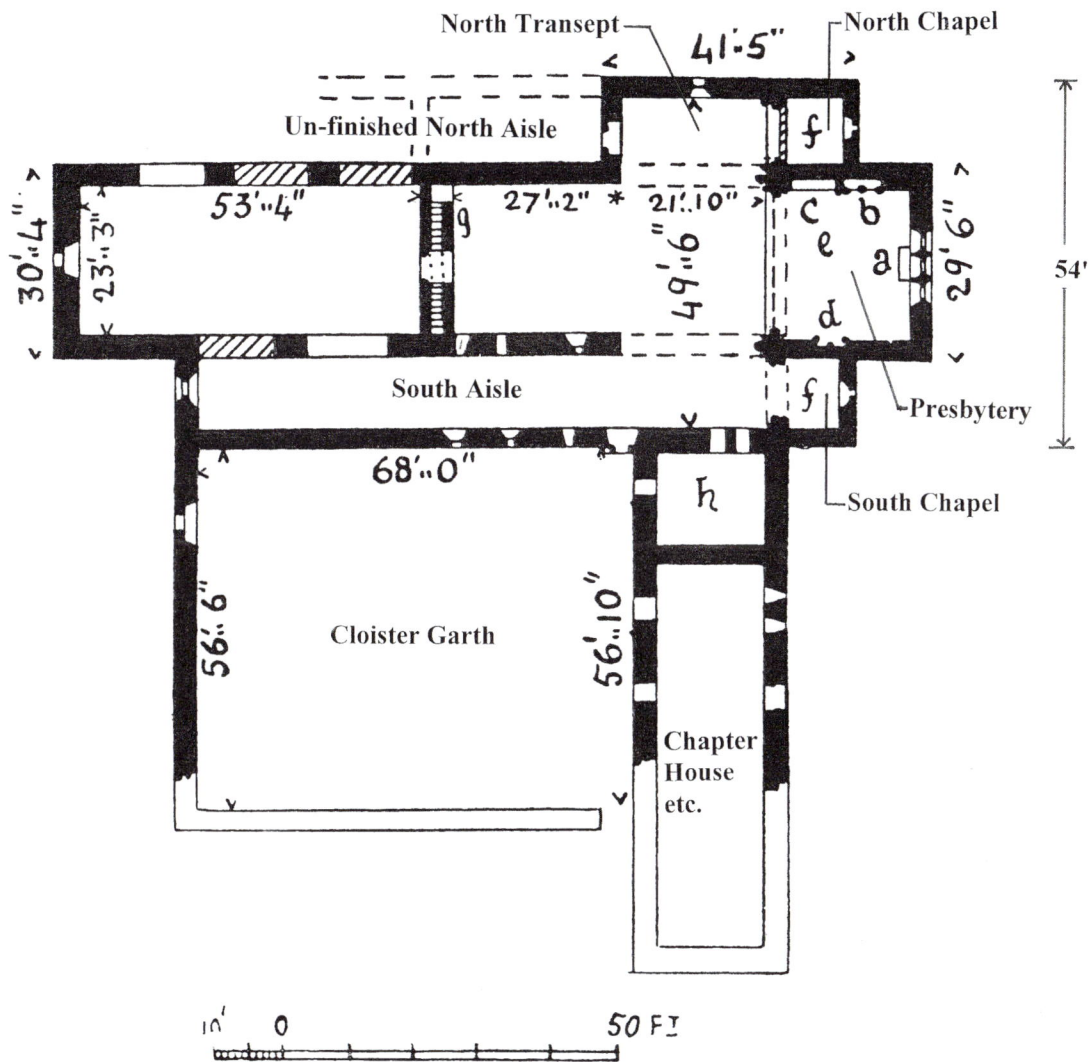

Figure 120
Plan of Corcomroe Abbey.

The plan shows measurements: North Transept, 41'·5", North Chapel, Un-finished North Aisle, 53'·4", 30'·4", 23'·3", 27'·2", 21'·10", 49'·6", 29'·6", 54', South Aisle, 68'·0", 56'·6", 56'·10", Cloister Garth, Chapter House etc., Presbytery, South Chapel, Sacristy (h), staircase (g), altar (a), sedilia (b), tomb (c), recess (d), slab (e), chapels (f).

Scale: 10' 0 — 50 FT

Figure 121
The presbytery of Corcomroe.

The first part of Corcomroe to be constructed, and certainly the finest, is the easternmost end, the presbytery. The roof is supported by a spectacular ribbed vault decorated with herringbone chevrons.

The Cistercians frequently used a system of two related squares to lay out the proportions of their buildings. At Corcomroe, two squares appear to have been used as a rough guide, one with sides of 42 feet and the other with sides of 56 feet. These squares can be seen in many measurements around the abbey including the measurement from the exterior of the north chapel to the exterior of the south chapel at 54 feet and the east-west measurement from the exterior of the north transept to the exterior of the north chapel which at 41' 5" is close to 42 feet. a – altar, b – sedilia (seats for the clergy to use during intervals in the service), c – King Conor O'Brien's tomb, d – recess (which formerly held a wooden cross), e – O'Loughlin slab, f – chapels, g – staircase to bell tower, h – Sacristy.

Figure 122
Architectural details in Corcomroe Abbey.

Many of the capitals in the eastern end of the church are richly decorated with human heads, flowers and foliage. Some of the flowers have been identified as poppies, lily-of-the-valleys and lotus. This profusion of decoration is not typical in Cistercian abbeys where such fanciful carvings were generally thought to distract the monks from their prayers.

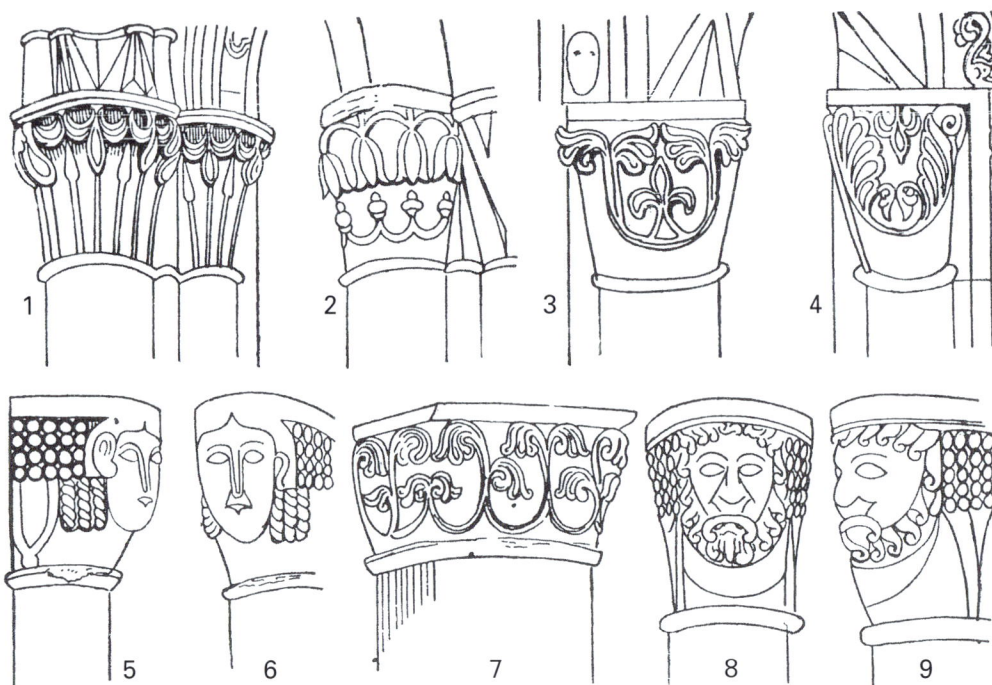

Figure 123
King Conor O'Brien's tomb.

King Conor O'Brien died in 1268 at the nearby battle of Suidaine. The Kings of Thomond were the founders and benefactors of Corcomroe. Thomond was the Medieval province which equates with the modern county of Clare.

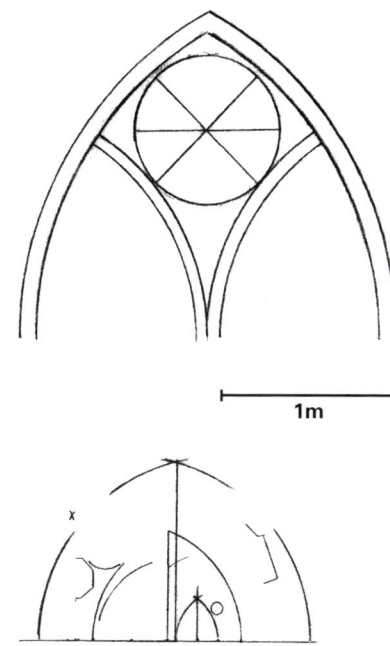

1m

Figure 124 ▶
Architectural sketches incised in the plaster at Corcomroe.

In the Medieval period both walls and floors of buildings which were under construction were sometimes used as convenient surfaces for architectural sketches. Two instances of this practice can be seen at Corcomroe where there are sketches faintly incised in the plasterwork. As the building work progressed, these sketches would have been covered with additional layers of plaster but the later layers of plaster have eroded away leaving the sketches visible once again.

The upper sketch in this figure can be seen high up on the north wall of the north transept. It is drawn at full scale (presumably by someone standing on a scaffold) and is almost two metres wide. Its design is similar to the tomb recess in the presbytery but they are not identical. The lower sketch in this figure shows a series of exercises that are inscribed in the north wall of the south chapel. It consists of several arcs drawn with a large compass and the marks where the pointed end of the compass drilled into the plaster are visible as well. The five-sided outline at the left of the sketch may be the profile of a chamfered pier. On the same wall (but not pictured here) there is also a crude sketch of a boat with a central mast.

◀ Figure 125
Corcomroe Abbey and its lands.

The rectangular fields of the monastery can be seen clearly here stretching away from the abbey and ending at the curving line of the outer monastic enclosure. Surrounding the abbey more closely, the roughly square inner monastic enclosure with the church at its centre can also be seen. Although not visible in this photograph, several other monastic buildings can be seen on the ground. The ruined gatehouse is located where the modern road (following the Medieval approach) passes through the inner enclosure wall, about 100 metres west of the church (just before the car park). Today the gatehouse appears as a ruin located just north of the road, with the high wall of the inner enclosure extending off it and running up the hill to the north, as well as continuing to the south on the other side of the road. The ruined building standing adjacent to the car park may be an infirmary and a very overgrown and collapsed ruin in a field to the east of the church may be the Abbot's house.

Figure 126
Ogee-headed window at Killilagh.

The S-shaped curves that form the tops of these windows identifies them as a type of later Medieval window known as 'ogee-headed' windows. The distinctive 'punch dressing' consisting of a regular pattern of small pits punched into the surface of the stone is also indicative of a later Medieval date and the rectangular hood moulding over the top of the window indicates that the window was built some time in the late fifteenth or sixteenth centuries.

Killilagh and Toomullin Churches in Doolin

Killilagh Grid Reference R 078 978

Toomullin Reference R 084 971

These two medieval churches lie less than a kilometre apart in the parish of Killilagh in Doolin on the west coast of the Burren. Both churches are mentioned in the Ecclesiastical Taxation list of 1302 and the large difference in their evaluations suggests that Toomullin may have been a dependant chapel to the parish church of Killilagh.

The church at Killilagh is a medieval parish church consisting of a nave with a later chapel extending off to the south. An antiquarian photograph taken of the east window before it collapsed shows a tall, round-headed lancet window that was probably Transitional in style. Assuming this window was original, it would indicate an early thirteenth-century date for the construction of the church. The beautifully detailed windows which remain in the church show that it was modified in the late fifteenth or sixteenth centuries, which is probably when the south chapel was added.

The church of Toomullin is located across the road on the north bank of the Aille river. A holy well close to the church is dedicated to St Brecan, a fifth-century saint and so it's possible that this site began as an early ecclesiastical foundation. The church itself appears to be a chapel with living quarters on its west end. The living quarters consist of two small, ground floor rooms with another room(s) above. The church is associated with lands that were traditionally held by the Mac Clancy clan. The Mac Clancys were the hereditary *brehons* (judges) of the area and so it is possible that Toomullin was a private chapel of the clan. This is by no means certain, however, as Toomullin is larger than other chapels in the area and burials, a feature not normally associated with chapels, were found during phosphate mining adjacent to the site in the 1940s.

Figure 127
Toomullin Church with living quarters on the west end.

Carran Church

Grid Reference R 240 974

The name of Carran church is derived from the word 'carn' or cairn, a heap of stones. The particular cairn for which the church is named may be a small one to the south of the church around which coffins were traditionally carried before burial. The church is recorded in a taxation list of 1302, but other than a few re-used cut stones, the church that stands today appears to date to the sixteenth century. There is an elaborate south door and the remains of a belfry on the west gable. There are windows high up in the south wall and corbels on the inside of the west wall that indicate the former presence of an upper storey which may have been living quarters for a priest. A machicolation (a small protruding wall supported on corbels which allowed defenders to drop things on attackers below while remaining covered themselves) on the north-west corner shows that some attempt was made to make the church defensible.

Figure 128
West gable of Carran church showing the defensive machicolation.

Figure 129
Carved head of a warrior inside Carran church.

At one time there were also carved heads of a king and a woman in the church.

Noughaval Church and Settlement

Grid Reference R 209 967

A few kilometres north east of Kilfenora is the site of Noughaval, or 'new settlement'. At the core of Noughaval is a medieval church and a market cross, while just south of the church are the remains of a settlement consisting of the ruined remains of several houses and other buildings. The site appears to have begun as an early ecclesiastical foundation that then developed into a small settlement with a market in the Medieval period and then continued as a settlement in the post-Medieval period up to the nineteenth century.

The earliest phase of the church is represented by the cyclopean masonry visible in its south wall. This early church was probably a single-celled building roughly equivalent with the present nave and with a door to the west. Other features on the site may date to this early phase as well. Within the graveyard, just south of the church, is a *leacht*, a small rectangular stone mound. These are often found on early sites and they may have been open-air altars or special graves. In many cases they are associated with pilgrimage. The *leacht* at Noughaval is topped by a small, early-style stone cross. Another possibly early feature is the base of a very substantial wall that curves around the site approximately 60 metres to the south west of the church beyond the graveyard. It is most visible as the southern boundary of the open field south of the modern church and it may be the remains of an early monastic enclosure wall surrounding the site. Subsequent to these hints of early activity, there is a major phase of refurbishment and building on the site in the late twelfth century. At this time the church was rebuilt, the south door was inserted into the earlier masonry and the chancel and chancel arch were added to the eastern end of the church. The small chapel in the graveyard is the mortuary chapel of the O'Davorens and it dates to the early eighteenth century (see *The O'Davoren Law School at Cahermacnaghten*).

Just south of the church and outside the graveyard are the small fields, houses and other buildings which are the remains of the settlement. In 1990 one of the houses was excavated by a research team headed by Sinéad Ní Ghabláin of the University of California, Los Angeles. The excavation revealed the house was a small, two-roomed building with two opposing doors and a hearth against one wall. Several large stones (including the reused base of a well-carved window, possibly from the church) formed a low stone bench adjacent to the hearth. This house seems to have been constructed and occupied in the post-Medieval period, some time in the seventeenth to nineteenth centuries, and it seems likely that most of the visible archaeology of the settlement probably dates to this period as well. There were also, however, indications of an occupation level below the post-Medieval house which suggests that settlement on the site began earlier in the Medieval period. Among the finds from the excavation was a small bone playing-dice.

Figure 130
Noughaval church.

The south door can be seen here inserted into the earlier cyclopean masonry of the nave. Further east along the wall, the smaller masonry of the later chancel can be seen. The elaborately carved south door is decorated with a pattern of tubular chevrons. It dates to the late twelfth century and its style is transitional between the earlier Romanesque and the later Gothic style. It is similar in style to the rib vaulting in the presbytery at Corcomroe Abbey which may indicate that some of the same masons worked on both sites.

Figure 131 (left)
Early ringed cross set in the *leacht* **at Noughaval.**

Figure 132 (right)
Base of the market cross at Noughaval.

Figure 133
Excavation underway on one of the houses in the settlement at Noughaval.

Relics and Pilgrimage on the Burren

ENSHRINING THE REMAINS OF IMPORTANT PEOPLE is a feature of many religions around the world. In Christianity, this practice appears to have first developed when the bones of early Christians who had been buried in the catacombs of Rome were removed and preserved as relics. There are two types of relics, corporeal and associative. Corporeal relics are parts of the saint's body while associative relics are objects which were used by a saint or associated with them during their life such as croziers (staffs) and bells. The relics were often preserved in reliquaries, elaborate containers made from precious metals and stones which were sometimes fashioned in the shape of the relic they contained. Relics were used in many different ways. Often they were brought on procession around the countryside to provide miraculous cures after an outbreak of plague or a failure of crops. At other times they were brought on circuit to enforce the 'laws' of the saint they were associated with and to assert the supremacy of the church that held the relics and thereby levy taxes. Relics were also used as objects on which oaths were sworn, as talismans carried into battle to ensure victory and as a means of attracting pilgrims, a valuable source of income for churches.

When the missionary Palladius was sent to Ireland by the Pope in the early fifth century, he carried with him relics of various saints, including relics of the apostles Peter and Paul. In the centuries that followed the introduction of Christianity to Ireland, relics of local Irish saints and martyrs were enshrined and venerated as well. A large number of Irish reliquaries date to the eleventh and twelfth centuries and this seems to be due to the politics of the era. At this time both ecclesiastical and secular powers were becoming concentrated in the hands of a small group of dynastic families. In the church, this was achieved by centralising power into a system of hierarchically organised dioceses (see *Medieval Churches and Society on the Burren*). As the dioceses were being formed, different churches competed to be made the capital of the diocese and thus the seat of power and wealth in the region. In this competitive climate, relics held by a church were an important asset that boosted the prestige of the church and thus enhanced its chances at becoming the capital of the diocese.

We can see this process in action at Killaloe in south-east Clare. At Killaloe, the body of St Flannan as well as a book, a bell and a crozier associated with St Flannan were all enshrined in the twelfth century. At the same time a 'Life of St Flannan' was written and at least two churches were built or refurbished at Killaloe. All this activity paid off and Killaloe was made the capital of a diocese. On the Burren, the process is not as well documented but at Kilfenora in the twelfth century there was a burst of activity along with the possible use of relics represented by the erection of several high crosses and in 1152 AD Kilfenora became the capital of the diocese which encompasses the Burren (see *Kilfenora*).

Pilgrimage to holy places, many of which housed relics, was a popular form of devotion in Medieval Europe. Pilgrims travelled to both local sites and to places far away such as Santiago de Compostela in Spain and to the Holy Land. Rome was also a very important pilgrimage destination and the seven hills of Rome were sometimes mimicked at other pilgrimage destinations by the use of the number seven. Various accounts suggest that Kilfenora may have originally had seven crosses and if so, it's likely that the seven crosses were meant to relate to Rome. Additionally, the possible depiction of a reliquary on the base of the Doorty cross and the gable-shaped void at the base of the West cross suggest these two crosses may have originally been associated with relics.

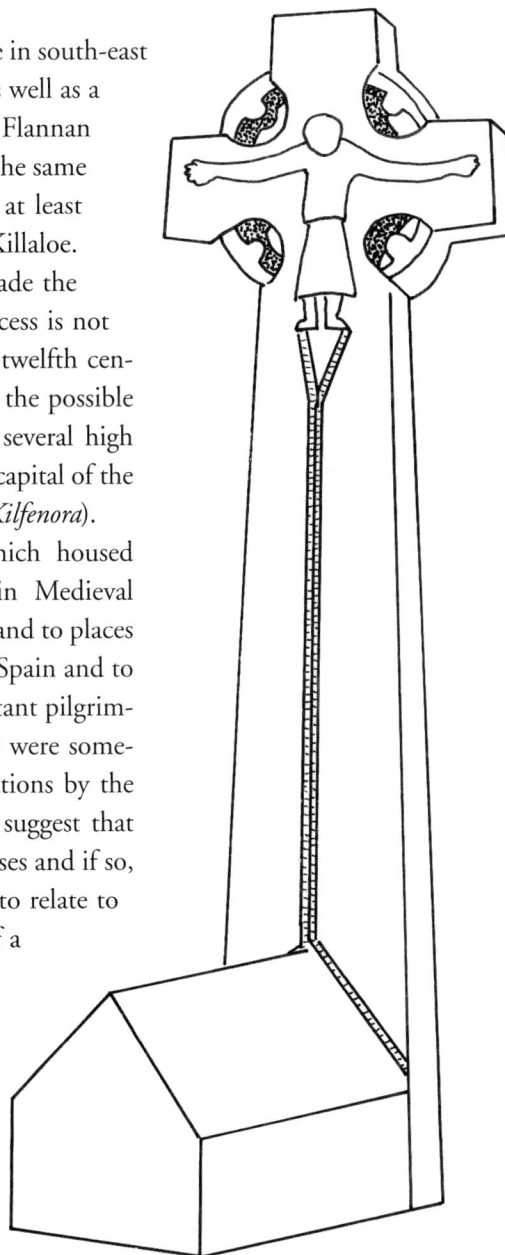

Figure 134 ▲

Possible depiction of a tomb-shaped reliquary at the base of the Doorty cross at Kilfenora.

At the base of the west face of the Doorty cross is a depiction of a peaked structure in the form of a gabled roof that may be a representation of a type of relic container known as a tomb-shrine. Tomb-shrines appear to have developed from above-ground sarcophagi in the Mediterranean region and miniature versions, tomb-shaped reliquaries, were also constructed from metal and precious stones to act as portable relic containers (see *The High Crosses of Kilfenora*).

◄ Figure 135

Hypothetical position of a tomb-shaped shrine at the base of the West cross at Kilfenora.

At the base of the east face of the West cross at Kilfenora is a blank area with a peaked, gable-shaped profile (see Figure 118). Although by no means certain, it is possible that the area was left blank intentionally because it once had a tomb-shaped shrine abutting it. In this simplified sketch it can be seen that the rope moulding connects the figure of Christ to the area that may have been occupied by a tomb-shrine, a potentially powerful connection.

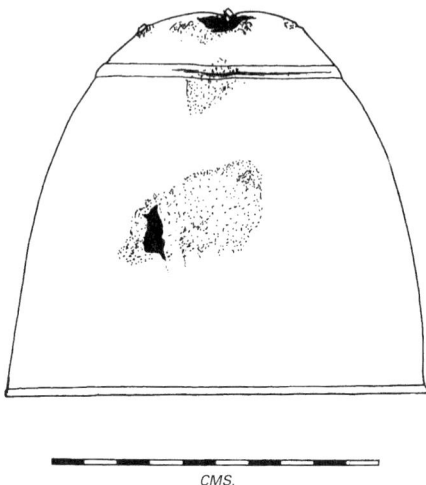

Figure 136 ▲

The bell of St Cuana from Kilshanny.

Several relics and reliquaries are known from Clare, and on the Burren a bell from Kilshanny is attributed as a relic of St Cuana. St Cuana was an early saint who may have lived in the seventh century and there is an account of him miraculously receiving his bell which appeared from the heavens. The bell of St Cuana is, therefore, an associative relic – an object associated with the saint during his lifetime. Unfortunately for the story of St Cuana and his bell, the metalwork of the bell appears to be twelfth century in date and it is possible that the 'bell' was actually originally a chalice subsequently inverted and refashioned as a bell. As noted above, a large number of Irish reliquaries were manufactured in the eleventh and twelfth centuries as churches vied with each other for the prestige of owning a saint's relic. The Kilshanny bell shows that it wasn't just the reliquaries that were being manufactured at this time, relics were being made as well. St Cuana's bell may be pictured on a grave slab at Killinaboy along with another local relic, a T-shaped crozier (see Figure 145).

Killinaboy

Grid Reference R 272 916

The church at Killinaboy was reconstructed some time in the fifteenth or sixteenth century, but it incorporates fragments of an earlier church dating to the late twelfth or early thirteenth century. In its earlier phase, Killinaboy may well have housed important relics and been a popular destination for pilgrims. At least three relics may have been associated with Killinaboy: a fragment of the True Cross (see Figure 137), the Bell of St Cuana (see Figure 136 and Figure 145) and the T-shaped Crozier (see *The Veneration of the T-Shaped Crozier in North Clare*).

The west gable of the church appears to have been re-assembled with most (but not all) the stones in their original positions as is shown by a very large, double-armed cross carved in relief on the gable end. This gable also has projecting *antae* on both sides which are a feature of early churches. Other fragments of the earlier church were not rebuilt in their original positions and one of these fragments can be seen just inside the door on the left. Here there is an ornate Romanesque carving of a beast with its tongue hanging out and its teeth bared. It is now lying on its side but it would have originally stood upright, perhaps as part of the surround of a doorway. At some point the church began to be used for burials and there are several interesting seventeenth-century grave slabs and inscriptions inside the church.

Figure 137 ▶

Double-armed cross on the west gable of Killinaboy church.

The most significant feature of the earlier church is the double-armed cross protruding in low relief from the west gable. The shape of the cross imitates Byzantine reliquaries which contained a fragment of the True Cross and it is likely that the church at Killinaboy once contained a relic of the True Cross as well. It is even possible that the church at Killinaboy was built specifically to house a relic of the True Cross. Many fragments of the True Cross were brought back to Europe from the Near East by Medieval Crusaders.

Figure 138
Base of a round tower at Killinaboy.

The round tower at Killinaboy is the only one on the Burren but there is a complete example which was partially restored in the nineteenth century not far to the east at Kilmacduagh near Gort. Round towers date to the tenth – twelfth centuries and are another indicator of relatively early ecclesiastical sites. Their name in Irish, *cloigteach*, means 'bell house' which suggests their primary function may have been bell towers but they were probably also used to store valuables, probably relics. When complete, the round tower at Killinaboy would have tapered as it rose and would have been capped by a conical stone roof. The tallest round towers are around 30 metres high but the diameter of the Killinaboy tower suggests it was smaller.

The door on a round tower is almost always above ground level and it would have been reached via a ladder, while inside there would have been several levels of wooden floors connected by ladders. The top floor of round towers had four windows facing the cardinal directions and hand bells were probably rung from these windows at appropriate prayer times.

The fact that the doors on round towers are almost always well above ground level has led some to speculate that the towers were intended as refuges from raiders, particularly Vikings. Against this argument, however, it has been pointed out that the number of references in the annals of round towers being burned indicates that they were particularly unsafe refuges. More recently it has been suggested that the primary function of round towers was to house relics and that their inaccessible doors were a precaution designed to keep the relics at a safe distance from over-eager pilgrims rather than from determined raiders. If the towers were treasuries for relics, their tall height would have also served as a beacon for pilgrims as they neared the monastery. On the Aran Islands, there is another base of a round tower at the important pilgrimage destination of St Enda's monastery (see Figure 195).

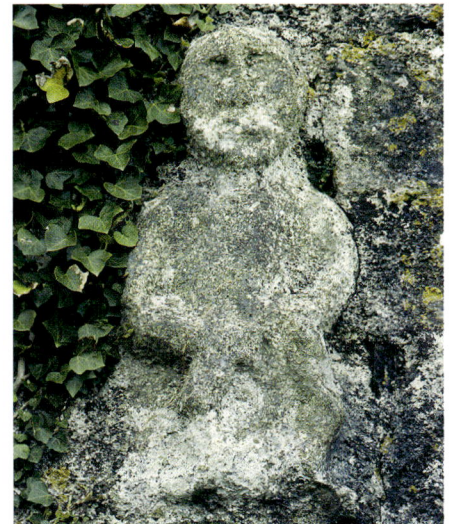

Figure 139
Sheela na gig at Killinaboy.

Sheela na gigs are stone carvings of women baring their genitals which are found on medieval churches and castles. The women are generally depicted in a grotesque manner with bald heads, grimacing mouths and sometimes bony ribs. In recent times many people have interpreted sheela na gigs as symbols of positive female power but they were certainly not intended to be viewed this way by those who fashioned them. They date to the period between the thirteenth and seventeenth centuries, hardly a period renowned for its feminist views. Rather than feminist icons, sheela na gigs appear to be warnings against the sin of lust (hence their grotesque appearance) and the fact that they are female rather than male is probably due to the fact that in the medieval church, lust was seen as mainly a female sin. Sheela na gigs and other 'exhibitionist' figures (which were also warnings against lust) are often found carved on churches on pilgrimage routes throughout Europe and this association with pilgrimage routes further emphasises Killinaboy's role as an important destination for pilgrims.

Temple Cronan

Grid Reference M 289 000

Temple Cronan is an early monastic site said to have been founded by St Cronan. The church itself is a small, single-celled oratory. It has features generally thought to be pre-twelfth century such as a lintelled west doorway and cyclopean masonry, but the incorporation of twelfth century carved Romanesque features throughout the church show that it was either built in an antiquated style or fairly thoroughly rebuilt in the twelfth century. A door inserted into the north wall shows that it was altered again in the fifteenth century.

There are two tomb-shrines to the east of the oratory which would have housed the bones of saints and which were probably objects of devotion for pilgrims to the site. These tomb-shrines are probably contemporary with the Romanesque carvings on the oratory and therefore

Figure 140
The oratory at Temple Cronan.

indicate a major refurbishment of the site in the twelfth century. As at Kilfenora and Killinaboy, it is the twelfth century that appears to be the focus of building projects designed to encourage pilgrimage.

Traces of enclosure walls circling the site have been detected on aerial photographs but they are harder to identify on the ground. Quite visible on the ground, however, are the remains of several buildings and a stone quarry in a field just north of the church. The foundations of these buildings appear today as low, grass-covered outlines and they are probably the remains of the secular buildings of the monastery. The quarry is a deep rectangular gorge cut into the bedrock just north east of the building foundations. This quarry presumably provided the large blocks used to build the church. It is interesting to contrast this medieval quarry which burrowed deep into the bedrock to obtain regular, unweathered blocks with the prehistoric quarrying activity on Roughan Hill which was restricted to prising weathered slabs from the surface of the bedrock (see *Building a Wedge Tomb*). There is a holy well a few hundred metres south of the church at the base of a small cliff, and the base of a cross which may have marked the original entrance to the monastery is located near the modern farm building on the hill overlooking the church to the west.

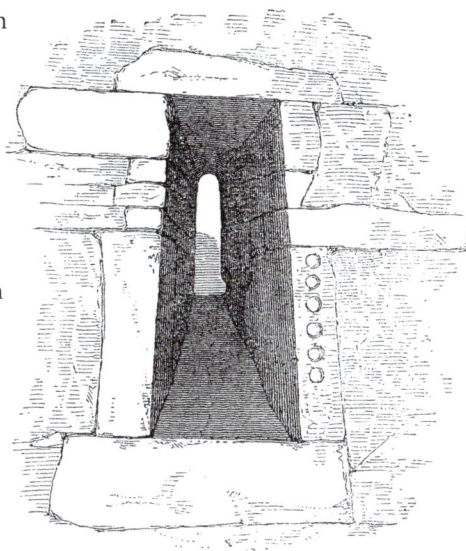

Figure 141 ▲
Tomb-shrine at Temple Cronan.

One of two tomb-shrines at Temple Cronan, the other is in the same position relative to the church on the north side, just over a field wall. This style of tomb-shrine developed from above-ground sarcophagi in the Mediterranean region. Although not present on the tomb-shrines at Temple Cronan, some examples have holes in their gable slabs so that pilgrims could reach inside and touch the bones of the saint (see Figure 223).

Figure 142 ▶
Romanesque east window at Temple Cronan.

Romanesque architecture had its origins during the latter eleventh century and early twelfth century on the continent and in England where the style emerged as a visible element of a period of reform and renaissance. Its appearance in Ireland coincides with the twelfth century Irish church reforms and so in Ireland as well, the architecture appears to be a visible symbol of these reforms (see *Medieval Churches and Society on the Burren*).

The Romanesque style is characterised by the use of round arches, decorative sculpture, high-vaulted ceilings and walls divided into distinctive 'storeys' but not all of these elements appear on all Romanesque churches. On the Burren, Romanesque architecture is restricted to the use of round arches and decorative sculpture. Romanesque architecture in Ireland generally dates to the twelfth century but in the west it continued in use into the early thirteenth century.

◀ Figure 143
Carved Romanesque-style head at Temple Cronan.

Temple Cronan is decorated with several carved heads of animals and people.

The Veneration of the T-Shaped Crozier in North Clare

There are depictions of a T-shaped crozier at several different locations in north Clare. It is depicted on the base of the high cross at Dysert O'Dea, on a grave slab at Killinaboy, carved as a free-standing sculpture known as the Tau Cross on the brow of Roughan Hill and in one of the scenes on the Doorty Cross at Kilfenora. These depictions may all illustrate the same venerated object which may have been brought on procession between all the sites where it is depicted, as well as attracting pilgrims from farther afield.

Figure 144 ▶

T-shaped crozier on the base of the Dysert high cross.

Grid Reference R 283 848

On the high cross at the site of Dysert O'Dea a little south of the Burren, there is a panel on the north side of the cross which may represent a procession with the T-shaped crozier in the central place of prominence.

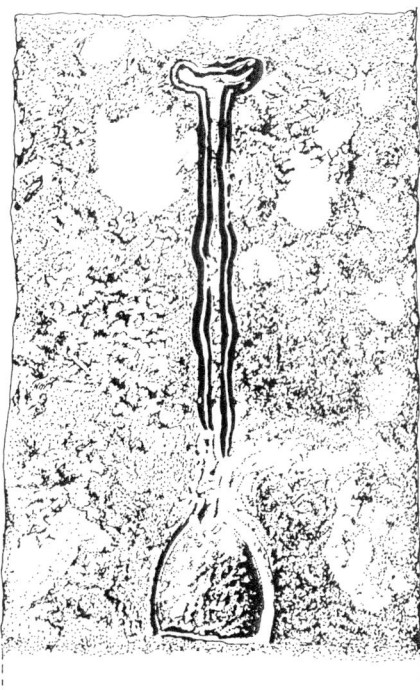

◀ Figure 145

Carving on a possible pilgrim's grave at Killinaboy.

This carving on a grave slab at Killinaboy is the clearest depiction of the T-shaped crozier. On the shaft are three knobs which suggest that the crozier being depicted was either made of bronze or it was a bronze reliquary encasing a wooden crozier. Also interesting is the roughly hemispherical carving beneath the crozier which could be a depiction of St Cuana's bell from Kilshanny, another local relic (see Figure 136). The Killinaboy grave slab is located in the graveyard south of the south-west corner of the church (see *Killinaboy*).

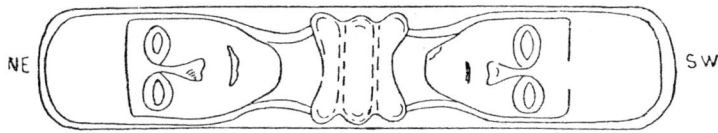

NE   SW

1899

0   6   12 INS

Figure 146 ▲
The Tau cross on Roughan Hill.
Grid Reference R 252 924

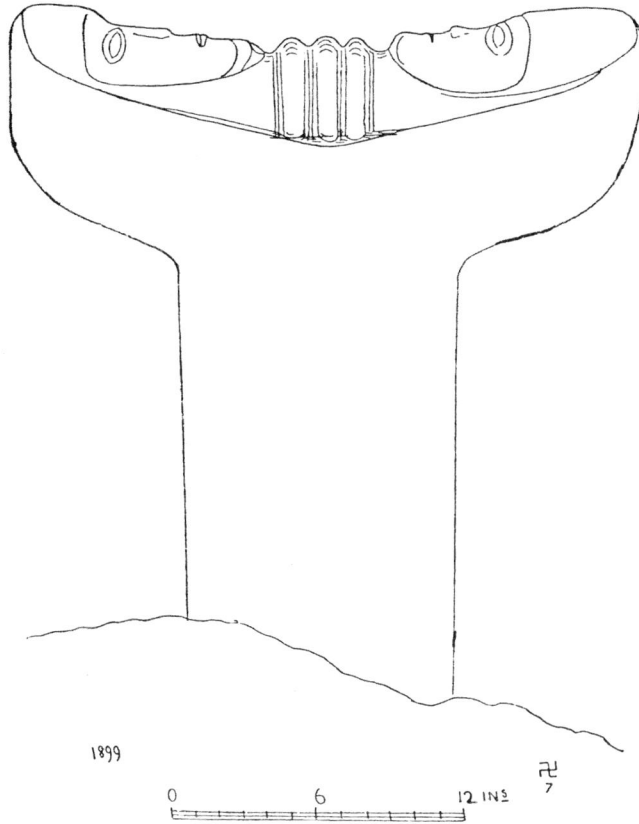

The Tau Cross is now in the Heritage Centre in Corrofin but its original location beside the road where it crosses the brow of Roughan Hill is marked today with a replica. It is likely that what survives today is just the top of the cross and that it originally had a much taller shaft, making it more like the other depictions of the T-shaped crozier. Its location beside the road at the brow of a hill, a good resting place, strongly suggests that the modern road is following the same path as a much earlier Medieval road used by pilgrims to travel between the holy sites of north Clare.

Figure 147 ▼
T-shaped crozier depicted on the Doorty cross at Kilfenora.

One of the scenes on the Doorty cross depicts two figures holding croziers. The figure on the left holds the typical crook-headed crozier while the figure on the right holds a T-shaped crozier (see *The High Crosses of Kilfenora*).

The Tower Houses of the Burren

THE PRACTICE OF BUILDING STONE CASTLES was first introduced to Ireland in the late twelfth century by the Anglo-Normans who built substantial stone castles, particularly at locations that became their principal seats of power. The Burren, however, never came under direct Anglo-Norman control. The Anglo-Normans occupied south County Clare by the mid-thirteenth century but after they were defeated at the battle of Dysert O'Dea in 1318, the areas they had colonised in Clare were taken back by the Irish. By the mid-fourteenth century there doesn't appear to have been any Anglo-Normans settled in Clare and so their direct influence in Clare appears to have lasted less than a century. During that brief time they built stone castles at three strategic locations in south-central Clare – Bunratty, Clarecastle and Quinn (although what stands at Bunratty today is a fifteenth century MacNamara castle).

The Gaelic lords did not respond to the Anglo-Norman stone castles by immediately building stone castles of their own. It's not certain what sort of sites the Gaelic lords did live in but they may well have been sites which, although fortified, are less visible to us today. These would be places such as low-lying sites surrounded by a moat, *crannógs* (artificial islands), natural island fortresses and ringforts. One reason that has been put forward to explain why the Irish didn't take up stone castle building very quickly is that their wealth was based on cattle, not the possession of land. Because it would be very difficult to feed and protect cattle during a prolonged siege, a better strategy for the Irish may have been one of strategic retreat and the use of the landscape for a mobile defence. Whatever the reason, we do not have any widespread evidence of Gaelic lords building stone castles until the period between the early fifteenth century and the mid-seventeenth century when they built tower houses.

Contemporary Travellers' Accounts of Tower Houses

We are come to the castle already. The castles are built very strong, and wth narrow stayres, for security. The hall is the uppermost room, lett us go up, you shall not come downe agayne till tomorrow . . . The lady of the house meets you wth. her trayne . . . Salutations paste, you shall be presented wth. all the drinkes in the house, first the ordinary beare, then aqua vitae, then sacke, then olde-ale, the lady tastes it, you must not refuse it. The fyre is prepared in the middle of the hall, where you may sollace yor. selfe till supper time, you shall not want sacke and tobacco. By this time the table is spread and plentifully furnished wth. variety of meates, but ill cooked and without sauce . . . When you come to yor. chamber, do not expect canopy and curtaines. – Luke Gernon c.1620

The castles or houses of the nobility consist of four walls, extremely high and thatched with straw; but to tell the truth, they are nothing but square towers without windows, or at least having such small apertures as to give no more light than there is in a prison. They have little furniture, and cover their rooms with rushes, of which they make their beds in summer, and straw in winter. They put the rushes a foot deep on their floor and on their windows, and many of them ornament their ceilings with branches. – M. Bouillaye le Gouz 1644 (a Frenchman travelling in Ireland)

Figure 148 ▶

Section through a typical tower house.

The advent of the tower house in the early fifteenth century may have been brought about by a merging of Gaelic and Anglo-Norman culture which occurred at this time due, in part at least, to the social turbulence of the preceding fourteenth century, a period marked by war, famine and the Black Death. The merging of the Anglo-Norman tradition of building stone castles and the Gaelic tradition of a mobile defence may have given rise to the tower house, a fortified residence for protection against raids that could still be abandoned if the occupants were faced with a superior force. Tower houses are often referred to as castles and in fact they are a type of castle, but they are modest castles – fortified houses rather than military fortifications. They provided the inhabitants with defence against small-scale raiding and warfare rather than defence against any prolonged military campaign.

The typical tower house is a tall, rectangular masonry tower, three to five storeys in height. The door is at ground level and it is usually protected with a machicolation, a projecting structure used by the defenders to drop things on attackers at the door or to pour water on fires set at the doorway by attackers. Long narrow holes called 'squints' also sometimes occur on one or both sides of the doorway. These were probably used both to shoot

Figure 149

Gleninagh tower house on Galway Bay.

Grid Reference M 193 103

The tower house at Gleninagh was built by the O'Loughlins in the late sixteenth century and it was inhabited up until the mid-nineteenth century. It is unusual in that it is L-shaped rather than rectangular, with the projecting wing of the tower containing the entrance and the spiral staircase. Three of its corners are protected with projecting circular bartizans and there is a defensive machicolation directly above the doorway as well. On the side facing Galway Bay, two garderobe (toilet) chutes are visible letting out directly onto the wall.

There are several interesting buildings and other features in the vicinity of the Gleninagh tower house. Close to the shore in the field just north east of the tower house is a large lime kiln which was probably used to produce the lime for the mortar and the plaster used to build the castle. It is visible today as a large grass-covered mound with a flue hole at its top and the kiln door opening to the north (this is incorrectly identified as a *fulacht fiadh* on the OS map). Immediately south of the tower house is a covered holy well topped with a stone cross and entered through a late Medieval pointed arch doorway. Sixty metres to the south, where the road ends at the gate, there is a line of overgrown and ruined buildings. The fireplaces visible in some of the rooms show that some of these buildings were dwellings while others may have been animal stalls or sheds. These buildings seem to date to the post-Medieval period. The Medieval parish church of Gleninagh is located 250 metres south of the castle.

at people at the door and to speak to those outside the door without having to open the door. If an attacker made it past the front door, they would find themselves in a small lobby directly under a 'murder hole', a hole in the ceiling through which the defenders could continue to shoot and drop things on the attackers.

Most of the Burren's tower houses have three doors leading off the entry lobby. The door straight ahead leads into a ground-floor storage area, kept cool by the extra thickness of the walls at this level. The door to the right typically opens into a small guard chamber where the door-keeper would sleep while the door to the left leads to the spiral stairs that give access to the rest of the tower house. The stairs rise in a clockwise direction which gives right-handed defenders wielding swords the advantage of an unencumbered swing as they attack down the stairs.

The upper rooms were the living and dining quarters of the household. The uppermost room was termed the 'Solar' because it was the only room which was out of harms way enough to allow windows large enough to light the room well. Although the tower houses of the Burren appear today as romantic grey ruins that blend into the landscape, when they were occupied their exteriors would have been covered with a durable lime-based coating which served as waterproofing and would have made the tower houses bright white beacons in the landscape. None of the tower houses on the Burren have retained their white exteriors but a nearby and recently restored example can be seen at Ballyportry castle just east of Corrofin. (Grid Reference R 300 901).

Figure 150
Doonnagore tower house at Doolin.
Grid Reference R 069 957

[P] [symbol]

Round tower houses are very rare and the only three examples in Clare are all on the Burren. Doonnagore in Doolin, Faunarooska near Fanore and Newtown near Ballyvaughan. In the Medieval period, round towers were often used as an essential element in large military castles because their curved sides deflected projectiles better and their lack of corners meant they were more difficult to undermine. But because tower houses are essentially defended houses rather than military castles, the practical consideration of having square rooms seems to have usually overridden the defensive advantages of round towers. Square rooms are much more practical when one is trying to furnish the rooms with wall hangings and square furniture, such as beds and chests of drawers.

Figure 151
Ballynalackan tower house.
Grid Reference M 104 003

Carn Mhic Táil

Grid Reference R 125 921

Carn Mhic Táil is a large and impressive cairn located just south of Kilshanny on the bank of the Derreen River. Across northern and western Europe, mounds were used as inauguration and assembly sites in the past. Most of the historical references we have to this practice relate to the Medieval period, but the references do stretch back into Early Medieval times. These mounds were used as tribal assembly places, platforms for expounding the law to an assembly, sites for high-level meetings, sites for royal inaugurations and sites of assembly before battle.

Many of these Medieval inauguration mounds may be much earlier prehistoric burial mounds which were appropriated by emerging royal dynasties to legitimise their right to rule. In other words, by using a very ancient mound as a site for their inaugurations, they were establishing a link between themselves and an ancient leader, possibly a mythological leader. *Carn Mhic Táil* is named after *Táil*, the ancestor of both *Conchobhar* and *Lochlainn*, and it was considered to be the burial place of *Táil*. *Táil's* descendants, *Conchobhar* and *Lochlainn*, were then named as the founding ancestors of what became the two leading dynastic families of the Medieval Burren, the O'Connors and the O'Loughlins.

In the eleventh and twelfth centuries, the kingship of the chiefdom of *Corcu Modruad* fluctuated between the O'Connors and the O'Loughlins and by the fourteenth century the chiefdom was split in two. After the division the O'Loughlins ruled the east Burren and the O'Connors ruled the west Burren. We have two historical references to *Carn Mhic Táil*. In 1573 it was used as an assembly point for troops before a battle which had O'Connors and O'Briens on both sides and another reference mentions a meeting at the cairn between the leaders of the *Corcu Modruad* and another group, the *Tuadmumu.*

Figure 152
Carn Mhic Táil.

Leamaneh Castle

Grid Reference R 234 936

Leamaneh Castle is a two-part construction. The eastern portion is a fifteenth-century tower house while the western portion is a seventeenth-century manor house. The later manor-house, with its broad, mullioned windows, stands in stark contrast to the earlier tower house with its narrow, window slits and shows that style and comfort had become greater concerns than defence by the seventeenth century. The projecting gallery or 'bartizan' with its musket holes on the south-west corner of the manor house, however, shows that defence was still of some concern. A greater concern with style and pleasure is also evident in the extensive seventeenth-century remains surrounding the manor house. Stretching to the east of the manor house was a walled formal garden which included a fish pond, a summer house and a 'turret walk' along the wall, where one could stroll and view the garden. Beyond the formal garden is a very large area surrounded by a high and sturdy wall. This was probably the deer park that gave Leamaneh its name which translates as 'the deer's leap'.

Most of the seventeenth-century improvements at Leamaneh were probably carried out by Conor O'Brien and his wife Mary Ní Mahon, also known as Máire Rua or 'Red Mary', because of her red hair. There are many legends about Máire Rua, some with more truth than others. What can be said with certainty is that after her husband Conor was killed fighting the Cromwellians in 1651, she married a Cromwellian named Cooper in order to save the estate for her son.

The fact that Leamaneh was an O'Brien castle has a lot to do with why it is located where it is. In the late Medieval and post-Medieval periods, the O'Briens were expanding their power and land holdings at the expense of other dynastic families. At this time the Burren was a distinct territory under the control of the O'Loughlins and they located their capital in the centre of their territory (and therefore at the centre of the Burren) at Gragans Castle (Grid Reference M 204 036). The O'Loughlins may have located their capital well within their territory in order to protect it from the encroaching O'Briens, but the O'Briens constructed Leamaneh castle right on the edge of the O'Loughlin territory. Leamaneh Castle is, in fact, located at the junction of three territories: the O'Loughlin territory of Burren to the north which had not come under O'Brien control, the O'Connor territory of Corcomroe stretching out westwards to the Atlantic which had already come under the control of the O'Briens and the O'Dea territory of Inchiquin stretching out to the east which was also already under the control of the O'Briens.

Not only is Leamaneh Castle sited at the junction of these three territories, the castle is also sited to control one of the most important road junctions on the Burren. It sits at the junction where the main north-south road across the Burren joins the main east-west road

Figure 153
Leamaneh Castle.

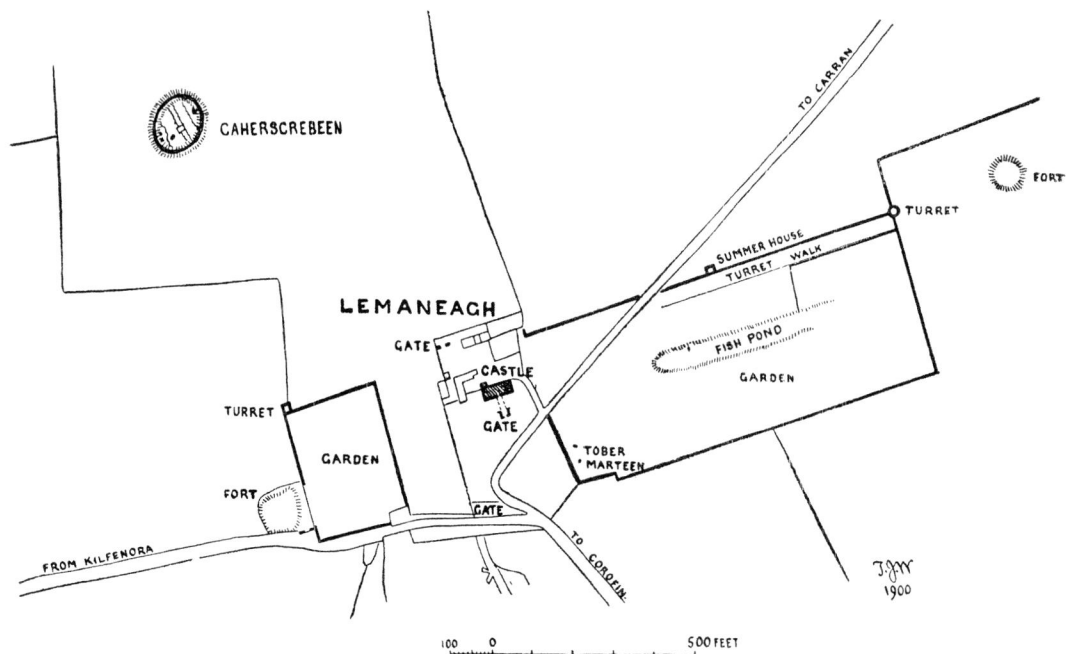

Figure 154
The gardens and grounds of Leamaneh Castle.

The remains of this formal garden can still be seen in the field just across the Ballyvaughan road to the east.

in the area. Both these roads are still in use today. The road approaching Leamaneh from the east was known as 'Sir Donat's Road' and travel along it was controlled by high stone walls and two sets of gates, the outermost of which stood two kilometres to the east of the castle. Portions of the well-built roadside walls can still be seen flanking the road as one approaches Leamaneh from the east.

By positioning their castle at the junction of three territories and at the junction of the most important crossroads in the area, it seems that part of the O'Brien's expansionist strategy was to control and possibly limit communication between the other dynastic families in the area. The O'Briens had already subjugated the two southern territories and now the northern territory of the Burren was clearly in their sights, so it seems that one consideration in the siting of Leamaneh Castle may have been the prevention of a military alliance between the O'Loughlainns, the O'Conors and the O'Deas.

Figure 155
The ornamented gateway of Leamaneh.

The ornamented gateway that once stood in front of Leamaneh Castle is now a garden ornament at Dromoland Castle near Newmarket-on-Fergus. The gate bears an inscription which states *'This was built in the yeare of our Lord 1643 by Conor O'Brien and by Mary Ní Mahon, wife of the said Conor.'* Above the inscription is the coat of arms of Conor O'Brien and the gate also bears the coat of arms of Conor's son, Donat.

Nineteenth-Century Military Fortifications on the Burren

IN THE LATER YEARS OF THE EIGHTEENTH CENTURY and the early years of the nineteenth century the British were continually worried about the possibility of a French invasion of Ireland which might enable an Irish uprising. These fears led the British to construct a comprehensive network of coastal defences around Ireland. Both the British and the French considered the sheltered harbours and beaches inside Galway Bay to be ideal landing spots for an invasion of Ireland, especially as Galway Bay is just under a week's march from Dublin.

To counter this threat, three Martello towers were built around Galway Bay. These towers are large, circular towers which were both gun platforms and living quarters for the soldiers. Of the three Martello towers built on the shores of Galway Bay, two were built along its south shore on the edge of the Burren, one at Finavarra Point and the other at Aughinish. The tower at Finavarra Point is clearly visible from the village of Ballyvaghan on the tip of the low peninsula that forms the north-east side of Ballyvaghan Bay. It is positioned so that its guns could cover all the nearby landing places. The other is located at Aughinish, five kilometres east of Finavarra Point. In addition to the guns mounted on the tops of the towers, there were probably additional guns arranged in batteries outside the towers.

Both towers are of the same design. The entrance is on the first floor and would probably have been accessed by a wooden ladder that could be raised and lowered quickly. Living quarters were on the first floor and were designed to accommodate a garrison of 39 men and one officer. The ground floor was the magazine for storing the gunpowder and the water tank was in the basement.

Figure 156
Martello tower at Finavarra Point.
Grid Reference M 241 116

The Aran Islands

The Colonisation and Early Settlement
of the Aran Islands

THERE ARE NO MONUMENTS ON THE ARAN ISLANDS as old as the Neolithic portal tombs and chambered tombs of the Burren. The earliest monuments on the Aran Islands are the Final Neolithic/Early Bronze Age wedge tombs and these wedge tombs may mark the first time there was a significant population on the islands. On the Burren, the Final Neolithic/Early Bronze Age seems to have been a time when the population was growing and expanding into areas that had been unoccupied or only sparsely populated earlier in the Neolithic (see *Competition and Social Upheaval on Roughan Hill*). On the Aran Islands, there are indications on a pollen core from Inisheer of tree clearances and farming earlier in the Neolithic, but the first significant peopling of the islands may well have been part of this expansion of population some time around 2300–2000 BC.

When the first colonists arrived on the Aran Islands from somewhere on the mainland, quite possibly from the Burren, it would have been a substantial undertaking. These first colonists were farmers and they would have to carry over their cattle, sheep, goats, pigs and seed corn with them. They would also have to arrive in fairly large numbers themselves in order to form a viable community. For a community to be viable in the long term it must be large enough so there are enough able, working adults to support the older and younger members of the community. Inbreeding must also be avoided if a group is to survive in the long-term and this poses problems for people living in small groups, especially isolated small groups such as islanders. For a group to avoid inbreeding each individual seeking a partner must have access to between 200–500 potential mates. Of course, there is no reason to suppose that mates were not exchanged between the islands and the mainland, but a group numbering several hundred is probably a fairly accurate estimate of the original colonising group.

Figure 157
Preparing to ship pigs in currachs.

Today currachs are made by stretching tarred canvas over a frame of wooden lathes. In the past they were made by stretching hides over a wicker or wooden frame and it's likely that the first people to arrive on the Aran islands made the passage in a similar sort of vessel. This early twentieth-century photograph shows the islanders preparing to ship pigs in currachs in much the same way as the first colonists would have had to do.

The Wedge Tombs of the Aran Islands

There are at least six wedge tombs on the Aran Islands. They are similar to the wedge tombs of the Burren and unfortunately, like the Burren wedge tombs, none of the Aran Island wedge tombs have been excavated. Evidence from excavated wedge tombs elsewhere in Ireland, however, suggests that the Aran Island wedge tombs were built *c.* 2300 – 2000 BC and that they were used repeatedly over a long span of time. Like all megalithic tombs, wedge tombs were not merely resting places for the dead. They were also sites where acts of worship and the veneration of the ancestors took place over many generations. The Aran Island wedge tombs are best viewed as fairly small ancestor shrines that served the spiritual needs of the local community and probably also served to mark that community's claim to the surrounding land.

Figure 158
Oghil wedge tomb, Inishmore.
Grid Reference L 850 099

The Oghil wedge tomb is the best preserved wedge tomb on the Aran Islands. It is located on the high ground in the middle of Inishmore.

Figure 159

Carrownlisheen wedge tomb, Inishmaan.

Grid Reference L 944 052

The collapsed remains of the Carrownlisheen wedge tomb located near to *Baile an Mhothair* on Inishmaan.

The intensive survey on Roughan Hill has shown that on the Burren there is a very close correspondence between the location of wedge tombs and contemporary prehistoric farmsteads. The same probably held true for the Aran Islands and so we can suggest that early settlement was probably in the immediate area of the wedge tombs. This would mean there was early settlement near the Carrownpholleen wedge tomb on the western side of Inisheer, early settlement in the general vicinity of the modern settlement on the northern side of Inishmaan, where there are the two wedge tombs at Carrownlisheen and Carrowntemple, and a cluster of early settlement in the middle of Inishmore where there are three wedge tombs at Oghil, Cowragh and Oatquarter. It is also interesting that there is one wedge tomb on Inisheer, two on Inishmaan and three on Inishmore. There may well have been other wedge tombs that are now destroyed, but the correlation between the numbers of wedge tombs and the size of the islands does suggest that Inisheer had the smallest population and Inishmore had the largest population. (Note: the 'wedge tomb' adjacent to Dún Eochla at the centre of Inishmore is a modern construction and there are no indications that a prehistoric wedge tomb was ever located in this area.)

The Cnoc Raithní Burial Mound, Inisheer

Grid Reference L 979 027

In the Early Bronze Age, a whole range of new burial customs were practised in Ireland. Megalithic tombs were no longer built and they seem to have lost their importance, although burials were sometimes still placed in them. More typically, however, individuals were buried in pits or stone cists, often accompanied by pottery vessels and sometimes accompanied by other grave goods as well. Some individuals were inhumed and others were cremated before they were buried. Sometimes, pottery vessels were placed beside the inhumation or cremation, in other cases cremated remains were placed inside pottery vessels that were then buried upside down in pits or cists. These Early Bronze Age burials are often found grouped together in flat cemeteries or in a cemetery mound.

The Cnoc Raithní mound, just inland from the beach on Inisheer, appears to have begun as one of these Early Bronze Age cemetery mounds. Today, Cnoc Raithní is a flat-topped, circular mound edged with a drystone wall. On top of the circular mound is a smaller square mound, once again edged with a drystone wall. Various slabs protrude from the top of both the circular mound and the square mound.

Cnoc Raithní is a complex monument. The square mound superimposed on the circular mound suggests at least two phases of construction. Some of the slabs protruding from the surface of the circular mound may outline slab-lined Early Medieval graves, and if so, Cnoc

Figure 160
Cnoc Rathní burial mound, Inisheer.

Raithní may be a prehistoric cemetery mound that was re-modelled and re-used in the Early Medieval period. Interpretation is made even more difficult by the fact that the site was 'restored' to an unknown degree in the nineteenth century.

In 1885 antiquarians excavated a mound close to the beach on Inisheer and although not well recorded, it is generally assumed that the mound was Cnoc Raithní. What they found within the mound were two Early Bronze Age cremations set within a circular stone cist approximately 1.5 metres in diameter. Both cremations were contained in pottery vessels and the cremated remains in the smaller pot were accompanied by a small fragment of bronze as well, probably the end of a pin or an awl.

Figure 161

Finds probably from the Cnoc Raithní burial mound.

Two Bronze Age pottery vessels and a small bronze fragment, possibly a pin or an awl, excavated from a mound (probably Cnoc Raithní) by antiquarians in 1885. The larger vessel is a Cordoned Urn and it is possibly the westernmost Cordoned Urn ever found. Cordoned Urns are essentially a Scottish pottery type which are most common around the Firth of Forth on the east coast of Scotland. Cordoned Urns seem to date to the centuries between 2000 BC and 1500/1400 BC. Their name derives from the distinctive raised cordons that encircle the pots. The occurrence of a Cordoned Urn on Inisheer shows that the Early Bronze Age inhabitants of the Aran Islands had far-flung contacts.

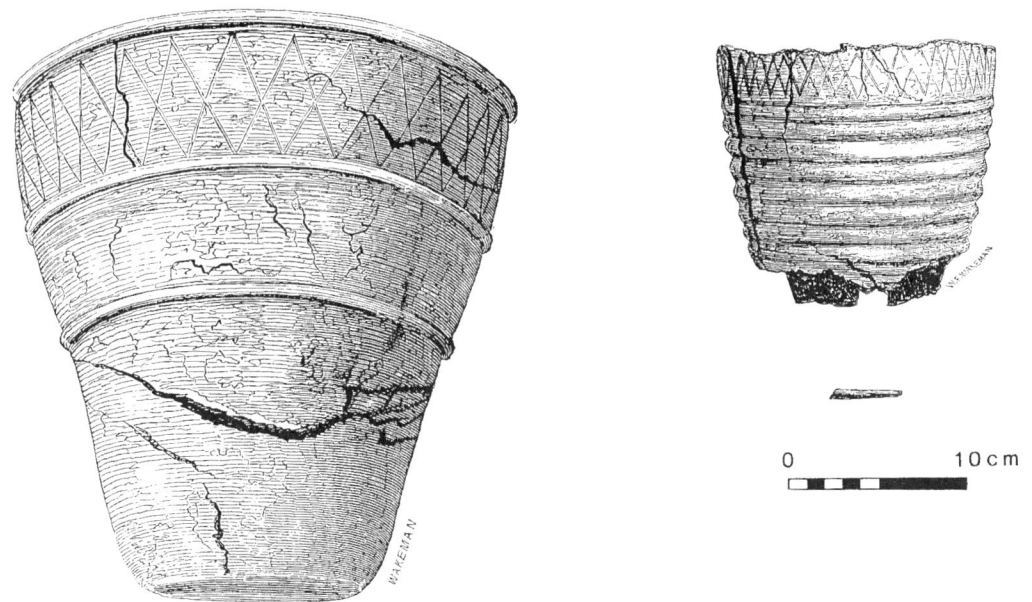

The Late Bronze Age Chiefdom of Dún Aonghasa

Hillfort at Dún Aonghasa on Inishmore: Grid Reference L818 098

[P] [人]

Prior to the Late Bronze Age, the people of the Aran Islands probably lived in what archae-ologists term a 'segmentary society'. This society would have been composed of several individual communities integrated into the larger society through kinship ties. No group would have held sway over any other and the settlements of the time would have been loosely clustered hamlets and scattered farmsteads. In the Late Bronze Age, however, this segmen-tary society appears to have developed into a hierarchical chiefdom. This chiefdom would have integrated the various local groups on the islands into a single, unified group under the rule of an individual leader or perhaps a council of leaders. The central site of this chiefdom seems to have been the impressive hillfort at Dún Aonghasa on Inishmore.

Like other Bronze Age chiefdoms in Ireland, the chiefdom of Dún Aonghasa would have been a kin-based organisation which had expanded into a regional governing body. Kinship and personal bonds would have been central to the political organisation of the chiefdom and each individual's rank in this society would have been determined by how closely he/she was related to the chief. At the top of this hierarchical society would have been the chief's family and a warrior elite who dominated the economic, social, political and religious realms.

The hierarchical society on the Aran islands in the Bronze Age was probably reflected in a hierarchy of settlement types ranging from humble farmsteads up to the massive hillfort at Dún Aonghasa. Indeed, the hillfort at Dún Aonghasa was probably as much a symbol of the power of the chief and his family as it was a defensive structure. It has often been pointed out that the area encompassed by the outer rings of many hillforts is much too large to defend efficiently. It's possible, therefore, that the outer rings had a role that was more symbolic than defensive. The extent and scale of the multiple rings of walls was certainly dependant on the amount of labour that the chief could call upon and this was perhaps one of their purposes – to visibly and dramatically reflect the strength of the chief's power base amongst the people.

Many chiefdoms develop a system of wealth and commodity re-distribution as a way to support the upper stratum of the society. In these 'redistribution' systems, food and craft goods are collected by the chief as a type of tax or rent and the chief then re-distributes the products as he sees fit, skimming off a profit to support the elite. Cattle have played an important role in the Irish economy ever since the Neolithic and it is possible that many Irish hillforts may have served as collection points for cattle tribute demanded by a chief from his subjects. Vast herds of cattle could have been gathered within the outer circuits of hillforts which the chief could then redistribute amongst his people. If this did happen, it may have been timed to coincide with various community ceremonies staged at the hillfort. The sight of a vast herd of cattle within the outer walls of the hillfort, if only for a short time, would have been a vibrant, smelly and noisy advertisement of the chief's wealth and power. At Dún Aonghasa, sheep seem to have been more important than cattle but a similar effect could have been achieved by bringing large flocks of sheep within the outer enclosure wall.

The Form of the Original Late Bronze Age Hillfort

Much of what is visible today at Dún Aonghasa is the result of later remodelling of the fort, probably in the Early Medieval period (see *The Stone Forts of the Aran Islands*). Figure 162 shows the most likely layout of the original Late Bronze Age hillfort based on the results of the Discovery Programme excavations.

Along the western portion of the innermost wall, Wall 1, Late Bronze Age occupation deposits were found to continue part-way under the wall but not all the way to the exterior of the wall. This suggests that the western portion of Wall 1 follows the line of an earlier, Late Bronze Age wall. Unfortunately, the archaeologists were unable to excavate a section all the way through Wall 1 because of the engineering difficulties but a small cutting at the eroded and rebuilt cliff-edge end of Wall 1 did reveal an earlier wall encased within Wall 1 and this may be the Late Bronze Age wall.

The line of the Late Bronze Age wall and Wall 1 appear to diverge on the north side of Wall 1. Excavations here revealed the foundations of a wall connecting Wall 1 to Wall 2A. A radiocarbon date from occupation material that butted up against the interior of this wall segment showed that it was a Late Bronze Age wall. The stratigraphy also showed there was occupation inside this wall but not outside it. The foundation of this Late Bronze Age wall can still be seen on the ground today if you look closely between Walls 1 and 2.

Another interesting clue found by the archaeologists in this area was that the Late Bronze Age occupation material continued under both sides of Wall 1 at this point, although once again, they were unable to excavate a section completely through the wall. The presence of Bronze Age occupation material extending under both sides of Wall 1 at this point does suggest there may not be a Late Bronze Age wall encased in the eastern portion of Wall 1. There is, however, an earlier wall encased within Wall 2A which is presumably the continuation of the Late Bronze Age wall.

Nothing that could date Wall 4 was uncovered by the archaeologists but its wavy outline that sometimes follows the contours of the hill and the large area it encompasses, make it morphologically similar to other Late Bronze Age hillforts and dissimilar to all the other Aran Island stone forts.

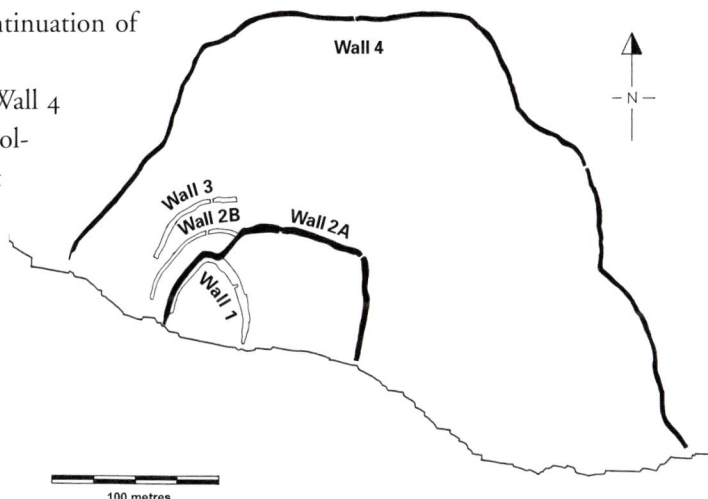

100 metres

Figure 162
The likely form of the original Late Bronze Age hillfort at Dún Aonghasa.

The walls which are most likely to have formed the Late Bronze Age hillfort are shown in solid black. Later walls are shown in outline only.

Figure 163
Bedrock platform on the cliff edge at the centre of Dún Aonghasa.

This platform appears to have been created by quarrying away the surrounding bedrock. It is unclear whether the platform is contemporary with the original Late Bronze Age hillfort or the much later, probably Early Medieval, remodelling of the site. Whichever period it dates to, it provides a dramatic stage and one should probably envisage various important rituals taking place here, such as the inaugurations of chiefs and the marriages of elite couples to cement alliances.

Figure 164

Dún Aonghasa from the air.

The prominent locations of hillforts such as Dún Aonghasa may have been chosen in part for their defensive advantages, but it also means that the views from hillforts are extensive and conversely, hillforts are visible from far away. Hillforts in other parts of Ireland are sometimes sited to overlook major prehistoric route ways and sometimes to command extensive views over a hinterland that was presumably under the control of the occupants of the hillfort. Dún Aonghasa certainly commands extensive views over a wide hinterland of both land and sea and it is possible that it is sited to command views over prehistoric sea routes.

Controlling Production at Dún Aonghasa

A large number of fragments of clay moulds which were used to produce swords, spearheads, bracelets and pins were recovered from the excavation of Dún Aonghasa. A chiefdom must develop some sort of system to finance the elites at the top of the society and one way to do this is through 'wealth finance'. Wealth finance involves the control of the production and distribution of valuables by the chief. These valuables are used as symbols of status that define a person's political and economic position in society. By controlling the production and distribution of valuables, the chief has the power to grant status and privilege and thereby motivate people to obey and work for him. The presence of these clay mould fragments, along with crucible fragments and a large hearth area within the fort, shows that the valuable bronzes being produced, as well as the craftsmen who produced them, were being directly controlled by the chief. It is also significant that many of the moulds found at Dún Aonghasa were used to produce weapons. Individuals and local communities may not have always submitted to the chief willingly but by controlling the manufacture and ownership of weapons the chief could monopolise the use of force. Controlling the production of metalwork, therefore, benefited the chief in two ways – by directly controlling the production of valuables, the chief controlled access to wealth and status and by controlling the production of weapons the chief ensured others could not usurp him by force or ignore his demands.

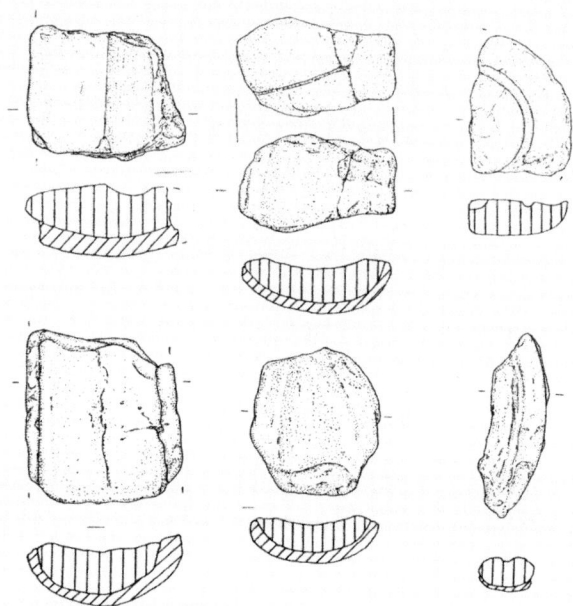

Figure 165
Clay mould fragments from Dún Aonghasa.

Fragments of Late Bronze Age clay moulds for swords, spearheads, bracelets and pins were recovered from the excavations at Dún Aonghasa.

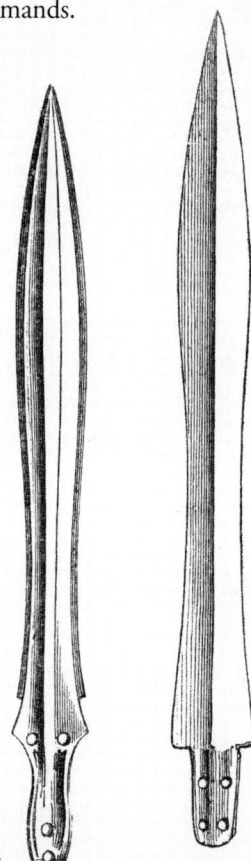

Figure 166
Bronze Age weapons and ornaments.

Weapons similar to these swords and spearheads, as well as ornaments similar to this pin were produced at Dún Aonghasa.

Excavating Dún Aonghasa

Portions of Dún Aonghasa were excavated under the direction of Claire Cotter in the 1990s as part of the 'Western Stone Forts Project' funded by the Discovery Programme of research. The main focus of this project was to shed more light on the date and function of a group of stone forts along the western seaboard of Ireland, of which Dún Aonghasa is one example. At the outset of the Western Stone Fort Project it was generally assumed that these forts were Iron Age constructions and, as far back as the nineteenth century, antiquarians viewed the stone forts as key elements of a Celtic past in Ireland.

In fact, although the excavations revealed some Iron Age activity at Dún Aonghasa, no definite evidence for a sustained occupation of the site during the Iron Age was found. Instead, the excavations revealed fairly extensive Late Bronze Age occupation, some Iron Age activity, and a renewed (but less intensive) occupation of the site in the Early Medieval period. The form of the fort and most of the upstanding walls that are visible to the visitor today probably date to the Early Medieval period (see *The Stone Forts of the Aran Islands*) but evidence for Bronze Age habitation was found throughout the Bronze Age inner enclosure (see *The Form of the Original Late Bronze Age Hillfort*). In particular, a series of hut foundations, paved areas and other features were found in the western portion of what is today the innermost enclosure. These huts and other features seem to relate to the occupation of the hillfort in the period between about 1300–800 BC. There were some traces of occupation underneath some of the huts, but radiocarbon dates from these layers place them firmly in the Bronze Age as well.

Other than the evidence for bronze working (see *Controlling Production at Dún Aonghasa*), the Bronze Age finds from Dún Aonghasa were mainly normal domestic debris. Out of the approximately 1,500 pottery sherds that were recovered all but 1 per cent were undecorated and therefore most were sherds from mundane pots for everyday use. Other finds included bone pins (probably clothes fasteners), a bone needle, bronze tweezers, a bronze chisel, whetstones, pin-sharpening stones, quern stones and rubbing stones, a few personal ornaments made from shale, and a few glass and amber beads.

The mammal bone assemblage from Dún Aonghasa was quite interesting as it showed a higher reliance on sheep and a lower reliance on cattle than most prehistoric sites in Ireland. Additionally, the cattle present were smaller than normal. The greater reliance on sheep seems to be an adaptation to the harsh and exposed climate of the Aran Islands and it also seems that the sheep were reared primarily for their meat rather than their wool. This is shown by the fact that about one-third of the sheep at Dún Aonghasa were killed at less than one year and less than a quarter lived past three and a half years. Altogether, sheep/goat makes up about half of the mammal bone assemblage from Dún Aonghasa, cattle approximately a third, pigs an even smaller number and red deer a very small amount. Other food remains found in the excavations were bird bones, fish bones, limpet and periwinkle shells, and the occasional cereal grain.

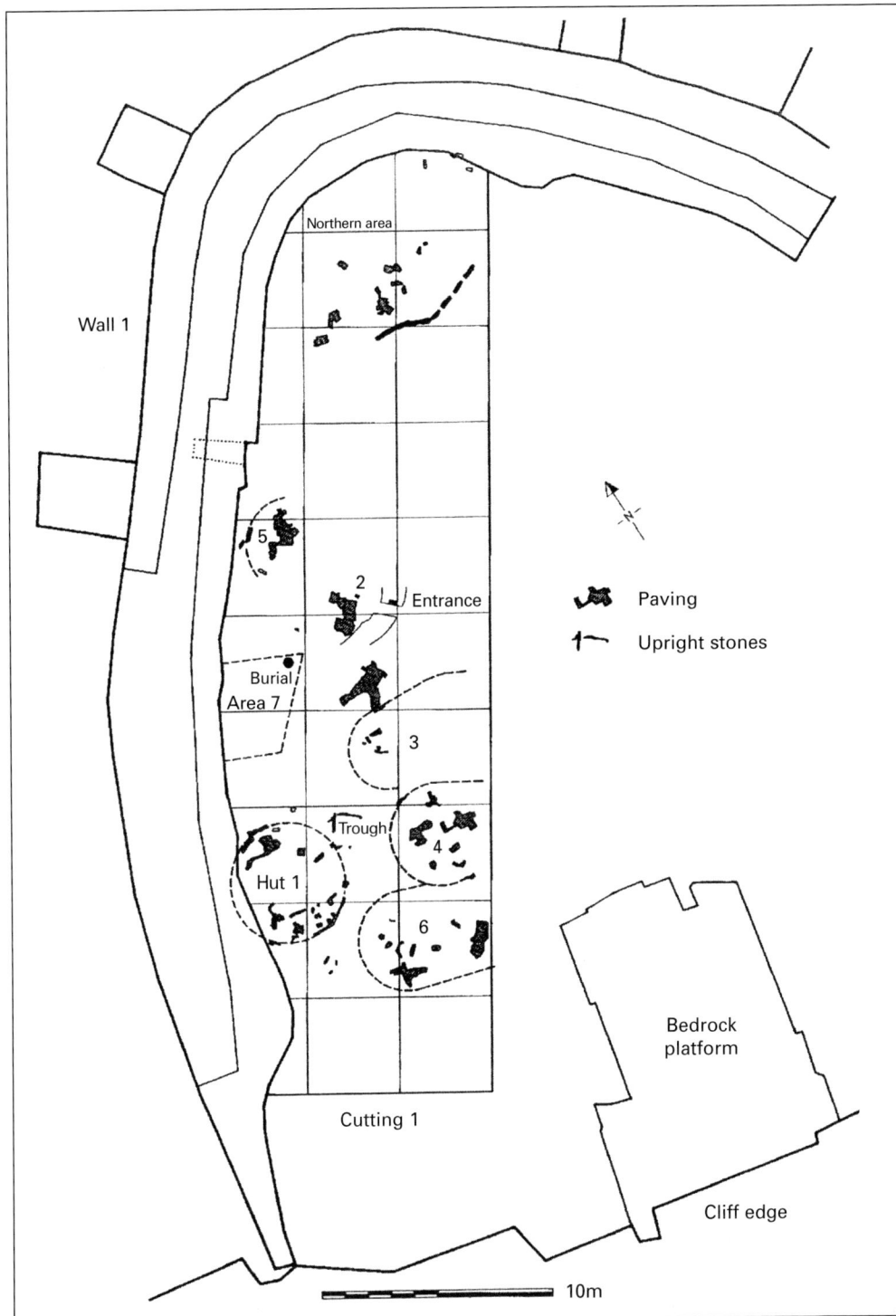

Figure 167
Hut foundations and other features at Dún Aonghasa.

Most of these hut foundations and other features belong to the Late Bronze Age occupation of the hillfort in the period between about 1300–800 BC.

Northern area

Wall 1

5

2

Entrance

Burial
Area 7

3

Trough

4

Hut 1

6

Bedrock
platform

Cutting 1

Cliff edge

Paving

Upright stones

10m

Figure 168
Late Bronze Age domestic pottery from Dún Aonghasa.

Many of the potsherds have some sort of plant or grass impressions on their surfaces and it's possible that the pots were wrapped with grass when they were fired so that they would heat up more gradually and therefore have less chance of cracking during the firing.

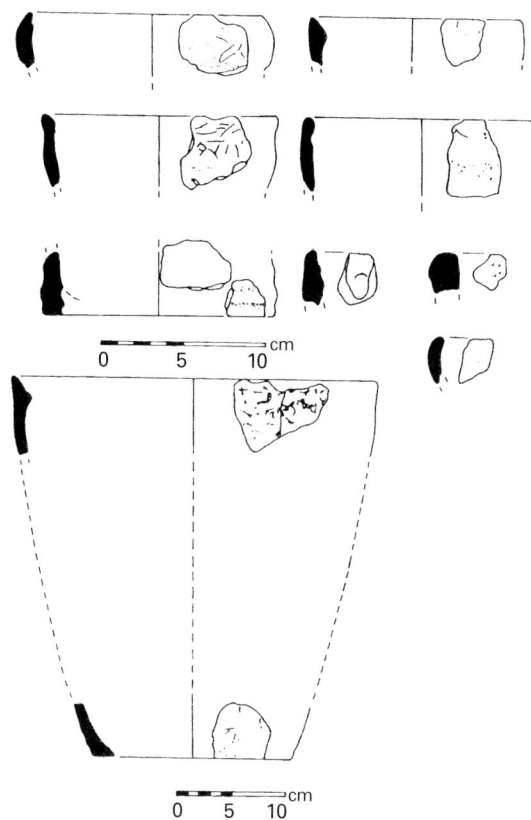

Figure 169
Bone pins, a bone pin/needle and a pin-sharpening stone from the excavations at Dún Aonghasa.

Bone pins with decorated heads may well have been used to fasten clothes while undecorated and more expediently manufactured examples may have been used as tools such as needles or awls.

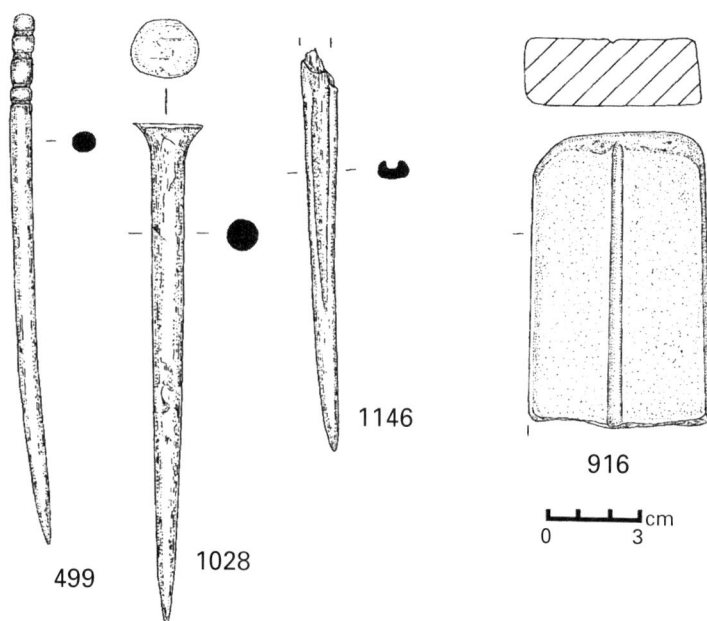

499   1028   1146   916

The Stone Forts of the Aran Islands

THERE ARE SEVEN LARGE STONE FORTS on the Aran islands: Dún Aonghasa (in its post-Bronze Age form), Dún Dúcathair, Dún Eoghanachta and Dún Eochla on Inishmore; Dún Chonchúir and Dún Fearbhaí on Inishmaan, and Dún Formna on Inisheer. These Aran Island forts are part of a spread of large stone forts all along the western seaboard of Ireland which are distinct from the more common cashels (stone ringforts) and earthen ringforts which also occur in large numbers in this region and beyond. The large stone forts are distinguished by the massive dimensions of their walls, the presence of terracing and steps on the inside of the walls, the occurrence sometimes of chambers or passageways within the walls and the presence sometimes of a *chevaux de frise*. The names of all seven forts on the Aran Islands are also prefaced by the word '*Dún*' which means the fort of a king or chieftain.

All seven of the Aran forts were restored in the nineteenth century and although some pre-restoration descriptions, photographs and drawings do exist, it is not always clear to what extent the present form of their walls is original or reconstructed. One feature found on many of the forts today which in all cases are probably nineteenth-century additions are the large external buttresses supporting the walls. Two of the Aran forts were partially excavated in the 1990s by the Discovery Programme, Dún Aonghasa and Dún Eoghanachta on Inishmore. As discussed previously, Dún Aonghasa began as a Late Bronze Age hillfort but it was subsequently remodelled and reused (see *The Late Bronze Age Chiefdom of Dún Aonghasa*). Although the timing of the remodelling of Dún Aonghasa is not certain, it seems most likely that it occurred during the Early Medieval period

When Dún Eoghanachta was excavated, the finds recovered suggested that its original

Figure 170
Territorial divisions on the Aran Islands.

As is the case on the Burren, some of the
territorial divisions on the Aran Islands may
reflect Medieval (and possibly Early Medieval)
tribal and sub-tribal land divisions (see
*Medieval Churches and Society on the
Burren*). The smallest territorial divisions are
the townlands and on the Aran Islands there
is an interesting correlation of one large fort
per townland. It is quite possible that the Aran
townlands represent the territories of
the chiefs who resided in the forts.

construction and its first occupation both occurred in the Early Medieval period. So it
appears as though Dún Eoghanachta was constructed at the same time that Dún Aonghasa
was remodelled and that both were occupied in their present form in the Early Medieval
period. This is probably also true for most of the large stone forts along the western seaboard
of Ireland. Indeed, very similar artefacts were found at Dún Eoghanachta on Inishmore and
at Cahercommaun, another of the western stone forts which is located on the Burren (see
Cahercommaun and the Early Medieval Chiefdoms of the Burren). It also seems likely, given
the evidence for later occupation at Dún Eoghanachta (see below), that the occupation of many
of the Aran forts continued into the Medieval period.

Like Cahercommaun on the Burren, the stone forts of the Aran Islands seem to have been
residences of wealthy and powerful Early Medieval chiefs. On the mainland, the wealth of
most Early Medieval chiefs seems to have been based on cattle. The close spacing of the large
forts on the Aran Islands, however, suggests a greater concentration of wealth than one would
expect if the wealth of the chiefs was based solely on stocking the islands with cattle or sheep
(contrast, for instance, the seven large stone forts on the islands which probably date to the
Early Medieval period, with the Late Bronze Age situation, where there only appears to have
been one chiefly residence on the islands – Dún Aonghasa). How then did the Early
Medieval chiefs of the Aran Islands gain their wealth? The answer probably lies in the
control of seaways. Certainly by Medieval times, when the O'Briens controlled
the Aran Islands, they are reported to have been active in keeping
Galway Bay free of pirates on behalf of the merchants of Galway
city. As is so often the case with 'protection rackets'
though, the protectors are often the same as the
perpetrators and it seems likely some of the
wealth of the Aran Island chiefs was
gained either through acts of piracy
or by accepting payments of
'protection money' from
merchants to refrain
from piracy.

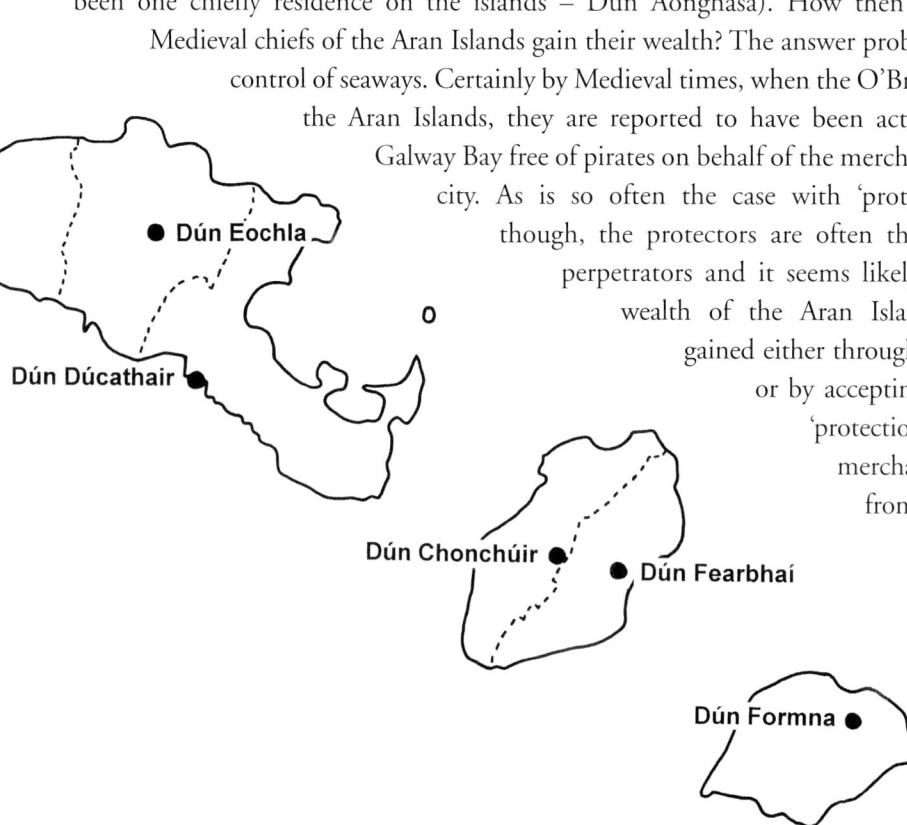

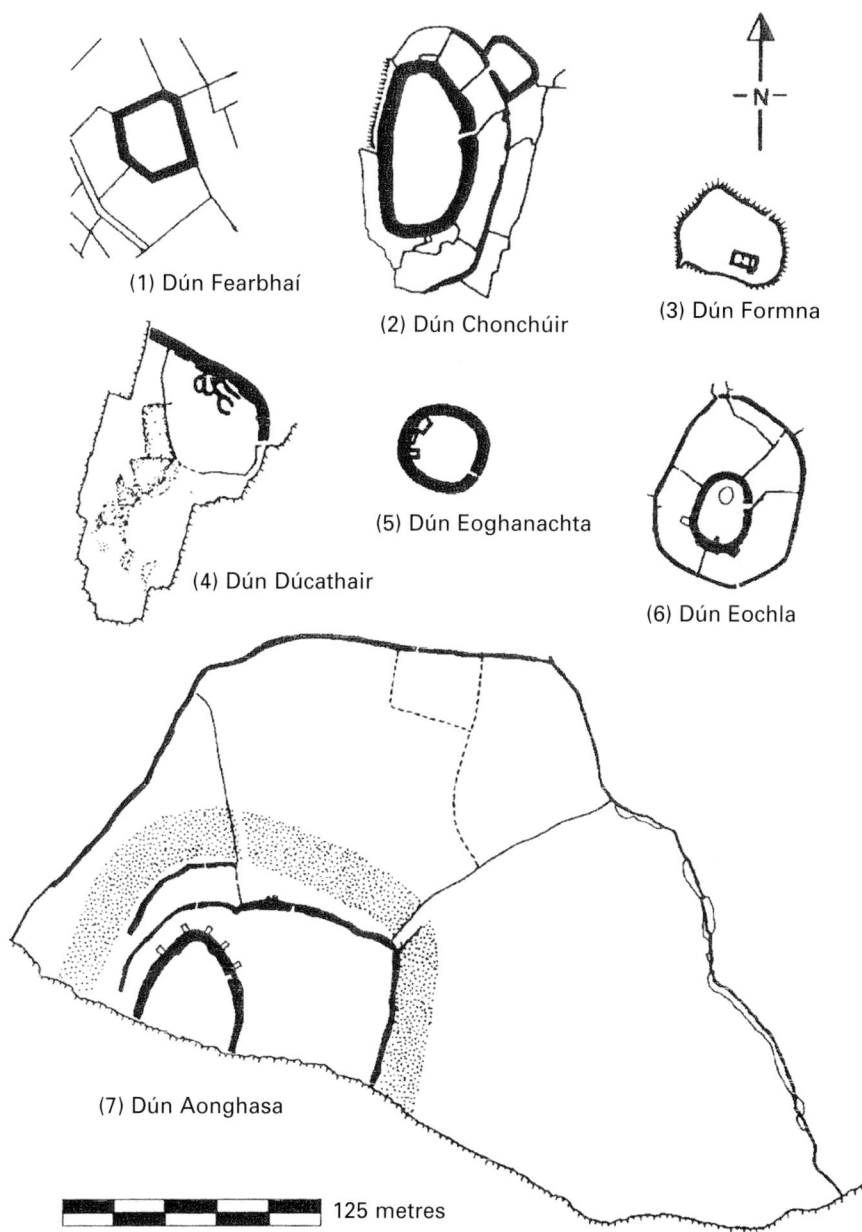

Figure 171
The seven large stone forts of the Aran Islands.

(1) Dún Fearbhaí

(2) Dún Chonchúir

(3) Dún Formna

(4) Dún Dúcathair

(5) Dún Eoghanachta

(6) Dún Eochla

(7) Dún Aonghasa

125 metres

Dún Aonghasa, Inishmore

Grid Reference L 818 098

⊡ 🚶

The appearance of the Dún as we first approach is that of a great chaos of ruins; but as it is reached, its general form soon develops itself – John Windele, *c.* 1854

. . . at Dún Aengusa the site and the building affect even the coolest mind as no blaze of mythic or historic association could do . . . All who have visited the spot feel the 'repellent attraction' of the gigantic precipice and the swirling abyss over which the fort is so airily poised. – Thomas Westropp, 1910

Most of what is visible at Dún Aonghasa today is the result of the Early Medieval remodelling of the earlier, Bronze Age hillfort (see *The Form of the Original Late Bronze Age Hillfort*). The Early Medieval fort (see Figure 173) consists of the massive inner enclosure or Wall 1, Wall 2 which completely encircles the inner enclosure, then a fragment of a third wall, next the wide band of the *chevaux de frise* and finally the outer or fourth wall which follows the outer line of the Bronze Age hillfort. The inner enclosure wall is truly massive. As it stands today, it is almost five metres high and just under six metres across at its widest. The external face of the wall has a marked batter that aids its stability. On the inside there are two terraces and various flights of steps. Wall 2 is not nearly as massive as the inner enclosure but it is still impressive. It has a single terrace and a few flights of steps. The western portion of Wall 2 is concentric with the inner enclosure but it then changes course at a noticeable kink where it starts to follow the older line of a Bronze Age wall (see Figure 162). Wall 3 is just a fragment of wall that runs roughly concentric to Wall 2. It is unclear if this fragment represents a wall that was never finished or a wall that has been robbed out. The next line in the defences is the *chevaux de frise*, the wide band of upturned stones. The outermost wall is Wall 4 which follows a course almost 200 metres outside of Wall 2 on the east, but runs much closer to the other walls on the west. This irregular outline is due to the fact that it follows the line of a Bronze Age wall.

Although it is during the Early Medieval period that Dún Aonghasa appears to have been remodelled into its present form, the Discovery Programme excavations on the site did not produce evidence for an intensive occupation at this time. Most of the habitation evidence revealed in the excavations dates to the original Bronze Age occupation of the site. There were, however, a few Early Medieval finds including a portion of a bone comb, several fragmentary iron objects and some animal bone which gave an Early Medieval radiocarbon date. A fragment of an Early Medieval ring-pin was also recovered from the site as a stray find unconnected with the excavations.

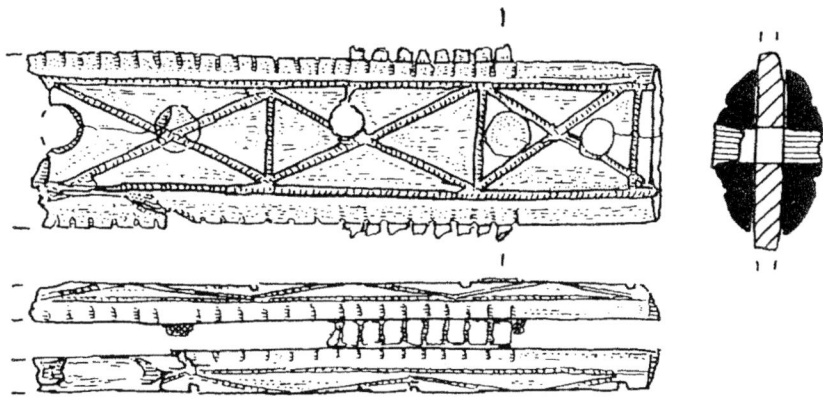

Figure 172
Portion of an Early Medieval antler comb from Dún Aonghasa.

This fragmentary comb is a composite piece with teeth-plates held between two decorated outer plates which are joined together with bone pegs.

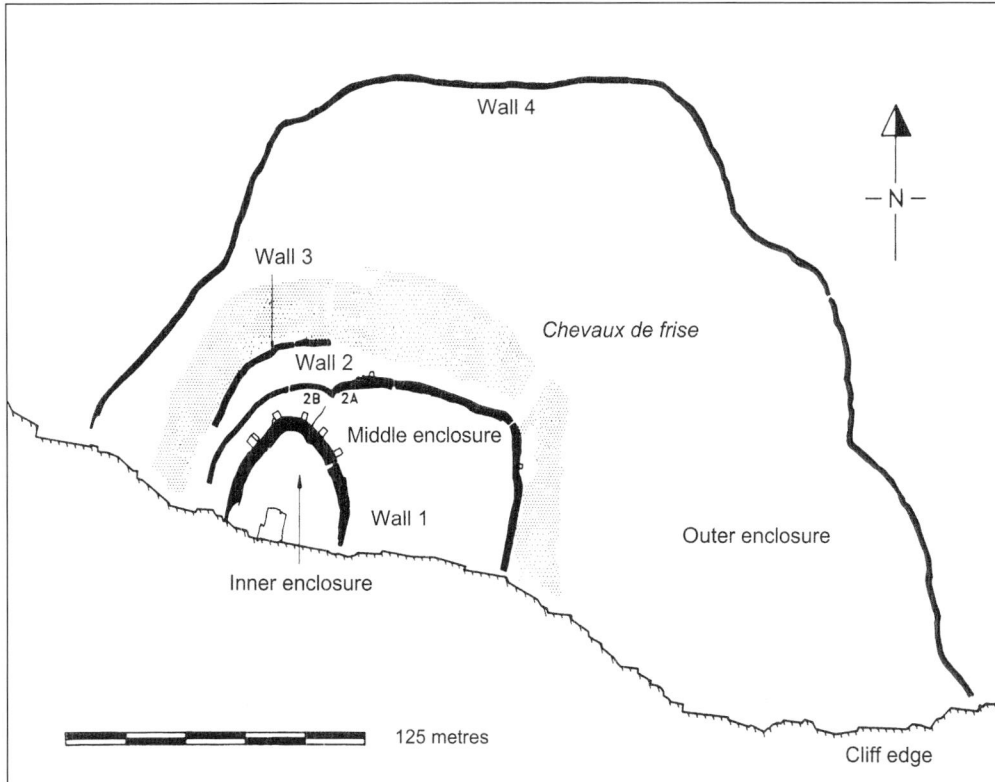

Figure 173
Plan of Dún Aonghasa.

Figure 174
Sections through the walls of Dún Aonghasa.

These section-drawings through the walls of Dún Aonghasa show the building technique that was used on all the large stone forts. As can be seen from the drawings, the walls were constructed of multiple sections which were built to different heights to form the terraces.

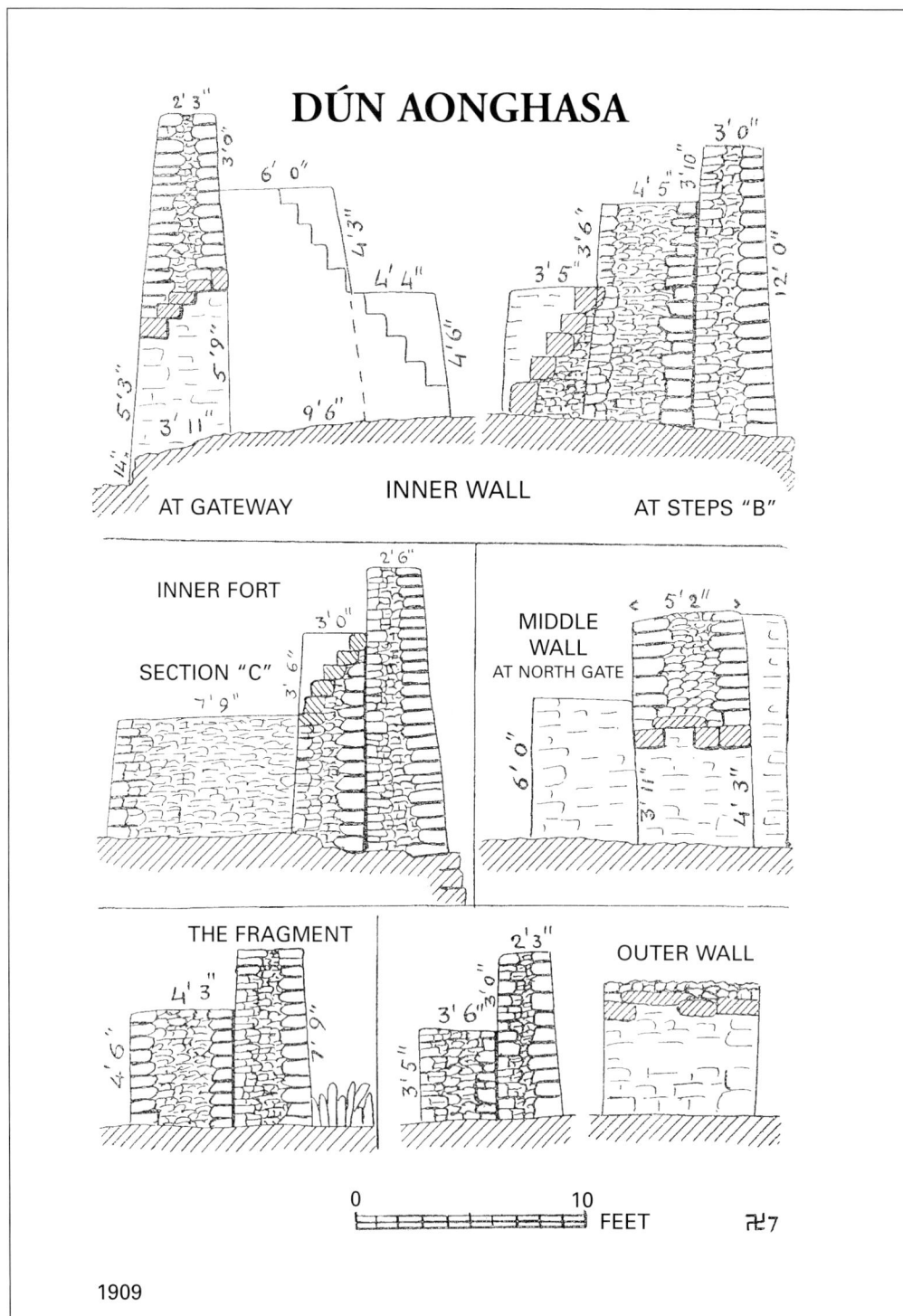

DÚN AONGHASA

INNER WALL

AT GATEWAY   AT STEPS "B"

INNER FORT

SECTION "C"

MIDDLE WALL
AT NORTH GATE

THE FRAGMENT

OUTER WALL

0   10
FEET

1909

Figure 175
Gateway through inner enclosure wall at Dún Aonghasa (Wall 1).

The outermost portion of this gateway is roofed with large lintels while the inner portion is an unroofed passage.

Figure 176
Gateway through the outer wall of Dún Aonghasa.

This well-built gateway is located in the northern portion of the outer wall (Wall 4). It is covered by massive lintels, the largest of which is 2.5 metres long.

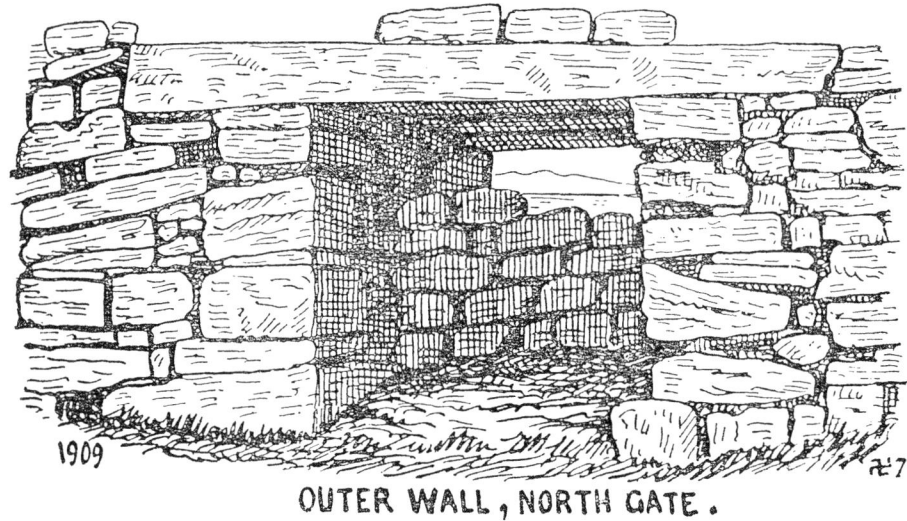

OUTER WALL, NORTH GATE.

Figure 177
Chevaux de frise at Dún Aonghasa.

The wide band of upturned stones outside the third wall is called a *chevaux de frise*. *Chevaux de frise* translates as 'horses of Friesland'. Friesland is a province in the Netherlands and the term is said to derive from the seventeenth century AD Friesian practice of setting up pointed timbers to defend themselves against cavalry charges, as they had few horses themselves. The *chevaux de frise* at Dún Aonghasa remains undated but it is possibily part of the Early Medieval remodelling of the site. *Chevaux de frise* defences are found on forts elsewhere in Ireland, Britain and farther afield in Europe, but the example at Dún Aonghasa is one of the most impressive. It measures 38 metres across at its widest and contains stones over 1.5 metres high.

Dún Eoghanachta, Inishmore

Grid Reference L 812 114

Dún Eoghanachta means the 'fort of the Eoghanachta', a tribal name. Dún Eoghanachta is located about 1.5 kilometres north west of Dún Aonghasa and the entire western third of Inishmore stills bears the name 'Eoghanacht'. Dún Eoghanachta is a univallate fort, that is, it has just one wall, but that wall is very impressive. The wall is up to five metres high and averages 4.75 metres in thickness.

Today, there are three buildings visible in the interior of the fort along the western side. The largest appears to have been a house while the two smaller structures appear to be out-buildings. When the site was excavated in the 1990s, midden from the original occupation of the fort was found to extend under the buildings and all three structures, therefore, appear to post-date the original construction and occupation of the fort. The date the buildings were built is uncertain, but a silver coin of Edward I, probably dating to 1300 AD, was found in the southernmost structure.

No structures which date to the original occupation were found within the fort during the excavations, but because only a portion of the interior of the fort was excavated, there may be buildings which have remained undetected. Where cuttings were opened, a midden layer was uncovered which contained limpet and periwinkle shells, along with lesser amounts of mammal, fish and bird bones. Although no structures were found that were contemporary with the midden, a possible hearth was found and two hollows in the bedrock that seem to have served as rubbish pits were found as well. The two pits contained cattle, pig, sheep/goat and red deer bones. Finds from the site were typical Early Medieval finds including a cake of iron slag, an iron ring-headed pin, part of a shale bracelet and an amber bead.

Figure 178
Plan of Dún Eoghanachta.

Terraces, flights of steps and internal buildings are all shown on this plan.

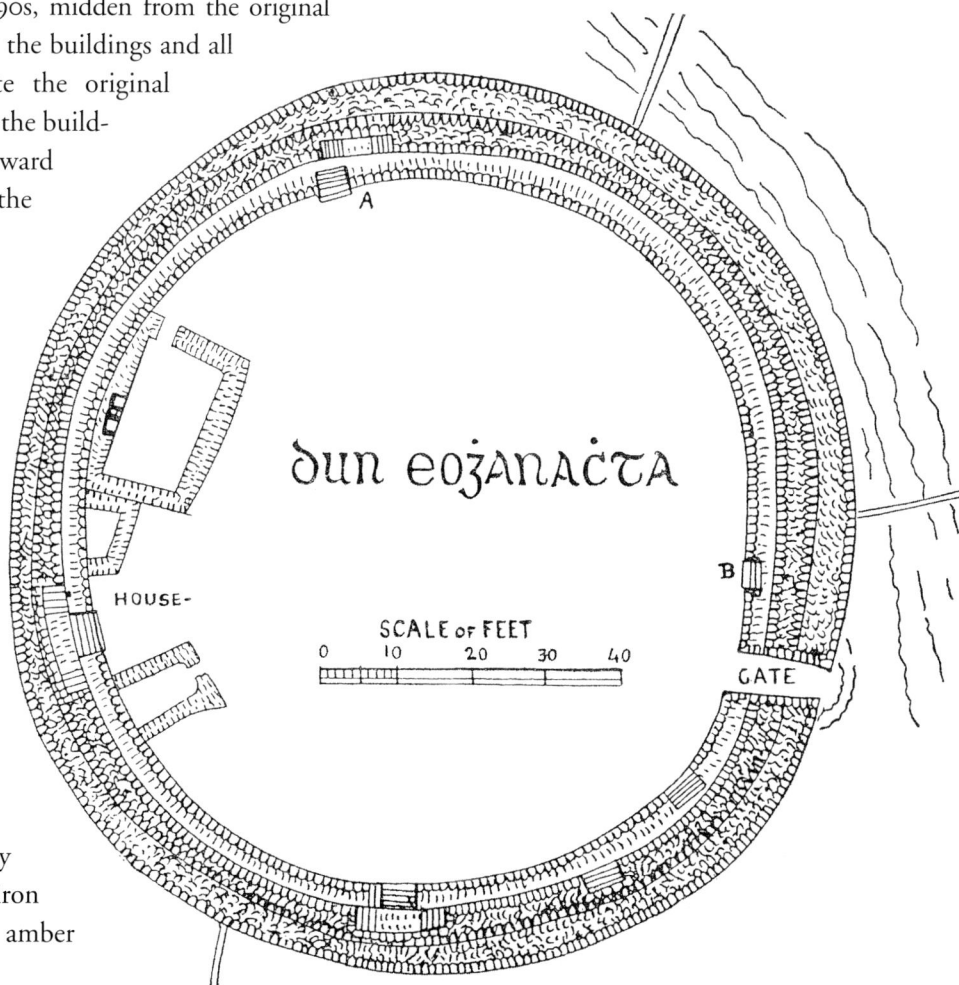

dun eoȝanaċta

SCALE of FEET

0   10   20   30   40

HOUSE

GATE

Figure 179 ▶
The interior of Dún Eoghanachta.

Visible in this photograph is a portion of the enclosing wall with terraces and flights of steps as well as the remains of the largest building inside the fort.

Figure 180
Plan of Dún Eochla, Inishmore.

Grid Reference L 863 098

Dún Eochla is a bivallate, that is, a two-walled fort located on the high ground in the middle of Inishmore. In one account, the name of the fort *eochla* derives from *oghil* which may be translated as 'oak wood'. So the full name may mean 'the fort of the oak wood' and as recently as 1821 dwarf-oak scrub was growing in nearby crags. It is an impressive fort with the inner wall approximately 5 metres high and 3.5 metres thick. This inner wall has a single terrace today but a sketch of the site from 1700 shows that it originally had two terraces. The outer wall is less massive and there are traces of a terrace around this wall as well.

The large circular stack of stones in the fort's interior appears to be the result of the nineteenth-century restorers' attempt to 'tidy up' the site. The stack of stones does, however, occupy the approximate position of a possible structure indicated on the sketch of 1700 and there is also a nineteenth-century description of the site, prior to its restoration, that describes a round heap of stones containing oval cells in this area. It's quite likely that this is a description of the collapsed remains of a group of conjoined huts similar to those that are still visible in Dún Dúcathair and Dún Chonchúir. ▶

The Other Stone Forts

Dún Aonghasa and Dún Eoghanachta are the only two of the Aran Island stone forts that have been excavated but there are five other large stone forts on the islands as well. By analogy with the excavated examples, we can say that these other forts were probably also constructed in the Early Medieval period as chiefly residences which may then have been occupied up into the Medieval period.

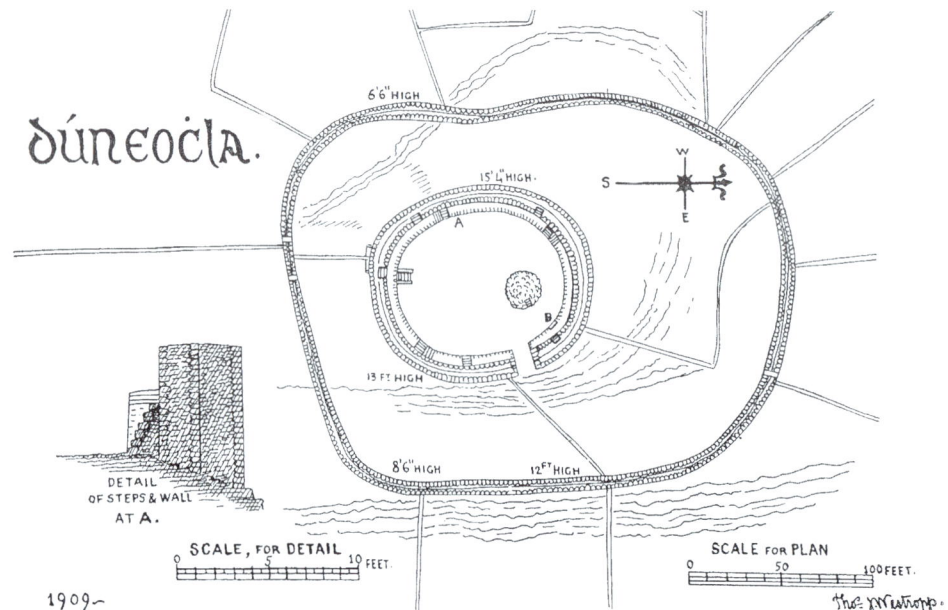

Figure 181
Dún Eochla from the lighthouse.

Figure 182 ▶
Dún Dúcathair, Inishmore.
Grid Reference L 870 073

P ⚐ (symbols)

Dún Dúcathair means the 'Black Fort', a name which reflects the darker colour of the limestone in this area. It is spectacularly located on a narrow promontory jutting out into the Atlantic from the southern side of Inishmore, south of Kilronan.

The rocks, dark grey, black in the shadow, are formed of huge strata of limestone, practically level, their seams often marked and their darkness relieved by close-packed rows of sea-gulls. The boom of waves into the great caverns can be heard through the rock inland with startling effect – Thomas Westropp, 1910.

Besides its spectacular location, there are several features of interest at Dún Dúcathair. The fort consists of a single wall cutting off a promontory and outside this wall is a *chevaux de frise*, an area of upended stones designed to impede an attack on the fort. This is a fairly rare form of defensive work. Dún Aonghasa is the only other fort on the Aran Islands to have a *chevaux de frise*, and only one fort on the Burren has one, Caherballykinvarga near Kilfenora (see *The Chiefdom of Corcu Modruad*). Other interesting features at Dún Dúcathair are the conjoined huts immediately inside the wall and the less obvious row of rectangular foundations further out on the promontory. Antiquarian accounts tell us that originally there was an entrance through the wall at its western end, but this fell into the sea in the early nineteenth century. There also seems to have been an entrance on the eastern side of the wall.

Figure 183 ▲
Inside Dún Dúcathair.

Figure 184
Dún Chonchúir, Inishmaan.
Grid Reference L 932 048

Dún Chonchúir is located near the centre of Inishmaan on the summit of the highest point on the island. It is a bivallate fort and is the most substantial fort on the island. The inner wall is a massive oval, rising to a maximum height of six metres and with a thickness of over five metres in places. The outer enclosing wall is less massive than the inner wall but still quite substantial on the fort's eastern side. On the western side of the fort, the line of the outer wall appears to follow less substantial walls until it disappears where the inner wall runs along the top of a small cliff. The name Dún Chonchúir is derived from the Early Medieval legend, which tells of a tribe called the *Fir Bolg* who settled on the Aran Islands with Aonghas on Inishmore at Dún Aonghasa and his brother Chonchúir on Inishmaan at Dún Chonchúir.

As you make your way up to the fort from the east you first pass through a substantial outer bastion which protects the entrance to the fort. The path continues through this bastion and passes into the fort through an entrance in the massive inner wall. Once inside the inner enclosure, the foundations of several conjoined huts can be seen along the southern wall. Based on analogy with the excavated site of Cahercommaun on the Burren (see *Cahercommaun and the Early Medieval Chiefdoms of the Burren*), these huts were probably the houses and sleeping quarters of the fort's inhabitants while the open spaces in the fort would have had less substantial structures for cooking, metalwork and other craftwork.

Figure 185
Dún Chonchúir, Inishmaan.

Figure 186
Dún Fearbhaí, Inishmaan.
Grid Reference L 942 045

The massive hulk of Dún Fearbhaí overlooks the landing spot occupied by the modern quay on the east side of Inishmaan. Dún Fearbhaí is a univallate, sub-rectangular fort with a single terrace running around the inside of the wall and several flights of steps.

Figure 187
Dún Formna, Inisheer.
Grid Reference L 982 023

Dún Formna is the roughly oval stone fort defined by the massive wall which surrounds the much later O'Brien's Castle on the hill that dominates the beach on Inisheer. The small rectangular turret that projects from the fort on the south west is probably a later modification contemporary with the medieval castle. The name 'Dún Formna' translates as 'the fort on top of the hill' (for O'Brien's Castle see *Power Struggles on the Aran Islands*).

Life Outside the Forts

EARLY MEDIEVAL AND MEDIEVAL IRISH SOCIETY was hierarchical and social hierarchy was reflected in a hierarchy of domestic site types. It was probably only the chiefs and their families who lived in the large stone forts so we must assume that most people lived outside the large forts and there is, in fact, evidence for this on the Aran Islands. Just as on the Burren, many of the homes of people below the chief in the social hierarchy were enclosed in a much simpler manner than the large chiefly forts. These enclosures are generally referred to as ringforts or cashels depending on whether they were built of earth or stone (see *The Ringforts of the Burren*). All the examples on the Aran islands are built of stone and are, therefore, cashels. These cashels were lightly defended farmsteads and there are at least eleven on the islands; seven on Inishmore, three on Inishmaan and one on Inisheer. There are also unenclosed house sites on the islands and these may have been the dwellings of people even lower in the social hierarchy than those who lived in the cashels.

Baile na mBocht, Inishmore

Grid Reference Oghil 1 – L 858 095, Oghil 2 – L 857 094, Oghil 3 – L 857 097.

(Important Note – These grid references mark three excavated house sites which are part of a settlement cluster first recorded in the nineteenth century but there is very little archaeology visible on the ground today. The three excavated house sites, Oghil 1-3, are now just grass-covered mounds and many of the other features recorded in the nineteenth century are nearly impossible to locate among the high field walls and brambles which presently cover the site. The area is important in the archaeological story of the Aran Islands, but only the most dedicated archaeology students will not be disappointed by a visit to the site.)

On the high ground at the centre of Inishmore in the townland of Oghil are the remains of an ancient settlement known as both *Baile na mBocht,* 'village of the poor' and also as *Baile na Sean,* 'village of the ancient ones'. The settlement is located 500 metres south west of the lighthouse in a shallow valley that dips to the south. The settlement consists of a scatter of collapsed structures, a few enclosures and various unclassifiable mounds. Excavation has shown that some of what today appear as grass-covered mounds of rubble are, in fact, the remains of stone and timber-built round houses. Other collapsed structures on the site appear to be clocháin, that is completely stone-built structures with corbelled stone roofs (see *The Clocháin of the Aran Islands*). The area is also covered by an intricate network of stone walls, most of which are later than the structures.

The settlement was first recorded by Henry Kinahan in 1869 and in the early 1950s three of the structures within the settlement were excavated by J.R.W. Goulden and subsequently published by John Waddell. The three excavated structures are known as Oghil 1, 2 and 3. Excavation showed them to be the collapsed remains of round houses. Even with excavation, the dating of these houses is not secure. It's most likely they date to the Early Medieval period but it is also conceivable that they are later (Medieval).

Although one of the three sites that Goulden excavated was very disturbed, the other two revealed floor plans of quite similar structures. What was revealed were circular houses with internal diameters of around seven metres. Both houses had a door opening to the east which was approached by a paved path. The houses consisted of a low circular stone wall, about 50cm high, which had an inner and an outer face of large stones and a rubble core. At the centre of the house would have been a wooden pole(s) to hold up a conical roof of thatch or sods. Just outside the doorways of the houses were small stone huts that may have housed animals. The small huts may have had corbelled stone roofs and one had a low lintelled doorway just 60cm high.

Mixed with the rubble of the houses was a fair amount of midden material which tells us something of the diet of inhabitants of *Baile na mBocht*. Goulden recovered cattle, sheep/goat, pig and fish bones as well as limpets and other shellfish. He also recovered the small shells which attach themselves to the edible seaweed dulse, suggesting that it too contributed to the diet. Two rotary quern stones were recovered indicating that some grain was ground on the site. Several pieces of human bone were also found amongst the midden material but it is not clear why they were there.

Craft activities at *Baile na mBocht* included wool spinning, indicated by spindle whorls, and antler working evidenced by several pieces of worked red deer antler. No deer bones other than antler were recovered so it seems likely the antler was brought from the mainland specifically for manufacturing items such as knife handles. A fair amount of charcoal was recovered from the site which provides us with a unique window on the ancient environment. Many species of smaller trees and plants that we would expect were found such as hawthorn, holly, hazel and ivy. In addition to the smaller trees and plants, however, several species of large trees (oak, ash, elm and alder) were present as well.

Figure 188
The house site of Oghil 2 during excavation.

Figure 189
Oghil 3.

One of the small stone huts just outside the doorway of the Oghil 3 house. It may have been used to house animals.

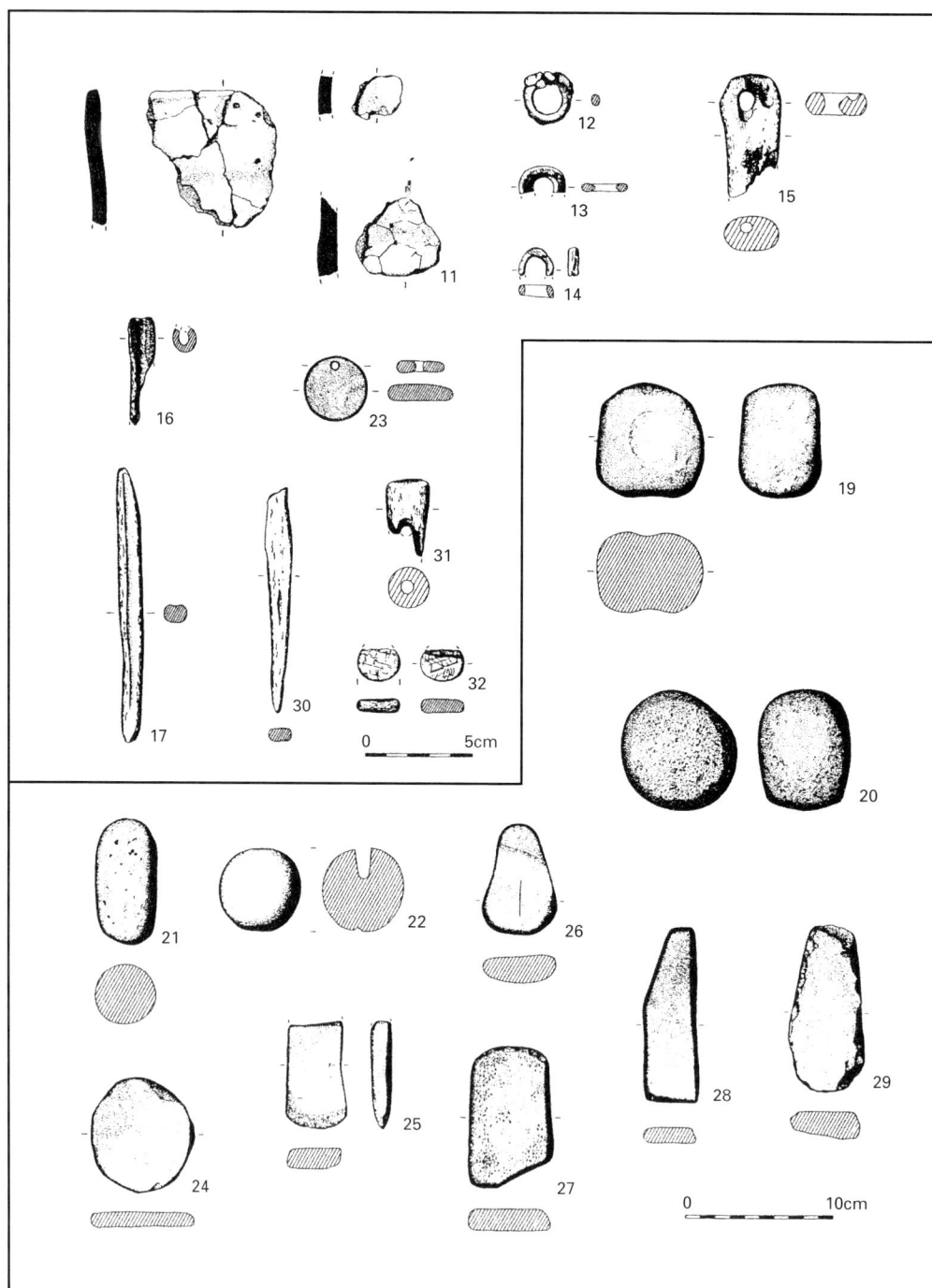

Figure 190
Finds from the Oghil excavations.

All the finds pictured are from Oghil 3 except
numbers 30–32 which are also from the Oghil
excavations but which do not have a more
specific context.
11 – pottery; 12 – iron ring; 13 – lignite
ring fragment; 14 – bone ring fragment;
15 – worked bone (knife handle?); 16 – bone
knife handle fragment; 17 – polished bone;
19, 20, 21 – hammer stones; 22 – partially
perforated limestone ball; 23 – perforated
stone disc; 24 – stone disc; 25 – small polished
stone axe; 26, 27, 28, 29 – smoothed and
polished stones; 30 – bone point; 31 – bone
knife handle fragment; 32 – stone disc.

Christianity and Pilgrimage on the Aran Islands

The isles of Aran are fameous for the numerous multitude of Saints there living of old and interred, or there trained in religious austerity, and propagating monasticall in other parts; venerable for many sacred churches, chappells, wells, crosses, sepulchres and other holy reliques of saints, still there extant, as monuments of their piety . . . frequently visited by Christians in pilgrimage for devotion, acts of penance and miraculous virtues there wrought.

Roderick O'Flaherty 1684

As we saw on the Burren (see *Relics and Pilgrimage on the Burren*), pilgrimage and the cult of relics was just as popular in Early Medieval and Medieval Ireland as it was in the rest of Europe. Pilgrims undertook their journeys both as an act of devotion to God and as a way of saving their souls. There were probably Irish pilgrims as early as the sixth century AD and when they were abroad they were sometimes referred to as *peregrini*. *Peregrini* translates as 'strangers who have left their own country' and it seems that many of these early *peregrini* never had any intention of returning home. Instead, they preferred to spend their time wandering abroad and visiting such famous pilgrimage destinations as Santiago de Compostela in Spain, Rome and the Holy Land. Eventually, authorities on the continent sought to control these wandering Irish *peregrini* and in the second half of the eighth century Charlemagne forbade the *peregrini* from travelling freely within his empire.

Around 800 AD, therefore, the Irish Church and its pilgrims had to find new pilgrimage destinations within Ireland and it seems the west coast of Ireland and its offshore islands were chosen as suitable pilgrimage destinations. Two factors were probably paramount in this decision. The first was probably the difficulty in traversing the rough and stormy Atlantic to reach the islands which would have made the journey a penitential hardship as great as that provided by travelling across the continent. The second important factor may have been the holy aura that many of the offshore islands would have already attained by this time because they had been the refuges of Christian hermits in the preceding few centuries. We have a much later, but relevant, account from the mid sixteenth century of a man who was instructed to visit sixteen separate sites around Ireland including 'Aran of the Saints' as penance for strangling his son.

Just as the Irish pilgrimages were starting to be established, however, the Vikings began raiding and this seems to have significantly curtailed pilgrimage activity, particularly along the Atlantic seaways. This drop-off was not permanent though and pilgrimage activity picked up again as the Viking raids died down. As on the continent, it was the eleventh and twelfth centuries that seem to have seen the most pilgrimage activity in Ireland. On the continent this upturn in pilgrimage was accompanied by the construction of many new churches such as those along the road to Santiago de Compostela and the same pattern appears to hold true for the Aran Islands. On the Aran Islands, many of the churches and the high crosses probably date to this time and it is likely that they were erected to cater for, and appeal to, the increased number of pilgrims (see *Radiocarbon Dating the Churches of the Aran Islands*). The eleventh and twelfth centuries appear to have been the zenith of pilgrimage activity in Ireland but pilgrimages continue to this day. Among the more well-known pilgrimages which are still practised are those to Croagh Patrick in County Mayo and Lough Derg in County Donegal.

All this pilgrimage and other ecclesiastical activity on the Aran Islands has left its mark in numerous sites scattered around the islands. These sites range from substantial monasteries incorporating multiple buildings, high crosses and relic shrines to more insubstantial sites consisting of little more than a church. What follows are accounts of the most substantial and interesting ecclesiastical sites on the islands.

St Enda's Monastery of Cill Éinne (Killeany), Inishmore

St Enda is the most famous of the Aran saints and it was Enda who founded the first monastery on the Aran islands some time in the early sixth century AD. This was located at Killeany, the original main harbour of Inishmore. St Enda is reputed to have been a student at the monastery of Candida Casa in south-west Scotland and two of his disciples are credited with founding other monasteries. St Ciarán at Clonmacnoise in County Offaly and St Finnian at Clonard in County Meath. His monastery on Inishmore developed such a widespread reputation that nearly all the early saints of Ireland are attributed with a visit to St Enda's monastery.

In the early seventeenth century the remains of six churches were recorded at Killeany but only two survive today because much of St Enda's monastery was dismantled to provide building stone for the seventeenth century Arkin Fort which occupies the waterfront at

Killeany (see *Arkin Fort, Inishmore*). It's likely that the four dismantled churches formed the core of the monastery which was probably located close to where Arkin Fort and the modern village of Killeany now stand. What remains of St Enda's monastery are the structures that were probably originally located towards the edges of the monastery. The buildings standing today are Temple Benan, the small oratory on top of the hill along with its ancillary structures, the base of a round tower near the bottom of the hill and Tighlagheany, the church set in the sand dunes to the south-east of the village of Killeany. These buildings have presumably survived because they were too far from the building site of Arkin Fort to be useful quarries (although the stones from the top of the round tower were obviously reused elsewhere). Other features of the monastery which still survive are fragments of two high crosses, St Enda's well and the 'Well of the Friars'.

Temple Benan

Grid Reference L 885 070

Temple Benan is the very small oratory that sits on the ridge line high above Killeany. Several features set this small building apart from more typical churches. One of the most obvious is its very small size which can only accommodate a handful of people at a time. On the inside it only measures a little over three metres long by just over two metres wide. Less obvious at first glance is the fact that the long axis of the building is oriented north-south rather than east-west. The single small window does, however, open to the east as is typical on churches but the orientation of the building means the window is on a long side of the building rather than on the east gable opposite the door, as is usually the case.

The exposed position of Temple Benan on top of the ridge also contrasts markedly with all the other Aran churches which are built on the lee side of sheltering high ground. The choice of this location for the small oratory may well be based on a desire to make it visible from afar. Its position on the ridge-top makes it clearly visible on the skyline from a number of different directions and it is particularly prominent when one is approaching by sea from the Galway coast. Since the visibility of Temple Benan seems to have been so important to its builders, its unusual orientation may be because its builders wanted to emphasise its profile from specific approaches.

But why the desire to make this small oratory so visible? Certainly a plausible explanation is that the primary role of Temple Benan was to attract pilgrims. Indeed, a radiocarbon date for the construction of Temple Benan (see *Radiocarbon Dating the Churches of the Aran Islands*) indicates that it was built in the eleventh or twelfth centuries, exactly at the time when pilgrimage activity in Ireland was at its height. Temple Benan may, therefore, have been primarily a reliquary – a structure built to house a relic. If this was the case, it probably held a relic of St Benignus, an early saint who is traditionally associated with the site. The relic may have been a bone of St Benignus or something associated with the saint, such as a bell or crozier.

There are a few features just outside the oratory. The terrace which survives downslope to the east may be a remnant of the lower portion of a small rectangular enclosure that may have originally surrounded the oratory on its east, south and west sides. Five metres north of the oratory is another small, rectangular structure formed by a natural corner in the bedrock with two drystone walls added. This structure was excavated in 1984. Underneath a layer of collapsed stones in its interior, a layer of soil was encountered that produced potsherds, clay pipe fragments, animal bones and some periwinkle shells. Both the pottery and the pipe fragments date to the seventeenth century. Although the structure could have been built earlier than this, it was certainly used in the seventeenth century and its use probably relates to pilgrims visiting the site or to the nearby lookout post known as 'The Watchman' (see Figure 237).

Figure 191
Temple Benan.

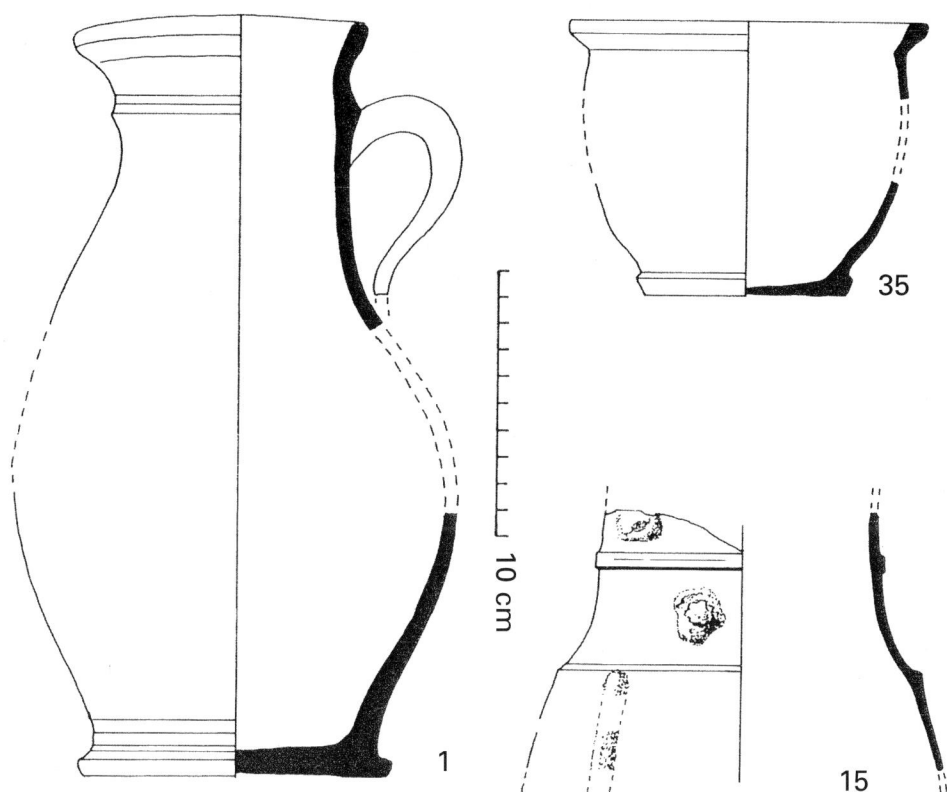

Figure 192
Finds from excavations in areas surrounding the oratory at Temple Benan.

Most of the finds are post-Medieval and most came from the area just north east of the oratory. They probably reflect visits to the site by pilgrims or by soldiers keeping a vigil at the nearby 'Watchman'. 1 – Post-Medieval jug; 35 – sherds from one or two small slipware vessels; 15 – Medieval jug; 11- clay pipe bowl *c.* 1660-1680; 48 – clay pipe fragment; 47 – clay pipe stem fragment decorated with *Fleur de Lis* in diamond-shaped frames, probably seventeenth century; 54 – clay pipe fragment, probably mid-seventeenth century. Also found (but not pictured) was a fragment of a nineteenth-century clay pipe decorated with a cock and the motto 'While I live I'll crow'.

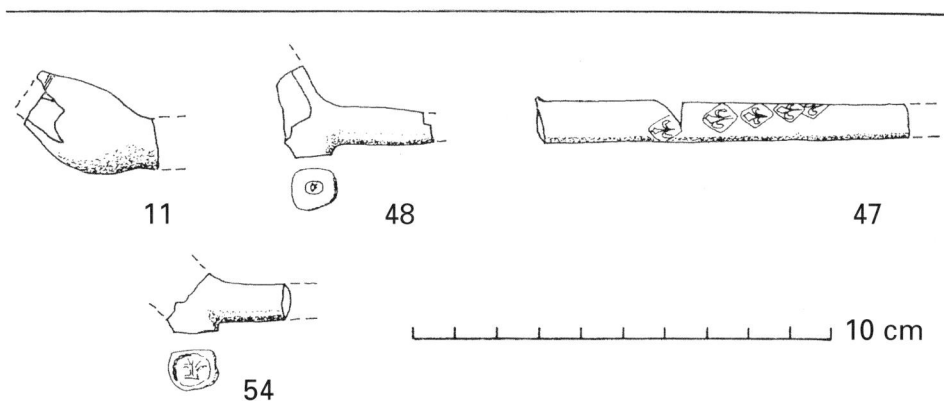

Figure 193
Cross-slab from Temple Benan.

There were at least five cross-inscribed slabs at Temple Benan at one time but they have subsequently been moved. This one was located on a small pile of stones a few metres south of the oratory.

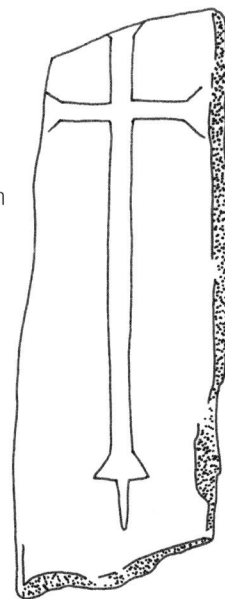

Figure 194 ▲
Tobar Éinne.
Grid Reference L 886 071

St Enda's Well (Tobar Éinne) is located just north of the round tower at Killeany. The water of this holy well is said to cure infertility. It is also reputed to be the place where St Enda's miraculous barrel was set in the ground. According to the legend, this barrel was actually responsible for Enda gaining control of the islands. When Enda first arrived he found the islands were controlled by a pagan chief named Corban. Corban put a barrel of seed-corn on the shore of the Burren and told Enda he would give up the islands if Enda's god could bring the barrel across the sea to Inishmore. Miraculously, the barrel made the crossing against the tides and currents and came ashore on a small beach on the eastern end of the island.

◄ Figure 195
St Enda's monastery.
Grid Reference L 886 071 (round tower)

At the bottom of the hill is the base of a high cross, further up is the base of a round tower and at the top of the hill is Temple Benan. When complete, the round tower at Killeany would have risen to a great height, perhaps as high as thirty metres. Although their Irish name *cloigteach* means 'bell house' which suggests their primary function was as bell towers, the fact that many important pilgrimage destinations in Ireland had round towers suggests they may have been more than bell towers. It has been suggested that round towers may have also functioned as beacons guiding pilgrims to their destination and as treasuries for the safekeeping of relics (see Figure 138).

Figure 196
Base of the high cross at Killeany.
Grid Reference L 887 071

The cross base shown here in an early twentieth-century photograph is probably in its original location but three other pieces of the same cross are now cemented together (in the wrong order) in the nearby church of Tighlagheany (see Figure 197). The other high cross of St Enda's monastery is represented by a portion of a ringed cross head found during excavations at Tighlagheany.

Tighlagheany

Grid Reference L 894 069

Like Temple Benan, the church of Tighlagheany was part of St Enda's monastery. Today, the graveyard surrounding Tighlagheany is the main graveyard on Inishmore and it seems it was also the graveyard for the monastery. A seventeenth-century account states that 120 saints including St Enda are buried in the cemetery. The eastern gable and a portion of the northern wall of the church have the distinctive early features of *antae* (projections on both sides of the gable) and massive cyclopean masonry. In fact, the enormity of the masonry is an illusion as what appear to be large blocks are actually thin slabs placed on edge while the core of the wall consists of rubble. On the outer face of the north wall, the large rectangular stone directly below the window has an inscription on its right hand side which today is sideways.

Figure 197
Fragment of a high cross from Tighlagheany.

This fragment depicting a hooded horserider is cemented to two others inside the church at Tighlagheany. They were brought here when they were found, incorporated into the wall of a local cottage but are actually fragments of the same cross whose base still stands just down-slope from the round tower (see Figure 196).

Figure 198
East gable of Tighlagheany.

As it stands today, the church of Tighlagheany is a two-phase structure. The large blocks of the cyclopean masonry in the northern wall and the eastern gable, as well as the projecting *antae* on both sides of the eastern gable, show that the eastern gable, and most of the north-ern wall belong to the earlier phase. Antae are short extensions of the side walls beyond the face of the gable wall. The *antae* would have helped to support the roof timbers and may, in fact, be an architectural translation into stone of wooden corner posts on earlier wooden churches (for further examples see Figure 137 and Figure 226, and for related projecting corbels see Figure 68).

Sir Morogh O'Flaherty was buried within the church in 1666 and the remodelling of the church evident may have been carried out around this time. This second phase is evidenced by the smaller masonry of the south wall and the west gable (with no *antae*), the late-style doorway in the north wall and all the windows except the eastern one which is contemporary with the east gable.

The inscription reads OROIT AR SCANDLAN which trans-lates as 'Pray for Scandlan'. The inscribed stone is in-situ in the earlier masonry of the church but because it is placed side-ways it probably pre-dates even the earliest phase of the church as it stands today.

There are several interesting features within the church which would have originally been located elsewhere on the site but which have been brought into the church over the years. At the west end are three fragments of a high cross cemented together which are fragments of the same high cross whose base is located near to the round tower (see Figure 196). There are also two bullaun stones inside the church which today are used for depositing coins and there are several cross-slabs and other carved pieces cemented together to form an altar at the east end of the church. Within the altar, the two stones at the bottom left of the front panel are reused architectural elements, the top left stone on the front is a cross slab with a simple cross and expanded terminals, the front right-hand stone is a cross slab inscribed with a ringed cross and on the south face of the altar is a cross slab with a simple cross with expanded ter-minals and an inscription (see *Cross-Decorated Stones of the Aran Islands*).

Cross-Decorated Stones of the Aran Islands

Many of the ecclesiastical sites on the Aran Islands have a variety of cross-decorated stones. Some but not all of these cross-decorated stones were probably grave markers. Other than grave markers, the cross-decorated stones reflect a variety of activities. Some seem to have functioned as boundary markers, some were used to record the dedication of a site to a particular saint, others were probably focal points for devotions and still others may have been commissioned by pilgrims on the occasion of their pilgrimage.

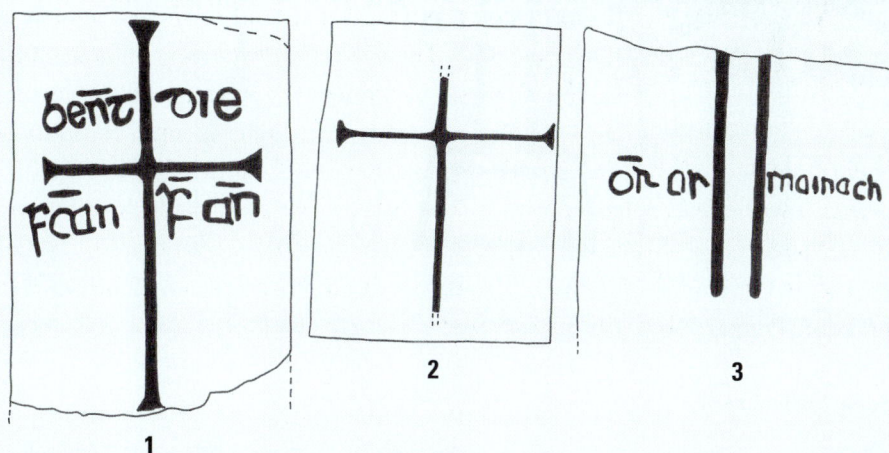

1

Figure 199
Inscribed cross slabs, Inishmore.

1. Cross slab with inscription now incorporated into the south face of the altar in Tighlagheany. The short horizontal lines above the inscribed letters indicate that the words have been contracted. When the words are expanded and read in a clockwise direction starting in the upper left corner, the inscription reads BEN(DACH)T DIE F(OR) AN(IM) S(AN)C(T)AN and translates as 'The blessing of God on the soul of Sanctan'. **2.** Uninscribed cross slab from Tighlagheany. **3.** Cross slab fragment at Temple Brecan (The Seven Churches). This inscription has also been contracted but when expanded reads OR(OIT) AR MAINEACH, which translates as 'Pray for Maineach'.

Cross slabs with inscriptions such as these may have been commissioned by pilgrims to commemorate their visit to the pilgrimage site. The two cross slabs from Tighlagheany have similar crosses but one has an inscription and the other does not. The cross slab without an inscription may have been a 'blank' manufactured by the monks of St Enda's to be inscribed at some point in the future when a pilgrim commissioned an inscription asking for a prayer for their soul. If pre-cut blanks were manufactured by the monks this might explain why so many of the inscriptions had to be contracted to fit onto the already existing cross slab.

Figure 200
Probable *tearmann* marker at Teampaill Chiaráin, Inishmore.

Good examples of cross-decorated stones as boundary markers for the *tearmann*, or sanctified land, of a monastic site, are the tall cross-inscribed pillars in the fields surrounding Teampaill Chiaráin. Three of these pillars may be in their original locations; one is less than ten metres west of the church, another is a little over 30 metres east of the church, and the third is approximately 40 metres to the east/north east of the church. Fragments of three more similar cross-inscribed pillars are located in a burial ground 40 metres to the north/north-east of the church. It's likely that these fragments were moved here after they were broken and then used as grave markers (see *Excavating St Ciaran's Monastery [Teampaill Chiaráin], Inishmore*).

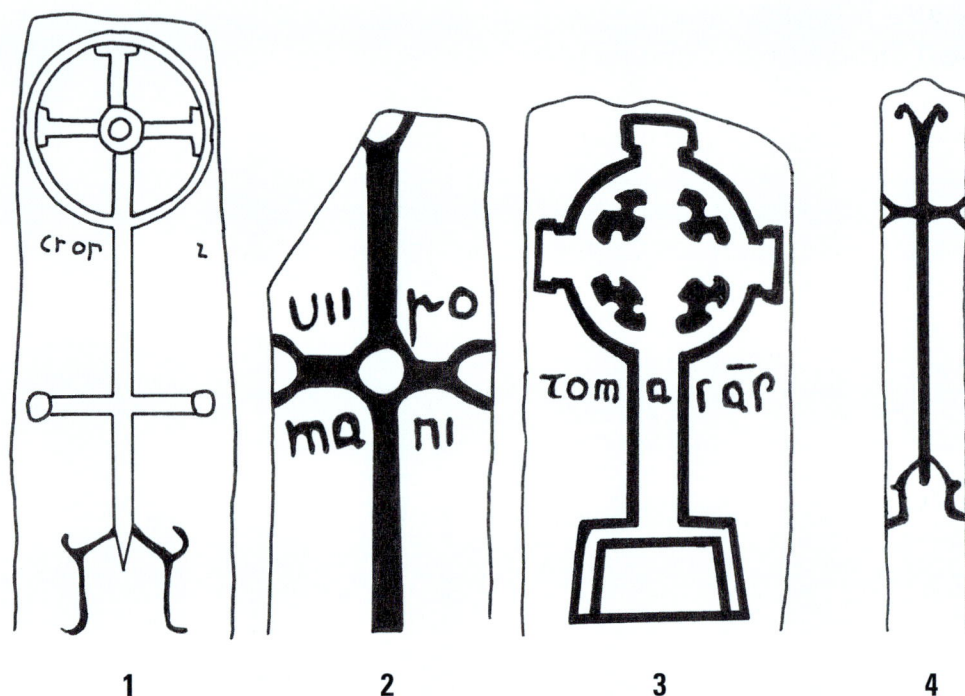

Figure 201
Four cross-decorated stones at Temple Brecan, Inishmore.

In the corner of the graveyard at Temple Brecan, approximately 25 metres south east of the church, four cross-decorated stones stand in front of a small rectangular area bounded by a low kerb of limestone slabs set on edge. The interior of this rectangular area is divided into what appear to be five slab-covered graves (see *Temple Brecan [The Seven Churches], Inishmore*).

1. What appear to be bent legs at the bottom of this cross may be a representation of a base which is holding a processional cross. The inscription on this stone is very worn but in the late nineteenth century it was recorded by the antiquarian George Petrie as the name CRONMAEL or CRONMAOL.

2. The inscription on this stone is broken into two lines, both of which read from left to right. It reads VII ROMANI and has been explained in various ways. It might have been commissioned by seven Roman pilgrims to commemorate their pilgrimage to the Aran Islands or it might have been commissioned by seven Irish pilgrims who had returned from Rome. It might be making reference to the pilgrimage circuit of Rome which incorporated seven churches (another name for Temple Brecan is 'The Seven Churches' which may reflect an attempt to associate Temple Brecan with the pilgrimage circuit of Rome). It might be that the VII ROMANI were part of the reformist or Roman element who were in favour of adopting continental reforms. It might even be making reference to the popular Early Medieval legend of the 'Seven Sleepers of Ephesus' who escaped persecution from the Roman Emperor by falling into a miraculous sleep and then awakening several centuries later.

3. This stone was found within Temple Brecan in the early nineteenth century but is now located to the south east of the church along with the three other cross-decorated stones shown here. The horizontal bar over the second word on the inscription indicates the word has been contracted. When the word is expanded, the inscription reads TOMAS AP(OSTALUS). This is a dedicatory inscription to Thomas the Apostle.

4. As with number 1, the bent legs at the base of this cross may be a representation of a base which is holding a processional cross.

Excavating St Ciaran's Monastery (Teampaill Chiaráin), Inishmore

Grid Reference L 873 104

P X

Teampaill Chiaráin is located one kilometre north west of the village of Kilronan on the slope overlooking *Port na Mainistreach* (Monastery Bay). It is traditionally believed to be the site of the sixth-century monastery of St Ciaran who is said to have studied under St Enda on Inishmore for seven years. Subsequent to this, St Ciaran is said to have founded the monastery at Clonmacnoise in County Offaly which became one of the most famous in the country. Visible on the site today are a church (Teampaill Chiaráin), a small chapel almost touching the north-east corner of the church, two nearby ruined buildings, a sundial, a holy well and several large cross-inscribed pillars.

In the late 1990s Dr Sinéad Ní Ghabhláin carried out excavations between the church and the base of the low cliff to the south. These excavations revealed a long and diverse history of occupation on the site. The earliest occupation was in the pre-Christian era. Only a few artefacts were found from this early occupation but a large pit filled with charcoal gave an Iron Age radiocarbon date of *c.* 40 BC – 230 AD. Then, very early in the Christian era, some time between the fifth and the mid-seventh centuries, a clay platform surrounded by a stone-lined ditch was constructed on the site. At the centre of this platform was a cobbled area with post holes and a small drain which suggests that a wooden building stood on the platform. The occupation of this platform seems to have lasted several centuries during which time debris slowly filled the surrounding ditch. Finds from the ditch included charcoal, animal bone, fish bone, several bone points, a bone pin with a bronze ring, fragments of worked lignite and a bronze pin with a silvered shaft.

The earliest phase of the present church appears to date to some time between the eleventh to mid-twelfth centuries (radiocarbon dated by charcoal in its foundation trench) but the archaeologists also uncovered evidence of an earlier foundation trench in the same location which suggests the present stone church was preceded by an earlier version. The round-headed window in the south wall appears to be an original window but the Transitional-style east window appears to have been inserted (probably in the early thirteenth century) and the early-style trabeate doorway in the west gable may have been inserted around the same time as well. The doorway in the north wall is a much later, fifteenth-century insertion.

The excavations also revealed that shortly after the church was built, a domestic building and courtyard were constructed abutting the south wall of the church (see Figure 205). Finds associated with this Medieval domestic building and with the construction level of the church include a bronze dress pin (see Figure 206), a fragment of a lignite bracelet, several bone points and toggles, two bone beads and sherds of coarse unglazed pottery. This domestic building seems to have been occupied up until some time between the mid-fifteenth to early seventeenth centuries.

Today, the area south of the church is dominated by the ruins of an even later, post-Medieval house (see Figure 208) which was built on top of the remains of the Medieval building. This house seems to have been built some time between the late sixteenth and the seventeenth centuries and had opposing doorways in the east and west walls, and a central hearth on the clay floor between the doors. The finds from this house were typical of what one would expect in a domestic context and included pottery (some imported from Germany and England), several large bone points which may have been used for weaving or making fish nets, grinding stones, hone stones for sharpening knives, a knife with a bone handle, clay pipe fragments, lead shot and iron nails. After this house had been abandoned and collapsed most of the rubble was removed from its interior and the house was reused as an animal pen.

Figure 202
Teampaill Chiaráin.

Surrounding the church in all directions, except to the south, are some tall, cross-inscribed pillar stones (see Figure 200). These cross-inscribed pillars probably mark the bounds of the *tearmann*, or sanctuary area, around the site to the west, north and east. The southern boundary may well have been marked by the cliff immediately south of the site. Three of the pillars are complete and standing and may, therefore, be in their original locations. One is in the field wall immediately west of the church, another is a little over 30 metres east of the church and the third is approximately 40 metres to the east/north east of the church.

Forty metres to the north/north-east of the church is a small burial ground in which four fragments of additional cross-inscribed pillars are located. Two of these fragments may be from the same pillar stone and all were probably broken before they were moved to the graveyard and reused as grave markers. There are also some chamfered stones from an unknown building reused on the site as grave stones. This graveyard was used into the twentieth century, mainly for infants. Across the road and east of this burial ground is a small hillock known as *Atharla* which was used up to the end of the nineteenth century as a burial ground for unbaptised infants. There are at least six cross-decorated slabs here though which may indicate quite early beginnings for this site.

Just west of the church beneath the small cliff are two wells, *Tobar Chiaráin* (St Ciaran's well) and *Tobar an Bhradáin* (the well of the salmon). St Ciaran's well can be identified by the enclosure of large limestone blocks that surround it. It is visited on the 9 September. The well of the salmon is located to the west of St Ciaran's well, against the cliff face and behind a concrete tank. Legend states that it is from this well that a huge salmon was sent by God to feed St Enda and all his comrades.

Figure 203 ▲
Excavation in progress at Teampaill Chiaráin.

Between 1996 and 1999, Dr Sinéad Ní Ghabhláin, a Research Associate at the Cotsen Institute of Archaeology UCLA, excavated at Teampaill Chiaráin. The project was a research excavation staffed by archaeologists and volunteers from Ireland and the United States. The excavation was funded by the University of California and the National Committee for Archaeology, Ireland.

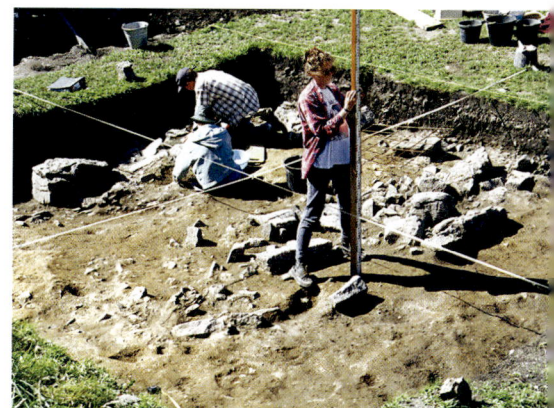

◄ Figure 204
Sundial at Teampaill Chiaráin.

The hole in the stone is designed to hold the gnomen, or upright pin, which would cast a shadow on the face of the sundial. No hours are marked on the dial's face and so it has been suggested that perhaps they were painted on. Similar sundials are known which are marked in three-hour periods. These three-hour intervals were the times at which prayers would be recited: Prime at six am, Terce at nine am, None at noon, Sext at three pm and Vespers at six pm In the more recent past, there are accounts of people passing rags through the hole which would then be used to effect 'cures'.

Figure 205 ▶

Medieval domestic building and courtyard south of the church.

Underneath the remains of the later house which is visible on the site today, the excavations revealed a domestic building and a courtyard built shortly after the church was constructed. The building is marked by its central hearth (052) and its western wall (028) which abuts the south wall of the church. The courtyard wall (064) runs due south from the south-west corner of the church. There is a gateway gap between the corner of the church and the start of the courtyard wall. The west wall of the later, post-Medieval house sits directly on top of the courtyard wall.

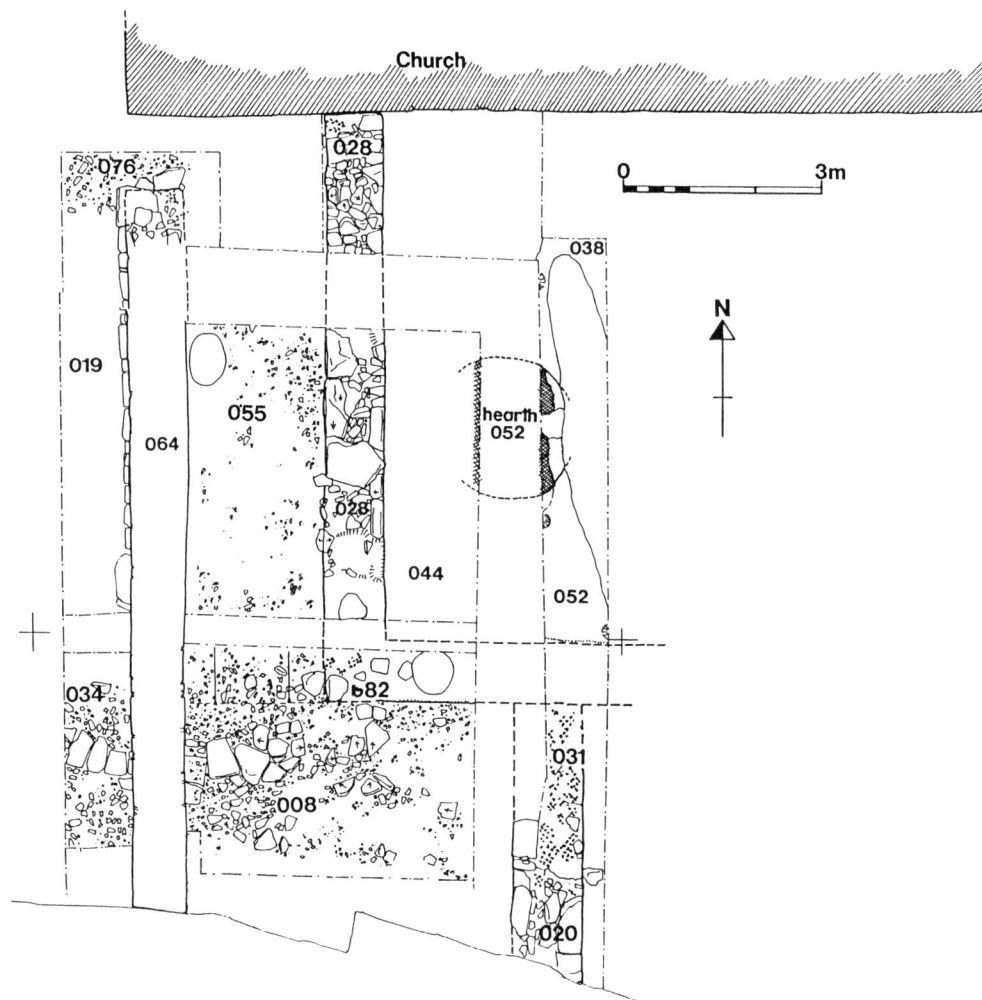

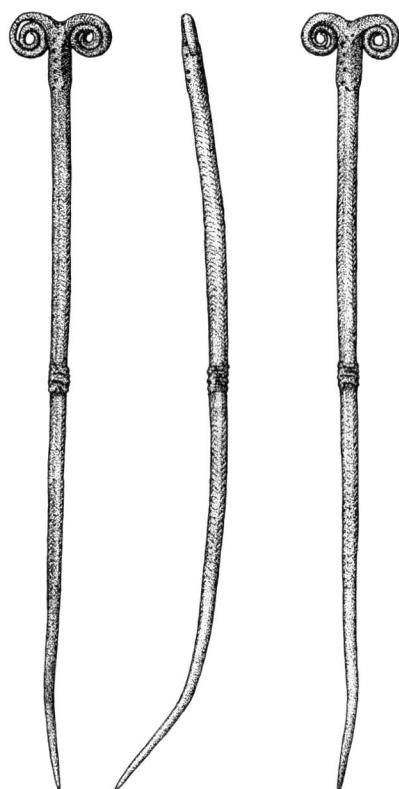

◀ Figure 206

Medieval dress pin from excavations south of the church.

This large dress pin would have been used to fasten an item of clothing such as a cloak. Its head is formed by a pair of scroll terminals while just below, the neck of the pin is decorated with two parallel rows of dots. Both the shaft and the pin's head are decorated with an incised herringbone pattern.

Figure 207
Burial at Teampaill Chiaráin.

Some time shortly before the Medieval domestic building was demolished, a pit was dug within it and the bones of at least two people were re-buried in it.

Figure 208
The excavated area as it appears today.

The area south of Teampaill Chiaráin was the focus of the excavations. The remains of the post-Medieval house are still clearly visible.

Temple Brecan (The Seven Churches), Inishmore

Grid Reference L 811 121

🅿 🚶

I came to Iubhar (of Aran) and established my settlement, everyone was pleased in turn when I expelled the devils.
Fierce Brecán Cláiringneach was in Iubhar before me, I undertook to expel him and I sanctified his place.
I got my seven requests, God was satisfied with my offerings, not least of them was that on an enclosed piece of land He created a sanctuary for pilgrims.

– verses from an anonymous Medieval poem in the voice of St Brecan (O'Sullivan 1983)

Temple Brecan is located towards the west end of Inishmore overlooking the small bay of Glenaghaun. The site is a remarkable group of churches, domestic buildings (some of which may be accommodation for pilgrims), saint's beds (known as *leapacha*), high crosses and cross-decorated slabs. Many of these features were probably penitential stations visited by pilgrims. Several holy wells have also been recorded at the site in the past but none are visible today. The presence of three high crosses and significantly more cross-decorated slabs at Temple Brecan than on any other Aran Island site suggest that it was one of the most important pilgrimage sites on the islands.

Despite being known as 'The Seven Churches', there are only two churches at Temple Brecan, the church of Temple Brecan itself and the smaller Teampall an Phoill. Reference to the 'seven churches' has been applied to a number of important Irish pilgrimage sites, often where the number of churches is obviously not seven. This practice may have stemmed from a desire to associate the Irish sites with the pilgrimage circuit of Rome which did incorporate seven churches or more generally with the number seven which had mystical significance. Brecan was apparently the name of a pagan god which St Brecan adopted upon defeating 'fierce Brecán'. Prior to this St Brecan was 'Bresal', the son of a king on the mainland in County Clare.

Although the site may at first appear disorganised, there is a structure to it. The central focal point is the church of Temple Brecan, the largest building on the site. Clustered around the north, east and south sides of this church are eight domestic buildings. Immediately west of the church is a line of at least two and possibly three *leapacha* (saints' beds) which appear to have been contained within a walled enclosure along with a high cross. Approximately 25 metres south east of the church, in the corner of the graveyard, is a group of what appears to be five important slab-covered graves along with four cross-decorated slabs. The building furthest from the church of Temple Brecan is the only other church on the site, Teampall an Phoill (Church of the Hollow) which is sited at the base of the escarpment about 50 metres to the south. The fragmented remains of three high crosses located to the north east, south and west of the buildings probably mark the bounds of the monastic enclosure.

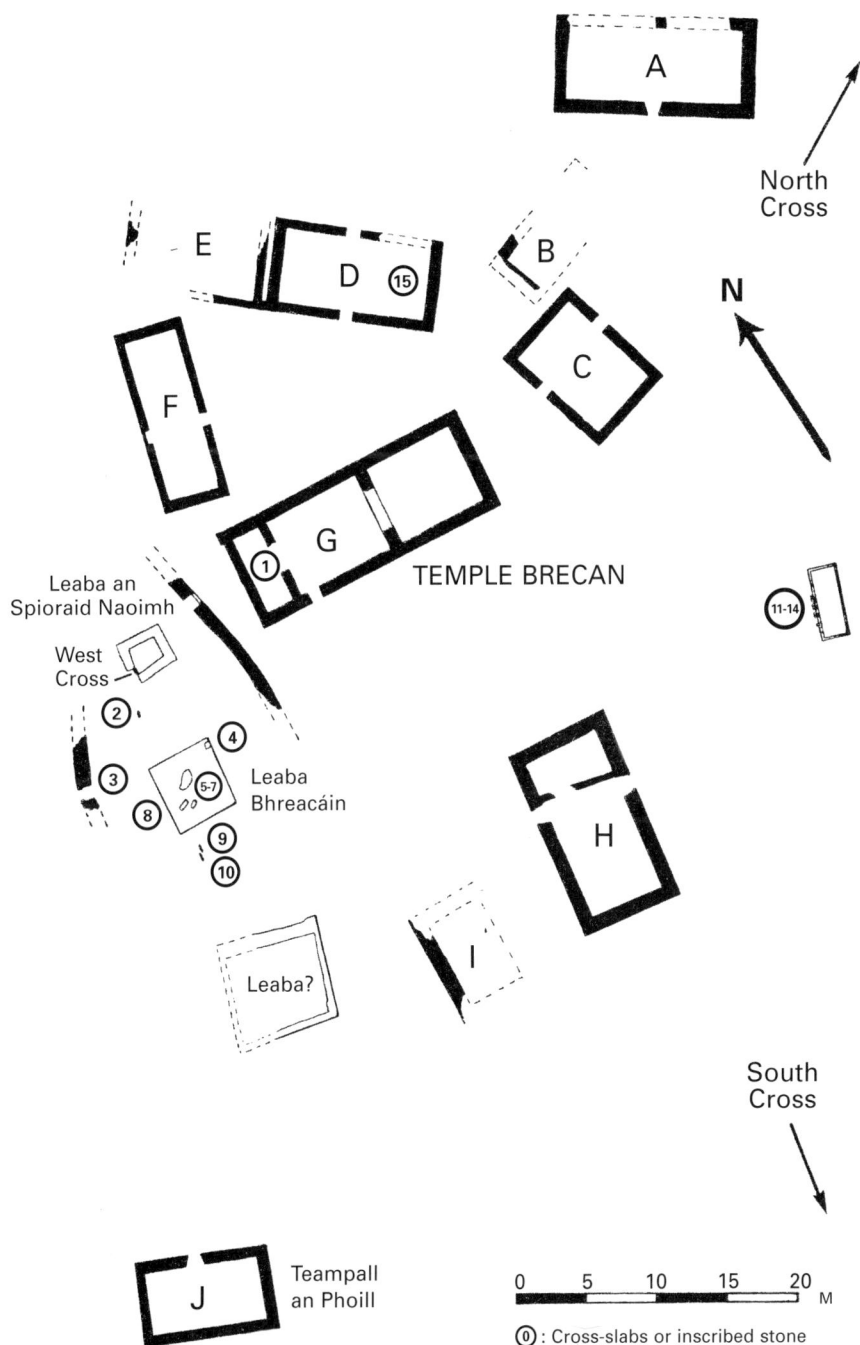

Figure 209
Temple Brecan.

At least three phases of construction (and probably more) are apparent in the church of Temple Brecan. The massive masonry of the north-west portion of the church and the single surviving *antae* projecting from the north-west corner are both indicators of an early date. At some later point in time the church was extended to the east and south and was divided by an arch into a nave and a chancel. The line between the older massive masonry and the later smaller blocks can be seen clearly in the north wall and the outline of the original gable can also be seen clearly in the present west gable. This extension of the church can probably be dated to the first half of the thirteenth century by the style of the slender lancet window which was used in the east gable. This window is made in a style known as Transitional because the style is transitional between the earlier Romanesque and the later Gothic style. The altar, the window and the doorway in the south wall of the nave and the partition wall at the west end of the nave are all later alterations, probably dating to the fifteenth or sixteenth centuries.

Figure 210
Inscribed stone at Temple Brecan.

This inscribed stone is located on the inside of the original west gable. It reads OR(ÓIT) AR II CANOIN which translates as 'A prayer for the two canons'. As one stands inside the church facing the west gable it is on the left-hand side of the original gable about two metres above the ground (approximately in the centre of the present gable).

Figure 211
Teampall an Phoill.

Teampall an Phoill (Church of the Hollow) is the only other church at Temple Brecan besides Temple Brecan itself. It is a small, simple church that seems to date to the fifteenth or sixteenth century.

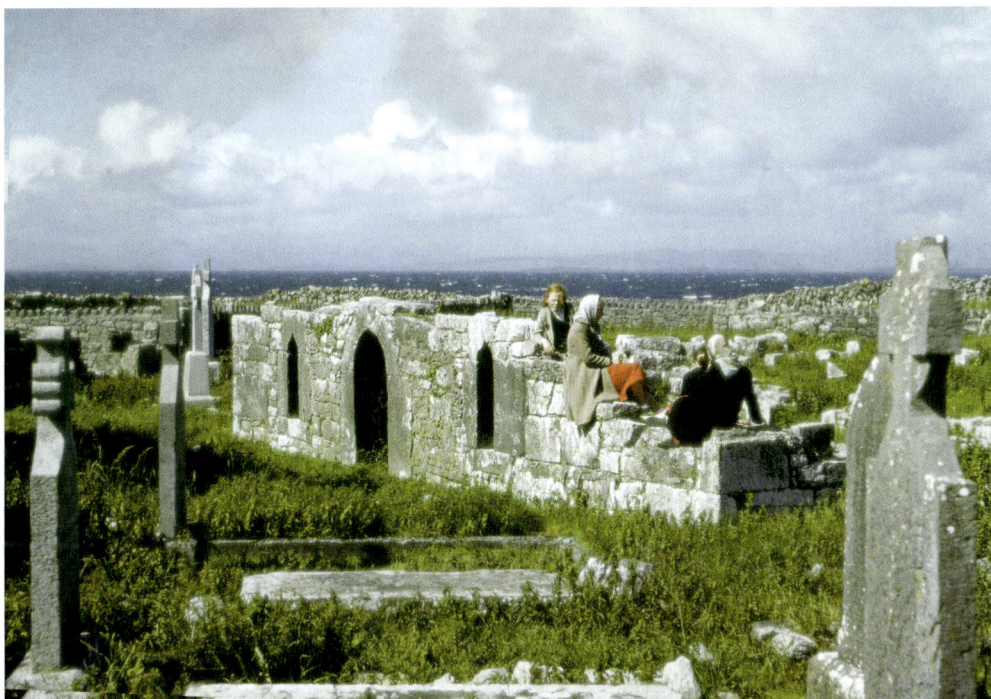

Figure 212
Domestic building at Temple Brecan.

Clustered around the church of Temple Brecan are eight other buildings which all appear to be domestic buildings. Some of the details of their windows and doors suggest these buildings date to the fifteenth and sixteenth centuries. These buildings probably provided accommodation for monks who were charged with supervising and administering the visiting pilgrims, as well as accommodation for the pilgrims themselves.

Figure 213
Group of slab-covered graves and cross-decorated stones at Temple Brecan.

In the south-east corner of the graveyard is a small rectangular area bounded by a low kerb of slabs placed on edge which seems to demarcate a group of important graves. Within this area are what appear to be five slab-covered graves along with four upright cross-decorated stones. For a full description of these cross-decorated stones see *Cross-Decorated Stones of the Aran Islands*.

Figure 214
The South Cross.

This cross is located approximately
80 metres south of Temple Brecan.
The fragments of the cross have been
cemented horizontally onto the bedrock
so that only one face is visible today.
The cross has an asymmetrical ringed
head and the decoration on the face
that is visible consists of interlace
and fret patterns.

The High Crosses of Temple Brecan

Large carved stone crosses known as high crosses were used for a variety of purposes.
Some marked the boundary of sacred areas, some may have been used as stations on
devotional rounds, and some may have been used for outdoor congregations. The
crosses are covered with relief-carved decoration. Much of the decoration is purely
ornamental but many Irish high crosses illustrate Bible stories or record important
events or agreements (see *The High Crosses of Kilfenora*).

There are three high crosses at Temple Brecan all of which probably date from the
late eleventh or the early twelfth centuries. Two of the crosses, the South Cross and the
North Cross, are located some distance from the buildings and therefore probably
mark the bounds of the monas-
tic enclosure within which
sanctuary was provided. The
West Cross may also
mark the bounds of
the enclosure but it
also seems to have
had an additional
role as it is incorporated into
the *Leaba an Spioraid Naoimh*
(see *The leapacha of Temple
Brecan*). It must be kept in
mind, however, that the
crosses are not necessarily in
their original positions.

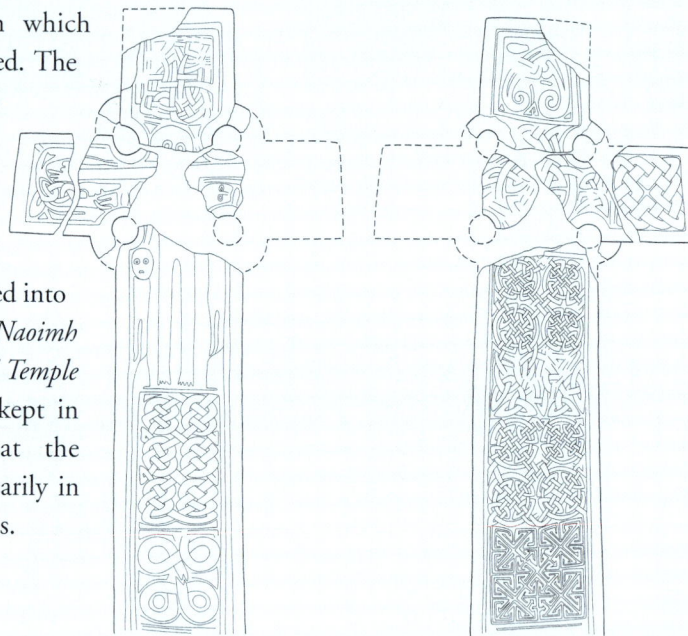

Figure 215
The West Cross.

The shaft of this cross stands at the south-west corner of the *Leaba an Spioraid Naoimh* while four fragments of its head lie nearby. There is a crucifixion scene on the west face. Christ is flanked by two figures
and there are also two further figures placed horizontally below Christ's outstretched arms. The details
of the figures are not sufficient to identify them. They could be the thieves, the spear-bearer and the
sponge bearer or possibly even the Virgin and St John. The bottom panel on the west face has a pair of
twisted animals who are biting each other. The remainder of the cross is decorated with interlace and
fret patterns.

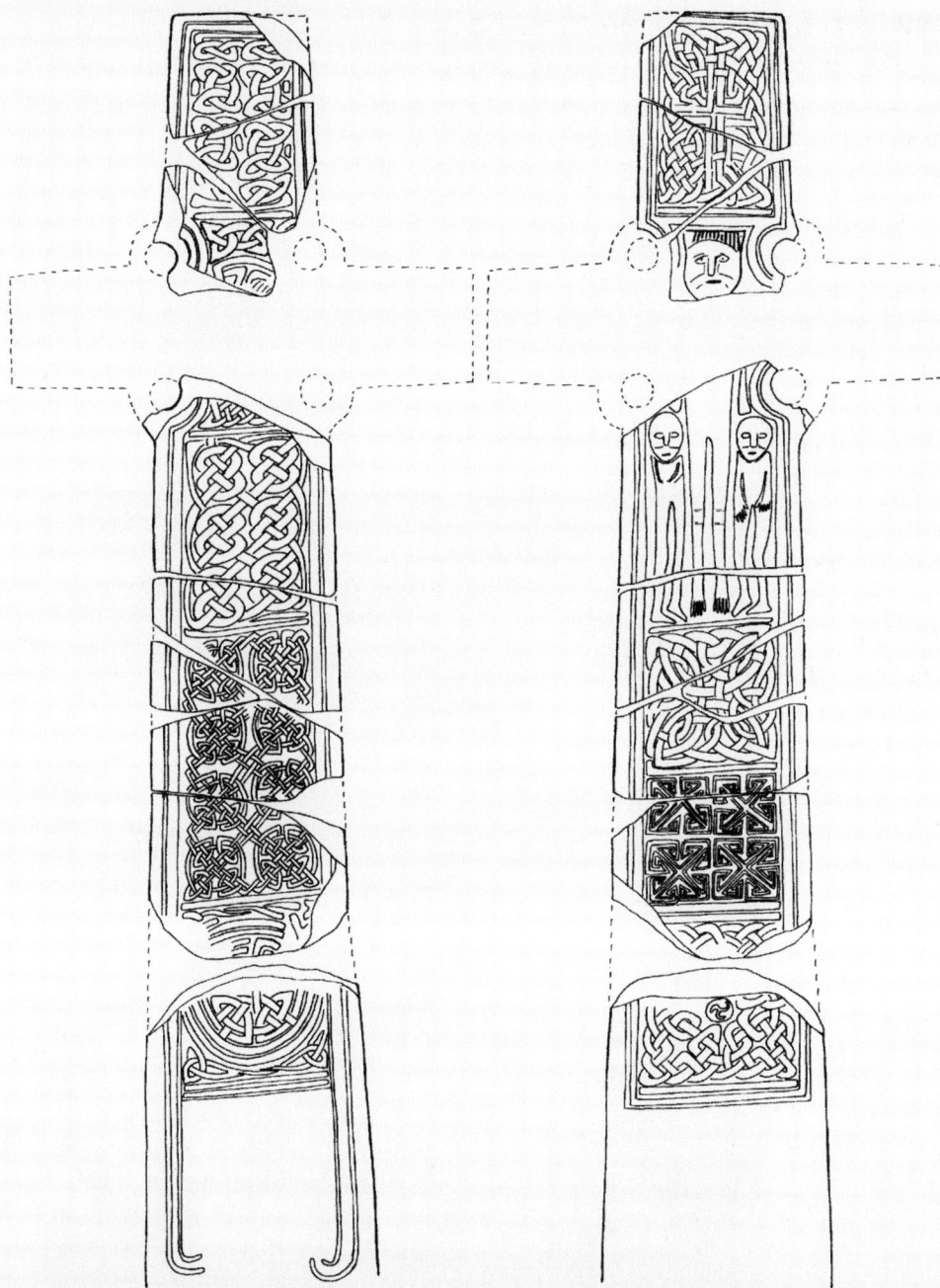

Figure 216
The North Cross.

This impressive cross would have originally stood a little over four metres high. Today, its fragments are laid horizontally in a small enclosure 80 metres north east of Temple Brecan. The east face of this cross bears a crucifixion scene where Christ is flanked by two figures but, as on the West Cross, their details are not sufficient to identify them. Interlace and fret patterns cover the remainder of the cross.

The *Leapacha* of Temple Brecan

When any member of a family falls sick, another member makes a promise that if the sick one recovers, the person promising will sleep one, two, or three nights in one of the saints' beds. One bed at the Seven Churches (probably St Brecan's bed) is said to be occupied pretty regularly.

– Haddon and Browne 1893

Leapacha, which is the plural of *leaba*, are saints' 'beds'. These are graves of saints (or sites purported to be graves of saints) which subsequently may have been used as penitential stations for pilgrims or places where 'cures' such as that described above were sought. There are at least two and possibly three *leapacha* at Temple Brecan. They are the low square stone enclosures placed in a north-south line just west of the church of Temple Brecan. To the east and to the west of the *leapacha* are the remnants of a wall that may have formed an oval enclosure around the *leapacha*, separating them from the rest of the monastery. There are several cross-decorated slabs both on and around the *leapacha*.

Figure 217
**Leaba an Spioraid Naoimh
(the bed of the Holy Spirit).**

This is the northernmost *leaba* and it is located just west of the western gable of Temple Brecan. It is a small, low, rectangular enclosure whose south-west corner is marked by the base of the West cross (see *The High Crosses of Temple Brecan*).

Figure 218
**Leaba Bhreacáin
(the bed of St Brecan).**

Leaba Bhreacáin is located immediately south of *Leaba an Spioraid Naoimh*. It is a low, rectangular grassy platform bounded by a kerb of limestone blocks. Several cross-decorated slabs are located on top of this *leaba*. In addition to the cure for a sick family member quoted above, there is also a tradition that women would pray at St Brecan's bed if they wanted children.

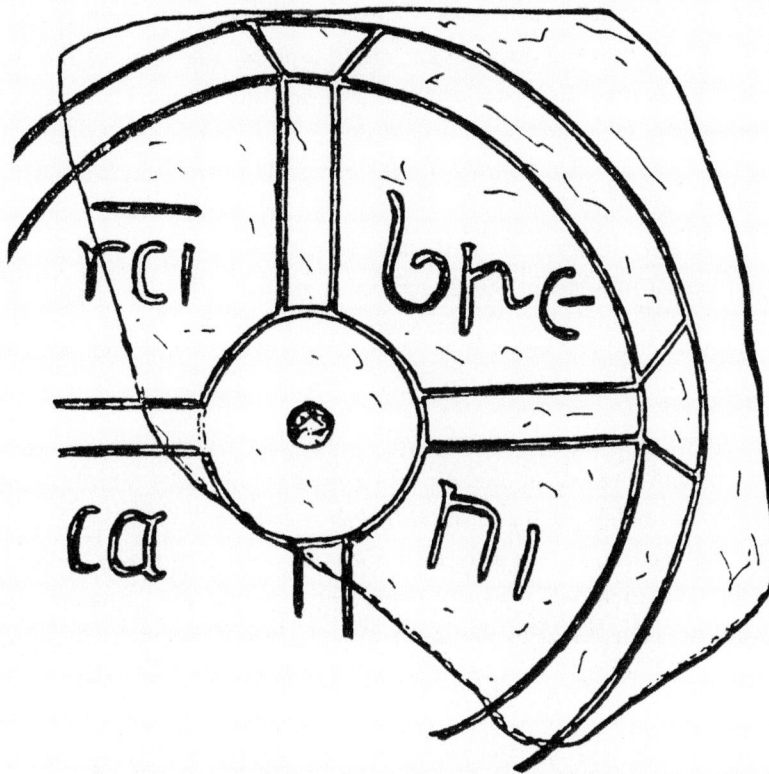

Figure 219
The grave slab of St Brecan.

This very large slab is decorated with a cross inside a double ring and bears the inscription SCI BRECANI (the horizontal bar above the first word indicates that it has been contracted on the carving). The slab therefore reads *Sancti Brecani* which translates as 'the grave/slab of St Brecan'. Today it is leaning against the edge of *Leaba Bhreacáin*. There is a nineteenth-century account that says the slab was actually found six feet underground when a circular enclosure known as St Brecan's tomb was opened up to inter an 'ecclesiastic' who had requested to be buried in the tomb, but today there is no visible trace of the circular enclosure.

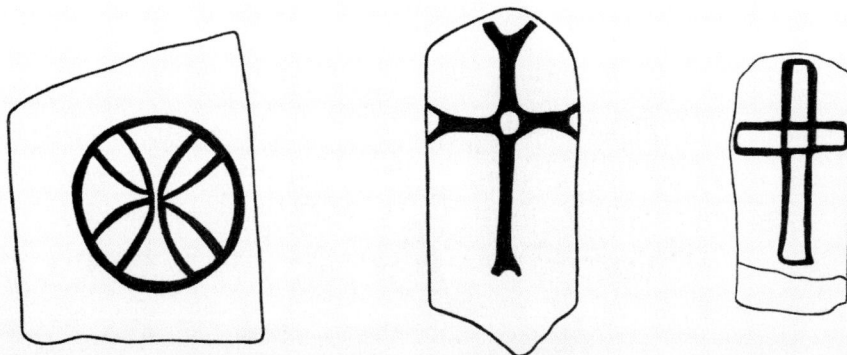

Figure 220
Other cross-slabs on Leaba Bhreacáin.

The cross of arcs on the far left seems to be a cross type that is associated with pilgrimage activity.

Cill Cheanainn, Inishmaan

Grid Reference L 944 045

This very small church is located just south west of the pier on the eastern shore of Inishmaan. It is a small single-celled oratory (measuring just over five metres long and just under four metres wide externally) with steeply pitched gables and projecting corbels at the corners. There is a lintelled doorway in the west gable, a small angular-headed east window and cyclopean masonry in its lower courses. The projecting corbels would have originally held barge boards which ran along the tops of the walls and out onto the corbels supporting the rafters. At some point the church was re-roofed with a less steeply pitched roof and in order to achieve this the north and south walls of the church were raised above the level of the corbels. The old line of the steeply-pitched roof can still be seen rising from the corbels in the masonry of the gable ends.

Approximately eight metres north of the church in the graveyard is a large triangular slab of limestone with a tenon on one side and a circular hole in its centre (a tenon is a projection designed to be inserted into the socket or mortise hole of another stone). This is the triangular gable end of a tent-shaped tomb-shrine similar to the two examples at Temple Cronan on the Burren (see *Temple Cronan*). The stone at Cill Cheanainn is now resting on its side and the edge raised to the south with the tenon is actually the base of the stone.

Figure 221
Antiquarian view of Cill Cheanainn.

Originally the tenon would have slotted into the mortise hole of a bottom stone for stability. Tomb-shrines housed the bones of saints which were objects of devotion for pilgrims to the site. The hole in the Cill Cheanainn slab was provided so that pilgrims could reach into the shrine and touch the bones of the saint. Another possible focus of pilgrimage at the site is a holy well marked by a large boulder and a low drystone wall 30 metres to the north west. Like many of the Aran pilgrimage destinations, Cill Cheanainn is located close to a good landing place, presumably to facilitate pilgrims travelling by sea.

Cill Cheanainn translates as 'the church of Cheanainn' and it is quite possible that the bones originally held in the tomb shrine on the site belonged to an individual named Cheanainn. There are conflicting accounts, however, as to who Cheanainn was. The antiquarian Thomas Westropp recounted the tradition that he was a zealous and violent preacher who was eventually killed but there is also a tradition that Cheanainn was a woman. In this tradition, Cheanainn was the mother of the 'seven sons of the king' whose memory is preserved in the name of another church site located in the centre of Inishmaan, *Teampall na Seacht Mac Rí* (the Church of the Seven Sons of the King, Grid Reference L 937 048). Not much remains at *Teampall na Seacht Mac Rí* other than *Leaba Chinndeirge*, a rectangular 'saint's bed' surmounted with a cross slab. Adjacent to *Leaba Chinndeirge* are the remains of a rectangular structure and although this structure bears no resemblance to a church there are a few hints of an early ecclesiastical site in the vicinity – 50 metres to the south west of *Teampall na Seacht Mac Rí* is a holy well and there is also a bullaun stone incorporated into the wall surrounding the nearby modern church, next to the gate.

Figure 222
The east window of Cill Cheanainn.

Figure 223
Gable end of tomb-shrine at Cill Cheanainn.

Teampall Chaomháin, Inisheer

Grid Reference L 986 025

It stands on a low knoll, much used for burial, and covered with the intruding sand – and is a beautiful object with its ivied gables and dark walls crowned with sea pinks and yellow vetches, rising out of the pale shifting sand – Thomas Westropp 1895

Teampall Chaomháin, or St Cavan's Church, is located about 300 metres south east of the beach on Inisheer and stands today partially buried in sand. St Cavan is known particularly for his intercessions on behalf of those in trouble in storms and fogs at sea and so the location of his church here near the shore is particularly fitting. This church is a multi-period structure which expanded through time. The earliest part of the church is the central portion which is now the nave. A radiocarbon date for this portion of the church places its construction some time between 1030–1217 AD (see *Radiocarbon Dating the Churches of the Aran Islands*). In its original form, the church would have been a single-celled structure entered through the trabeate door in the west gable.

Some time in the early thirteenth century the chancel with its Transitional style east window and pointed chancel arch was added to the east end of the church, thus converting the original church into the nave of the expanded church. At the base of the south pier of the chancel arch is a small carving of a human head. The original west door of the church now leads into a small sacristy which is a late alteration, as is the south door.

On the north face of the sandy hillock on which Teampall Chaomháin is situated, a fairly extensive midden can be seen eroding out of the dune face. It consists mainly of limpet shells but there are fish bones as well. It's possible that the midden is the result of monks inhabiting the site but without excavation it is impossible to know when the site was occupied or by whom it was occupied.

Figure 224
The cross-decorated slab of St Cavan's bed.

St Cavan's bed or grave is located just north east of the church in a small roofed building. The grave is marked by a recumbent cross-decorated slab.

There is a marble stone over his tomb, with a square wall built about it, on a plain green field in prospect of the sea, where sick people used to lye over night, and recover health of God, for his sake. I have seen one grievously tormented by a thorn thrust into his eye, who by lying soe in St Coeman's burying place, had it miraculously taken out, without the least feeling of the patient; the mark whereof, in the corner of his eye, still remains – O'Flaherty 1684

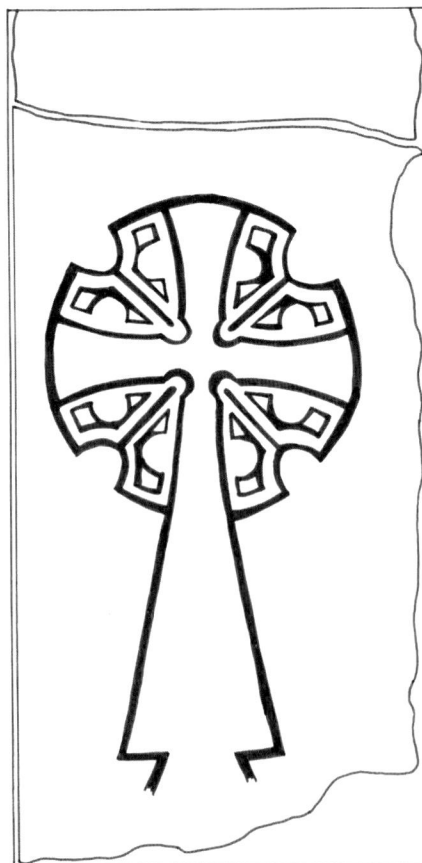

Figure 225
Teampall Chaomháin.

Other Interesting Church Sites

The sites discussed in the preceding pages included the largest and most significant ecclesiastical sites on the Aran Islands, as well as those which have been the subject of excavations. There are, however, many other ecclesiastical sites on the islands, of which a few of the more interesting are discussed here.

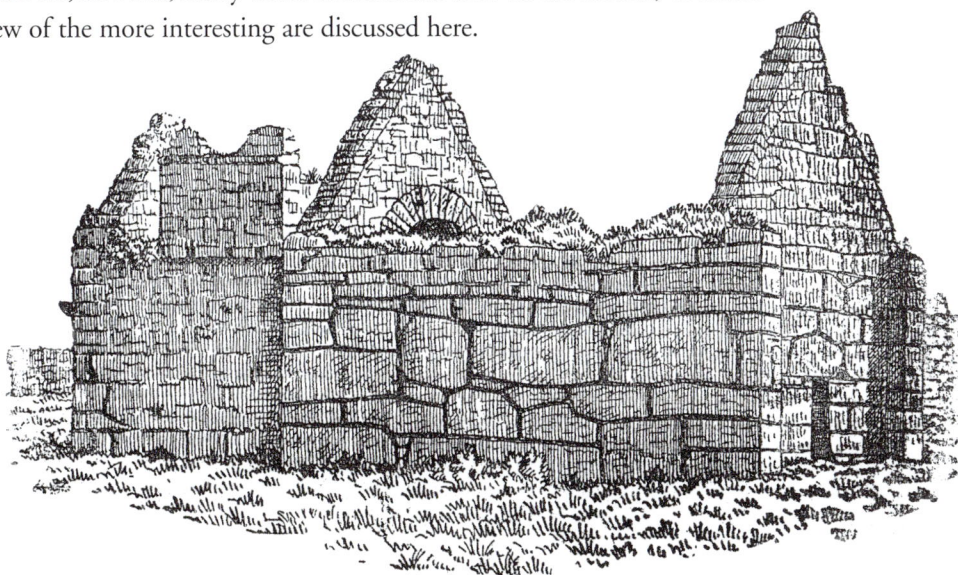

Figure 226
Teampall Mac Duagh, Inishmore.
Grid Reference L 823 103

The founding of this site is attributed to St Colmán Mac Duagh who seems to have been the same St Mac Duagh associated with at least two sites on the Burren, the hermitage at Keelhilla and the early monastery at Oughtmama (see *St Mac Duagh's Hermitage at Keelhilla* and *Oughtmama*). The site consists of a multi-period church, a cross-inscribed pillar stone just west of the church, another pillar stone to the north and a nearby holy well, *Tobar Mac Duach*, to the south behind Kilmurvey House.

Figure 227 ▲
The trabeate doorway of Teampall Mac Duagh.

As with so many multi-period churches, the earliest portion of Teampall Mac Duagh is the western part which was transformed into a nave by the addition of a chancel to the east. The original church would have been a single-celled building and several early features are still visible on the original, western portion of the church. These early features are the tra-beate door in the west wall, the projecting *antae* on either side of the west gable and the massive 'cyclopean' masonry used in this part of the church. A radiocarbon date for this phase of the church places it between 1030-1226 AD (see *Radiocarbon Dating the Churches of the Aran Islands*). Subsequent to this, probably in the early thirteenth century, the chancel and chancel arch were added to the eastern end of the church. The east window in the chancel is of the Transitional style. The third phase of construction at the church was the addition of the battlemented parapets to the top of the north and south walls of the chancel in the fifteenth century. The large carved stone lying outside the church to the east is probably the top of the original eastern window.

Figure 228 ▶
Carving of a 'horse' on Teampall Mac Duagh.

This is a rubbing of a very faint carving located on the outside face of the northern wall near to the north-west corner of the church in the upper right-hand corner of a very large block. It may be a horse.

◀ Figure 229
Cross-inscribed pillar stone at Teampall Mac Duagh.

This cross-inscribed pillar is located just west of Teampall Mac Duagh. The motif on its western face, a cross surmounting an orb, was used in Medieval Europe as a symbol of the rule of Christ over the earth as well as a symbol of ecclesiastical and secular office, particularly the office of kingship.

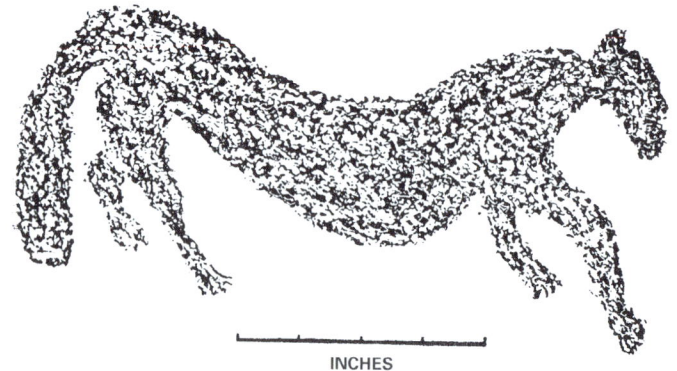

INCHES

Figure 230
Teampall an Ceathrar Álainn, Inishmore.
Grid Reference L 852 101

Figure 231
The Well of the Four Beauties at Teampall an Ceathrar Álainn, Inishmore.

This is the holy well that appears in John Synge's play *The Well of the Saints* and its water is reputed to be a cure for blindness.

Teampall an Ceathrar Álainn is a small fifteenth-century church which has a low rectangular enclosure containing five slab-covered graves attached to its eastern gable. This enclosure is a *leaba*, that is the bed or grave of the four saints after whom the church is named (Fursey, Brendan of Birr, Conall and Bearchán). Up until fairly recently people would sleep in the enclosure to obtain a blessing or effect a cure. Just south of the church at the foot of a small scarp is the Well of the Four Beauties and there are also two very large upright stones placed almost in a line with the church in fields to its west. The nearest is a little less than three metres high and 150 metres distant, the farthest is approximately 3.6 metres high and 420 metres distant (just 15 metres east of the nearer stone are several large slabs which are in some accounts reported to be the graves of the four saints rather than the *leaba* attached to the church). Today, people making the 'rounds' of *Teampall an Ceathrar Álainn* walk around the well and the church saying their rosaries but a raised path leading out towards the upright stones to the west suggests that these stones were included in earlier pilgrimage rounds at the site. Just upslope are a few *clocháin* including Cloghanaphuca which may be satellite structures of *Teampall an Ceathrar Álainn*, perhaps built to house pilgrims visiting the site (see *Clocháin*).

Figure 232
Cill Ghobnait, Inisheer.
Grid Reference L 975 028

This site consists of a small, single-celled church, three *leachtanna*, two bullaun stones and a possible trace of an enclosure. All these features are traditionally taken by archaeologists to suggest an early date for the site but a radiocarbon date indicates that the church was built in the late eleventh century (see *Radiocarbon Dating the Churches of the Aran Islands*). The church is named after St Gobnait, an early female saint. She is supposed to have originally come from Clare but fled from there to Inisheer to escape an enemy. Another story relates that she was a skilled beekeeper and once outwitted a robber who had taken her cattle by unleashing her bees on him.

The small church has a trabeate western door and a round-headed east window. Two of the *leachtanna* abut the south wall of the church and the third lies a few metres to the south. Inside the church, a cross-inscribed slab has been mounted on the altar. There is a bullaun stone just outside the church door and another next to the southernmost *leacht*. The graveyard wall curves around all these features and may, in fact, follow the line of an early ecclesiastical enclosure. Twenty-five metres to the west is a *clochán* built against a rock outcrop with its door facing the church.

Radiocarbon Dating the Churches of the Aran Islands

Without excavation, and sometimes even with excavation, it is often very difficult to date stone buildings. In the absence of any independent dating method, architectural features are often used to infer a date. This can lead to problems, however, as architectural dating usually relies on the assumption of some sort of typological progression which may not, in fact, be valid. It has often been assumed, for instance, that Irish stone churches progressed from small and simple buildings to larger and more complex structures. Based on this assumption it has been asserted that the small and simple church of Temple Benan on Inishmore was very early, possibly earlier than the eighth century AD. An innovative method of radiocarbon dating these early stone buildings, however, has now shown that Temple Benan, and several other Aran Island churches, date to the eleventh century at the earliest.

The method was developed by Dr Rainer Berger from the University of California, Los Angeles and relies on extracting charcoal encased in the buildings' mortar. The mortar used to bind the church stones was produced by heating crushed limestone with charcoal in a lime kiln. Often, the original fuel used to produce the burned lime was not totally consumed in the heating process and is preserved as charcoal particles in the mortar. These charcoal particles were removed from the mortar, purified in the laboratory and then radiocarbon dated. To avoid the possibility of dating a refurbishing episode in the church's history, wherever it was possible the samples were taken from behind blocks of masonry in the buildings' walls, which were temporarily removed for the purpose.

Four of the Aran Island churches were dated with this method. Temple Benan on Inishmore, which had been suspected of being earlier than the eighth century AD, gave a date of 1012-1160 AD. Teampall Mac Duagh on Inishmore gave a date of 1030-1226 AD. Cill Ghobnait Church on Inisheer gave a date of 1047–1093 AD and Teampall Chaomháin (St Cavan's Church) also on Inisheer, gave a date of 1030–1217 AD. Not only do these radiocarbon dates show that the Aran Island churches were built several centuries later than many had thought, the dates also show a remarkable flurry of church building some time between the early eleventh and the early thirteenth centuries. Rather than being the churches of the earliest saints, it seems more likely that the churches were built to capitalise on the growing popularity of pilgrimage to places associated with those early saints several centuries after the saints had died.

Cloghanaphuca, Inishmore.

Grid Reference L 852 100

[P] [X]

Cloghanaphuca means 'the stone hut of the pooka/ ghost' and it was sketched by Captain Stotherd of the Ordnance Survey in 1840 when it was still roofed. Since then the roof has collapsed but the walls are still standing to a height of around two metres. The *clochán* is roughly oval in shape with three niches on the inside. The original east and west doors shown in Stotherd's sketch have been blocked and a more recent entrance has been added in the north wall. The beginnings of the inward corbelling can still be seen on the inside of the south wall.

Cloghanaphuca is not an isolated site and in fact it appears to be part of a whole complex of structures and other features associated with the church site of Teampall an Ceathrar Álainn which is sited just down-slope. Moving down-slope and north west from Cloghanaphuca, there is a rectangular building of very poor construction in the next field and lying on top of the wall are two carved pieces of a Medieval trefoil-headed, two-light window, of a type often found in ecclesiastical buildings. This ruin has been tentatively identified by some as a church but it is more likely to be just the site of a church as the present building bears no resemblance to a church. Just down-slope from this site, approximately 50 metres to the north west are the remains of a completely collapsed *clochán* which today appears as a large circle of rubble with a small C-shaped annex off to one side. There is also another collapsed *clochán* just 30-40 metres south west and up-slope from Cloghanaphuca. All these structures seem to be satellite structures (possibly built to house pilgrims) of the main ecclesiastical/ pilgrimage focus of Teampall an Ceathrar Álainn farther down the slope (see *Other Interesting Church Sites*).

Clocháin

The Irish word *cloch* translates as 'stone' and a *clochán* is a structure built and roofed entirely in stone. *Clocháin* is the plural of *clochán*. *Clocháin* are built without mortar and their roofs are fashioned using the technique of corbelling, where each course of stones is laid so that it overhangs the course below, eventually bringing the sides of the structure together to form a roof. It is difficult to date *clocháin* on their architecture alone as the corbelling technique is an ancient, simple and practical technique which is well suited to rocky terrain. Excavations have suggested an Early Medieval date for a few *clocháin* while the association of many with Early Medieval ecclesiastical sites has reinforced the impression that many date to this period.

The distribution of *clocháin* is confined almost exclusively to the west coast of Ireland and it has been suggested that many were constructed as temporary habitations for pilgrims participating in a maritime pilgrimage route along the west coast and its islands. Dr Peter Harbison has characterised the *clochán* as '… Ireland's first and oldest surviving bed and breakfast establishments.' The densest concentrations of *clocháin* in the country are on the Dingle Peninsula in County Kerry where there is a large cluster west of Mount Brandon and another cluster on the western tip of the peninsula. These two clusters have been explained by Dr Harbison as accommodations for pilgrims waiting to ascend Mount Brandon and cross the sea to the Skelligs, both well-known pilgrimage destinations. As the Aran Islands were also well-known pilgrimage destinations it seems likely that many of the *clocháin* on the islands served as accommodation for visiting pilgrims as well.

Figure 234
Clochán na Carraige, Inishmore.
Grid Reference L 823 116

Clochán na Carraige translates as 'the stone hut of the rock' and it is probably named after the area in which it is sited north of the village of Kilmurvy which is known as *An Charraig,* 'the rock'. This *clochán* is still standing and it is the best preserved *clochán* on the islands. Externally it is oval but its interior is rectangular. It has two opposed doors in its long sides and a single window in one end. It is not obviously associated with any pilgrimage site.

Power Struggles on the Aran Islands

In the Medieval and post-Medieval periods, Galway city became an important trading port. As a result, large amounts of ships and goods flowed in and out of Galway Bay bound for France, Spain and other destinations. Because the Aran Islands are situated directly at the mouth of Galway Bay, they became strategically important to the flow of this trade.

In the Medieval period the Aran Islands were controlled by a branch of the O'Brien's of Clare and as early as the thirteenth century there are records of payments of large amounts of wine by Galway city to the O'Briens to keep the shipping routes in the area free from piracy. The O'Briens held the islands until 1582 when they lost them to the O'Flahertys of Connemara and for the next 70 years the islands changed hands several times. Piracy continued to be a concern and the islands were periodically garrisoned to try and thwart pirates at least as late as the eighteenth century. But the Aran Islands also took on an even greater strategic role in post-Medieval military campaigns. Particularly in the turbulent seventeenth century, but also as late as the nineteenth century, Galway Bay became a likely landing site for an invasion of Ireland. Because the Aran Islands were the key to controlling Galway Bay, they were contested, fortified and garrisoned by various competing powers.

O'Brien's Castle, Inisheer

Grid Reference L 982 023

There seem to have been two principal O'Brien castles on the Aran Islands in the Medieval period, one on Inishmore and one on Inisheer. Although there are historical records of the O'Brien castle on Inishmore at Killeany, no trace of this remains today, as it seems to have been completely dismantled to build the later Cromwellian-period Arkin Fort (see *Arkin Fort, Inishmore*). The two-storey rectangular tower on Inisheer known as O'Brien's Castle is, however, fairly well preserved.

O'Brien's Castle is the prominent tower on the high ground of Inisheer. It is set within the earlier, roughly oval, stone fort of Dún Formna (see *The Stone Forts of the Aran Islands*) and the earlier oval fort also seems to have had a rectangular turret added to its west side at this

Figure 235
O'Brien's Castle, Inisheer.

The people at the left of the photo are standing in the rectangular turret which was added to the earlier stone fort of Dún Formna at the time O'Brien's Castle was built, or perhaps even later.

time or perhaps later. In this way the earlier fort was reused as a bawn wall surrounding the much later two-storey 'keep' tower which is O'Brien's Castle.

O'Brien's Castle was probably built in the fourteenth century which makes it earlier than the tower houses of the Burren (which generally date to between the early fifteenth to mid seventeenth centuries) and later than the stone forts of the Aran Islands. The function of all three types of site, however, was the same. They were all fortified residences of local chiefs. Although O'Brien's Castle is not unique, it does date to a period before the widespread adoption of castles by Gaelic lords, when most were probably living in other types of fortified sites such as moated sites, *crannógs* and ringforts.

The castle consists of a ground floor basement which was probably used for storage, a large first floor hall (which may have occupied the entire first floor), and possibly further living quarters directly under the roof in the attic. The original doorway is directly above the present-day ground floor entrance in the north-east wall and the two beam holes that flank the original doorway would have held an external wooden stairway. The basement consists of three vaulted chambers and access to it seems to have been through an opening in the roof of the central chamber. There are two narrow windows on the ground floor (one of which is blocked) and there were at least two windows on the first floor including a finely carved trefoil-headed window in the south-west wall. A set of stairs contained in the thickness of the south-west wall leads up from the first floor to a wall walk protected by a parapet. The castle roof would have been steeply pitched and covered in either thatch or slate. Numerous spouts can be seen piercing the base of the parapet to drain the water from the roof which would otherwise have collected behind the parapet. Also of interest are two carved stone heads on the outside of the castle. One projects from the north-east wall and the other from the south-east wall. Their function is unknown but they may have been intended to ward off some form of evil.

Although not occupied by O'Brien's after 1582, O'Brien's Castle was used and occupied by others until the Aran Islands were surrendered by royalist forces to the Cromwellians in 1652. At that time the Cromwellians seem to have partially dismantled O'Brien's Castle and focused their garrison on Inishmore where they built Arkin Fort.

Arkin Fort, Inishmore

Grid Reference L 887 073

In 1649, the English Civil War ended with the Parliamentarians triumphant over the Royalists. Charles I was executed and Cromwell brought his New Model Army of Puritans to Ireland. One of Cromwell's goals was to control Ireland militarily but he had a social agenda as well. In addition to military control, Cromwell wanted to eliminate or remove all Catholic landowners and priests who had joined in an uprising against Protestant settlers in 1641, and he also wanted to convert the Irish population to Protestantism. The Cromwellian soldiers pursued these goals with a brutal zeal which has left a legacy of bitterness and animosity down to modern times. Cromwell's New Model Army was probably the most efficient army in all Europe at the time and the war in Ireland ended in 1652 with the Cromwellian forces victorious. When the Cromwellians took control of Galway city, the terms of surrender included the garrisoning of both Galway and the Aran Islands and it is the Aran Islands, garrison which began building the fort at Arkin on Inishmore in 1652 and finished the construction a few years later. Arkin Fort is located in the village of Killeany towards the southern end of Inishmore. The name 'Arkin' is the anglicised version of the Irish word *aircín* which means a small natural harbour, and Killeany, or Arkin as it used to be known, was originally the primary port of Inishmore before Kilronan took over that role.

Figure 236
Arkin Fort.

Not much remains of Arkin Fort, as most of it seems to have been dismantled to provide building stones for later structures. This, however, is only the latest recycling of the stones in Killeany as the stones to build Arkin Fort were apparently obtained by dismantling the nearby Franciscan friary, part of St Enda's monastery and presumably the earlier O'Brien castle which stood on the site as well. A late eighteenth century plan of Arkin Fort shows it as a roughly rectangular curtain wall with four towers surrounding several free-standing buildings. Two entrances are shown, one in the south wall opening onto the road and the other in the north wall opening directly onto the water. What remains of the fort today can best be seen by walking out on the modern quay and looking back at the fort. From here it can be seen that most of the north curtain wall remains, as well as a portion of the north-east tower. The entrance opening onto the water is still visible in the north wall and is protected by an overhanging machicolation.

The fort was garrisoned until 1685, holding up to a full company of 100 foot soldiers. After 1685 the fort was manned only occasionally, often to protect the islands from French privateers. Even this sporadic use of the fort seems to have stopped in the early eighteenth century after which it seems the fort was allowed to fall into disrepair.

Figure 237
View from 'The Watchman' over the harbour at Killeany.
Grid Reference L 885 071

A rough stone structure located on the ridge above Arkin fort about 50 metres north of Temple Benan is known locally as 'The Watchman' and it may well have been a lookout post for Arkin Fort. Excavation in 1984 revealed that it had been built in three separate phases. It's not clear why this was but the separate phases may have been successive attempts to enlarge it and make it more windproof. Finds from the excavation consisted of potsherds, clay pipe fragments, fragments from a heavy glass bottle, two musket balls, a melted piece of lead and two large iron nails. It's not hard to imagine a guard sitting in the lookout passing the time smoking, drinking and maybe casting a few musket balls.

Archaeology of the Eighteenth and Nineteenth Centuries

Signal Towers

In the early nineteenth century, at roughly the same time as the two Martello towers were built on the north shore of the Burren, two signal towers were built on the Aran Islands. As with the Martello towers, the signal towers were part of the comprehensive network of coastal defences built around Ireland by the British because they feared an invasion by the French, which might lead to an Irish uprising.

The two towers, one on Inisheer (Grid Reference L 982 022) and the other on Inishmore (Grid Reference L 861 099), were part of a network of signal towers built around the Irish coast between 1804 and 1806. Most of these towers were built with defensive features so that the signal crew and military guard could defend itself against attack. The signal towers formed a line of communication from Dublin on the east coast to Bantry Bay in the south west and then up along the west coast to Malin Head in the north west.

The towers were built to a fairly standard plan. They were square towers, generally with two storeys. The door was typically on the seaward side above ground level and it was accessed by a wooden ladder that could be quickly pulled up. Directly over the door was a machicolation for added defence and the two landward corners of the tower were generally defended with machicolations as well. The roof was flat and protected by a parapet. The ground-floor windows were relatively small while the upper windows were larger, again reflecting defensive concerns. Both of the Aran Island signal towers were covered in shingles for weather proofing.

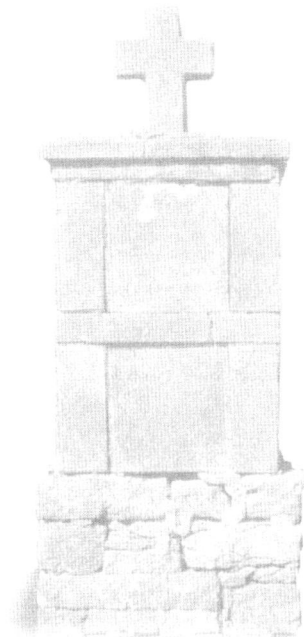

The towers were intended to be defensible guard houses and barracks. The actual work of signalling was carried out just in front of the tower where a large wooden signal post was erected on the seaward side of the tower. The signal post consisted of a 50-foot mast supported by a tripod of large timbers. The signals were conveyed by a system of balls and flags which were hoisted up the mast. In the chain of signal towers around the coast of Ireland, the next tower to the south of the islands is found on the Clare coast at Hags Head at the southern end of the Cliffs of Moher, and the next tower to the north is found at Golam Head on the north coast of Galway Bay.

Many of the signal towers were abandoned only a few years after they had been built. Maintenance was one problem, while the completion of other coastal defences seems to have made some of the signal towers obsolete. Interestingly, during the War of 1812 in America, some signal towers were brought back into use to help guard against American naval ships and privateers who at the time were capturing large numbers of merchant ships in Irish waters.

The signal tower on Inisheer is well preserved and is located on the highest point on the island, 500 metres south of the sandy beach. The building adjacent to it is the old National School. Similarly, the signal tower on Inishmore is located on the highest point on that island where it can be seen partially altered and incorporated into the slightly later lighthouse station, built in 1818.

Figure 238
Signal tower on Inisheer.
Grid Reference L 982 022

Roadside Cenotaphs and Wayside Cairns

A curious custom, seemingly now almost extinct, amongst the islanders of Arran, is the erection on the roadside of monuments to the memory of the dead – G.S. Brady 1866.

The tall stone monuments topped with a cross and faced with inscribed plaques that stand along the roadside on Inishmore are some of the most visible archaeological monuments to the casual visitor to this island. These roadside cenotaphs are nineteenth-century memorials to the dead. The cenotaphs typically have two inscribed plaques, one asking for mercy on the soul of the departed, the other recording the people who erected the monument. Like many memorials that date to the last few centuries, the inscriptions on these memorials often contain words that are split in odd places. It's quite likely this is because the masons who were carving the slabs were illiterate and were merely copying something they could not read.

Most of the dates on the cenotaphs fall between 1811 and 1876 and there are a few later examples with dates up to 1892. On the Aran Islands, the cenotaphs seem to be unique to Inishmore as there are no examples from the two smaller Aran Islands. There are, however, a few examples of similar monuments on the mainland. Although all the roadside cenotaphs are nineteenth-century monuments, there are also some similar eighteenth-century cenotaphs dedicated to the Fitzpatricks set away from the road on the high ground just south of the village of Killeany on Inishmore (Grid Reference L 888 069).

Figure 239
Roadside cenotaph, Inishmore.
Grid Reference L 868 101

This roadside cenotaph or *leachta cuimhne* near Oghil is only one of many which can be seen along the roadsides of Inishmore.

Figure 240
Wayside cairn, Inishmore.

Grid Reference L 825 110

Small wayside cairns can also be seen along the roadside in places. These wayside cairns are simpler than the cenotaphs and range from a few stones leaned up against each other to more substantial piles of stones over a metre in height. These small cairns were built by mourners at spots where it was traditional for the funeral procession to pause on its way to the cemetery.

Site Index

Site	Type	Page	Map
The Burren			
Ballyganner	cashel and tower house	110	D
Ballyganner South	megalithic tomb	66	D
Ballynalackan	tower house	146	A,C
Baur South	megalithic tomb	67	A,B,D
Cabhail Ti Breac	post-Medieval building	114	A,D
Caherballykinvarga	stone fort	108	D
Cahercommaun	stone fort	98	E
Caherconnell	cashel	112	A,B,D,E
Cahercottine	cashel	110	D
Caherfadda	rectilinear cashel	111	E
Cahermacnaghten	cashel	113	A,D
Caherminnaun	cashels	111	D
Cahermore	cashel	112	A,B
Caherwalsh	rectilinear cashel	110	D
Carn Mhic Táil	cairn	147	C,D
Carran Church	ecclesiastical site	130	D,E
Castletown	cashel	112	E
Cathair na mBithiúnach	cashel and megalithic tomb	110	D
Coolnatullagh	burial cairn	77	B
Corcomroe	ecclesiastical site	122	B
Creevagh	megalithic tomb	68	E
Doolin	stone axe site	40	C
Doolin	ring barrows	82	C
Doonnagore	tower house	145	C
Fahee South	fulacht fiadh	75	B,E
Finavarra Martello Tower	nineteenth-century military fortification	152	B
Glencolumbkille	ecclesiastical site	95	B,E
Gleninagh	tower house	144	A
Kilfenora	ecclesiastical site	116	D
Killilagh	ecclesiastical site	128	C
Killinaboy	ecclesiastical site	136	E
Knockstoolery	standing stone	75	C

Baile na mBocht	settlement	185	F
Clochán na Carraige	*clochán*	221	F
Cloghanaphuca	*clochán*	220	F
Dún Aonghasa	Bronze Age hillfort	161	F
Dún Aonghasa	Early Medieval stone fort	172	F
Dún Dúcathair	stone fort	180	F
Dún Eochla	stone fort	178	F
Dún Eoghanachta	stone fort	177	F
Oghil	wedge tomb	157	F
Roadside Cenotaph	mortuary monument	229	F
St Ciaran's monastery (Teampaill Chiaráin)	ecclesiastical site	199	F
St Enda's monastery (Killeany)	ecclesiastical site	190	F
Signal Tower	nineteenth-century military tower	227	F
Temple Brecan (The Seven Churches)	ecclesiastical site	204	F
Teampall an Ceathrar Álainn	ecclesiastical site	217	F
Teampall Mac Duagh	ecclesiastical site	215	F
The Watchman	military lookout	226	F
Wayside Cairn	mortuary monument	230	F

Maps

Site Symbols

Cairn		Megalithic Tomb	
Cashel		Prehistoric Farmstead	
Church		Rectilinear Cashel	
Clochán		Ring Barrow	
Cross-inscribed Pillar		Roadside Cenotaph	
Cross-inscribed Slab		Round Tower	
Prehistoric Field System		Signal Tower	
Fulacht Fiadh		Souterrain	ST
High Cross		Standing Stone	
Holy Well		Stone Cross	
Large Stone Fort		Tourist Information	i
Martello Tower		Tower House	
Medieval Building			

The Burren and the Aran Islands

Explorer Map Coverage

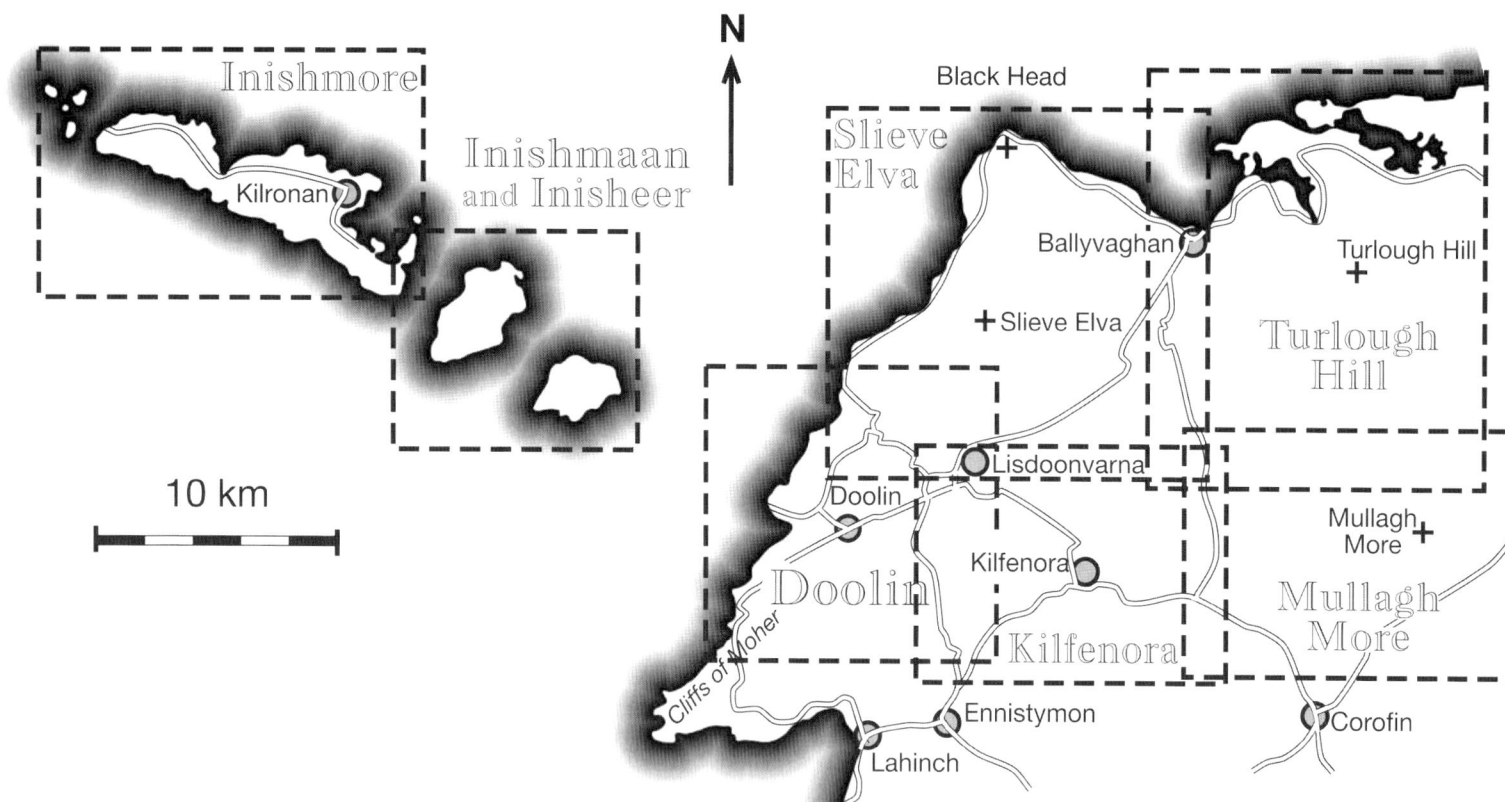

Inishmore

Inishmaan and Inisheer

Kilronan

10 km

N

Black Head

Slieve Elva

Ballyvaghan

Turlough Hill

Slieve Elva

Turlough Hill

Lisdoonvarna

Doolin

Mullagh More

Doolin

Kilfenora

Kilfenora

Mullagh More

Cliffs of Moher

Ennistymon

Corofin

Lahinch

Cartographic data taken from Ordnance Survey
Ireland West, Holiday Map, 1:250,000
Published by the Director at the
Ordnance Survey Office,
Phoenix Park, Dublin, 1998.

Slieve Elva

Lisdoonvarna to
Ballyvaghan to
Black Head

Explorer Map A

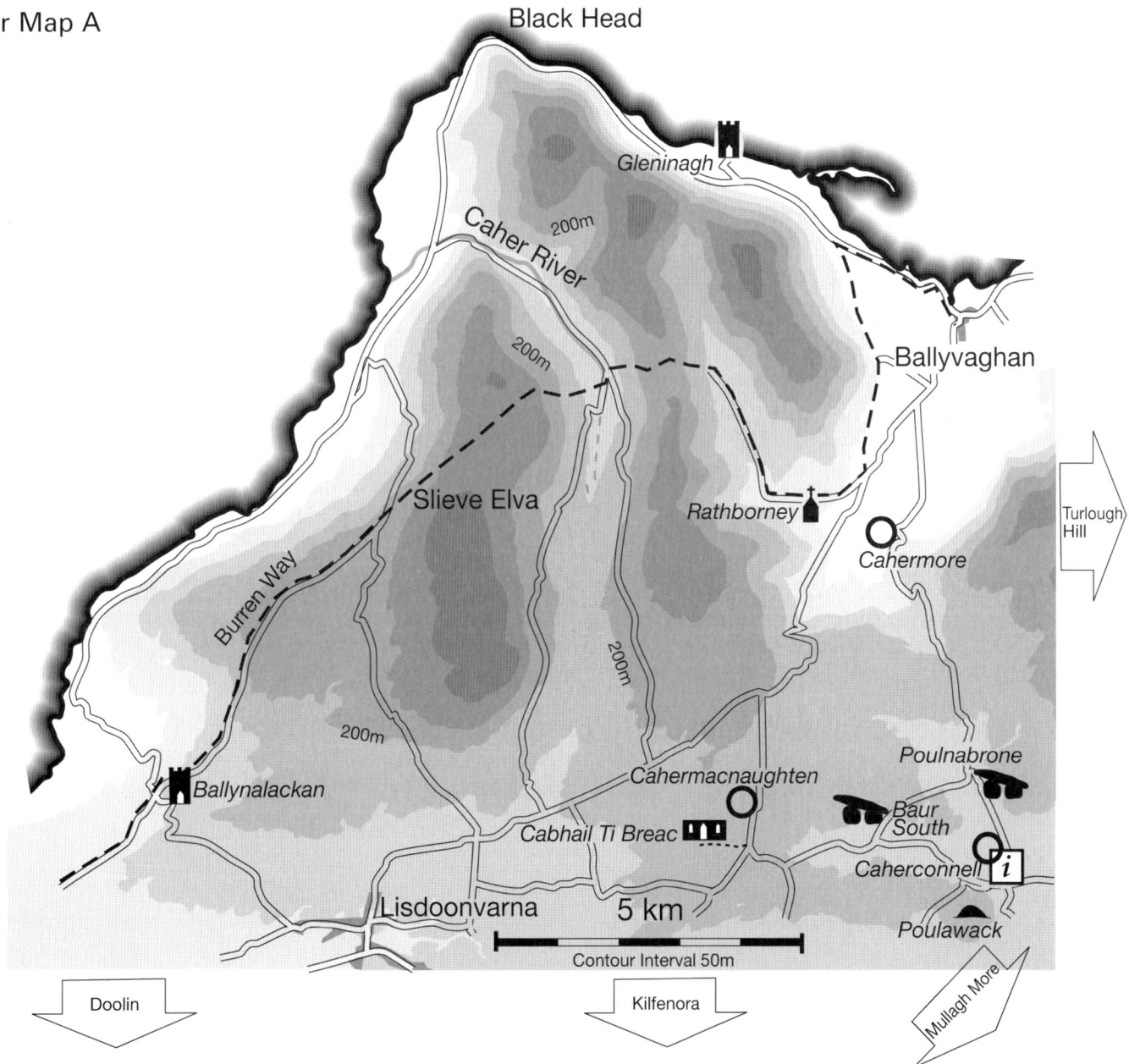

N

Black Head

Gleninagh

Caher River

200m

200m

Ballyvaghan

Slieve Elva

Rathborney

Cahermore

Burren Way

200m

Turlough
Hill

200m

200m

Poulnabrone

Ballynalackan

Cahermacnaughten

Baur
South

Cabhail Ti Breac

Caherconnell

i

Lisdoonvarna

5 km

Poulawack

Contour Interval 50m

Doolin

Kilfenora

Mullagh More

Turlough Hill

Carran to
Ballyvaghan to
Bell Harbour

Explorer Map B

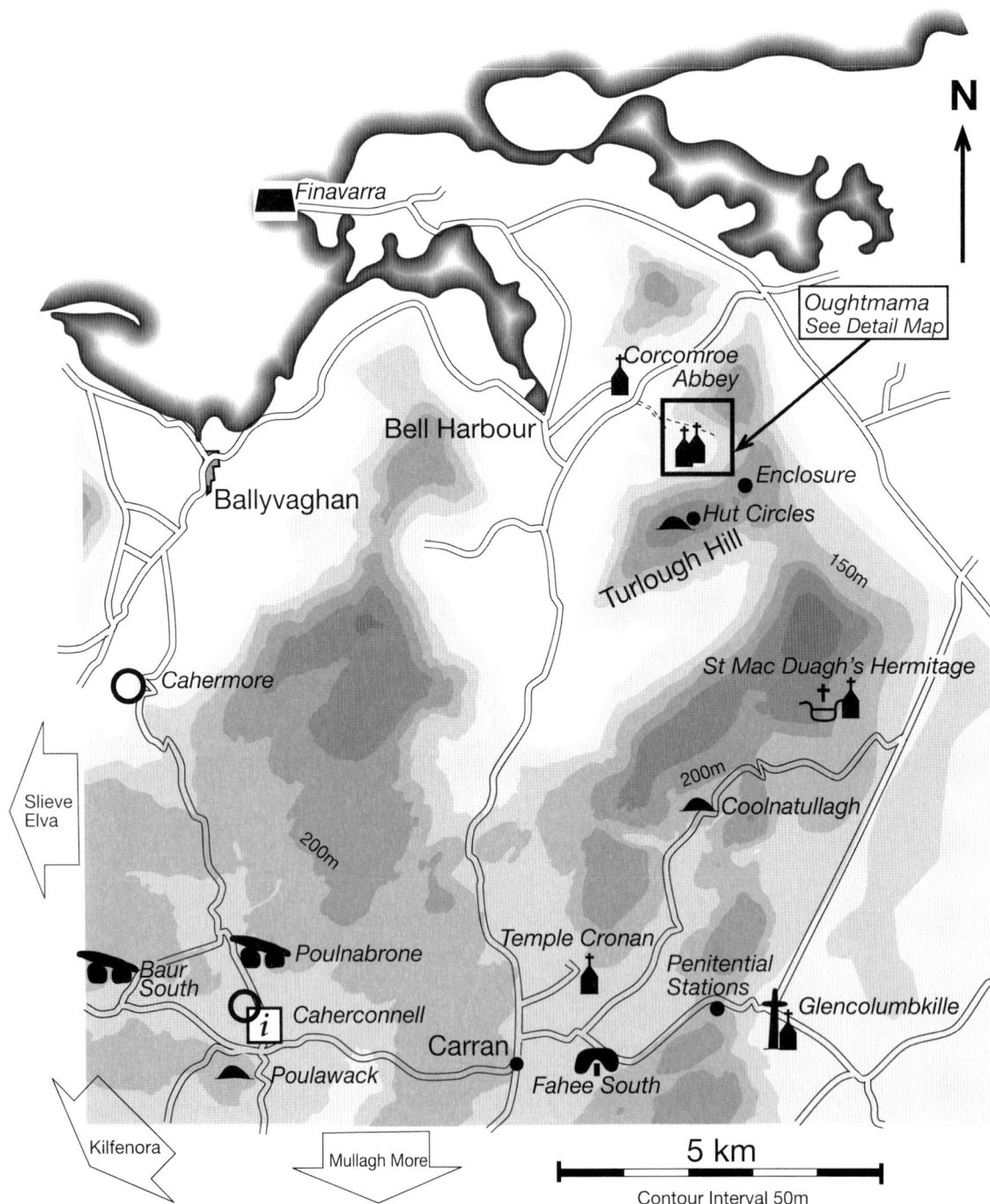

N

Finavarra

Oughtmama
See Detail Map

+Corcomroe
Abbey

Bell Harbour

Enclosure

Ballyvaghan

Hut Circles

Turlough Hill

150m

St Mac Duagh's Hermitage

Cahermore

200m

Coolnatullagh

Slieve
Elva

200m

Temple Cronan

Penitential
Stations

Poulnabrone

Glencolumbkille

Baur
South

Caherconnell

Carran

i

Poulawack

Fahee South

5 km

Kilfenora

Mullagh More

Contour Interval 50m

Doolin

Cliffs of Moher to Lisdoonvarna

Explorer Map C

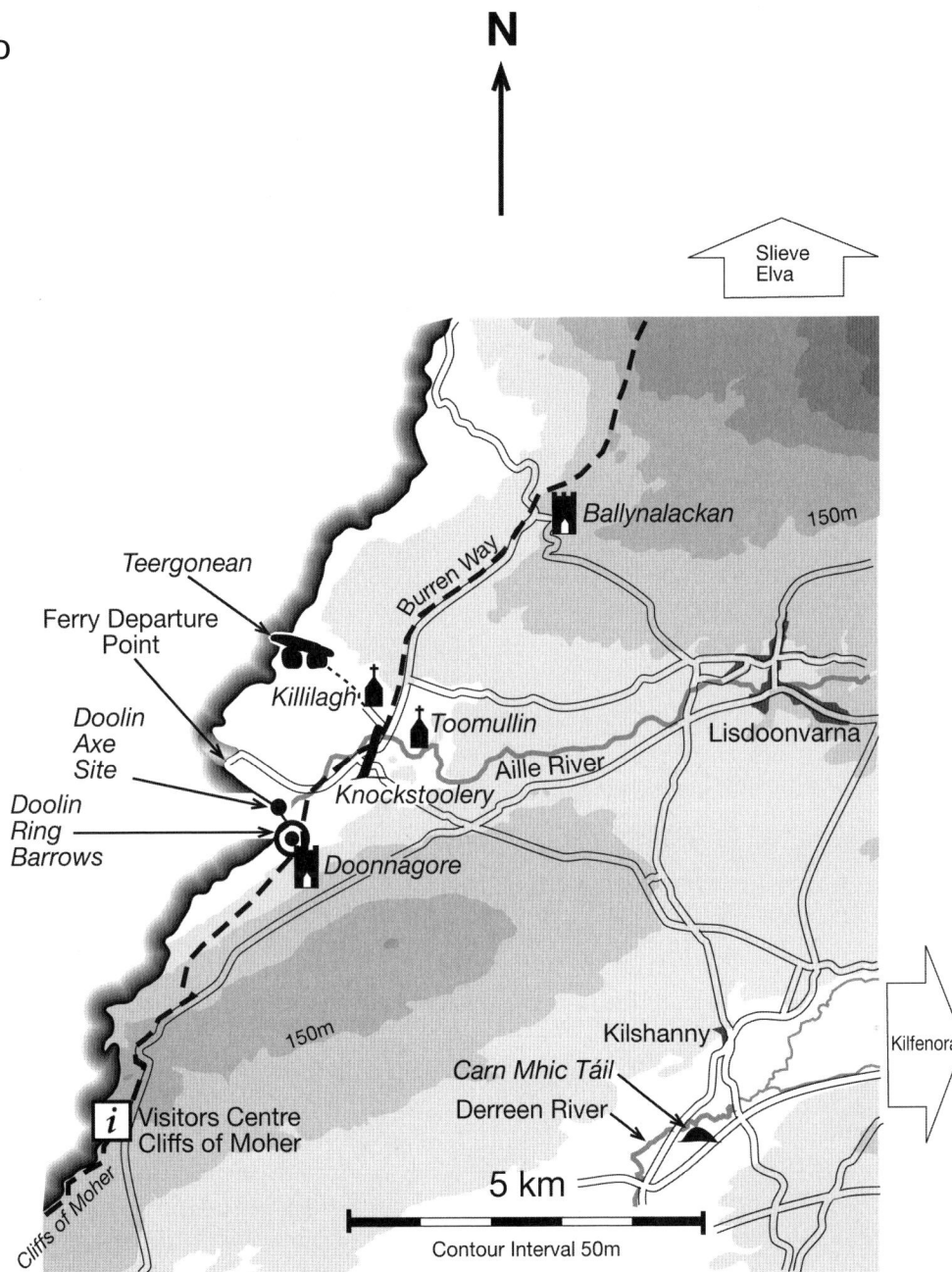

N

Slieve Elva

Ballynalackan

150m

Burren Way

Teergonean

Ferry Departure Point

Killilagh

Toomullin

Lisdoonvarna

Doolin Axe Site

Aille River

Knockstoolery

Doolin Ring Barrows

Doonnagore

Kilshanny

Kilfenora

Carn Mhic Táil

Derreen River

i Visitors Centre Cliffs of Moher

5 km

Cliffs of Moher

150m

Contour Interval 50m

Kilfenora

Lisdoonvarna to
Kilfenora to
Leamaneh Castle

Explorer Map D

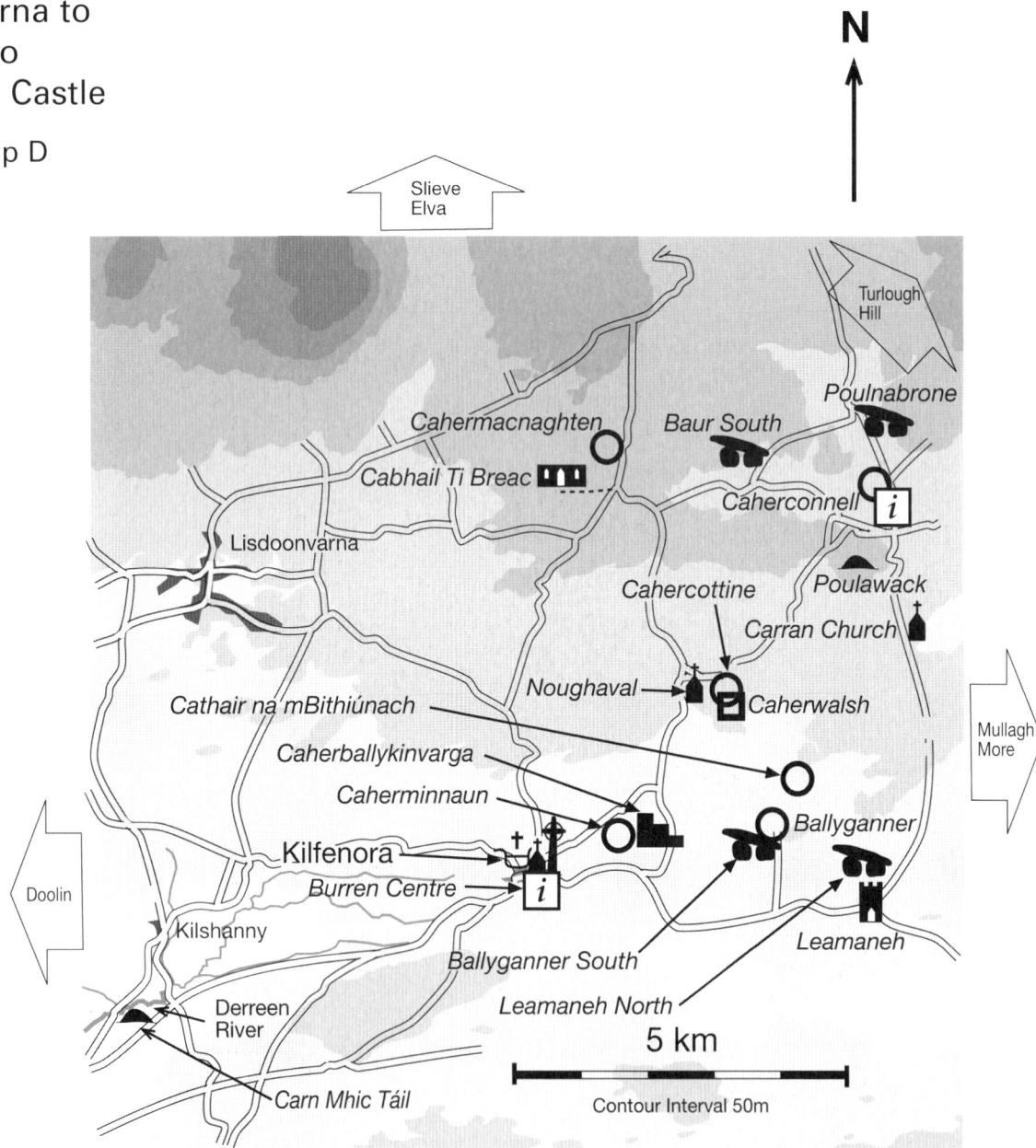

N

Slieve
Elva

Turlough
Hill

Poulnabrone

Cahermacnaghten

Baur South

Cabhail Ti Breac

Caherconnell

i

Lisdoonvarna

Cahercottine

Poulawack

Carran Church

Noughaval

Caherwalsh

Cathair na mBithiúnach

Caherballykinvarga

Mullagh
More

Caherminnaun

Ballyganner

Kilfenora

Burren Centre

i

Leamaneh

Doolin

Kilshanny

Ballyganner South

Leamaneh North

5 km

Derreen
River

Carn Mhic Táil

Contour Interval 50m

Mullagh More

Fergus River to
Carran to
Mullagh More

Explorer Map E

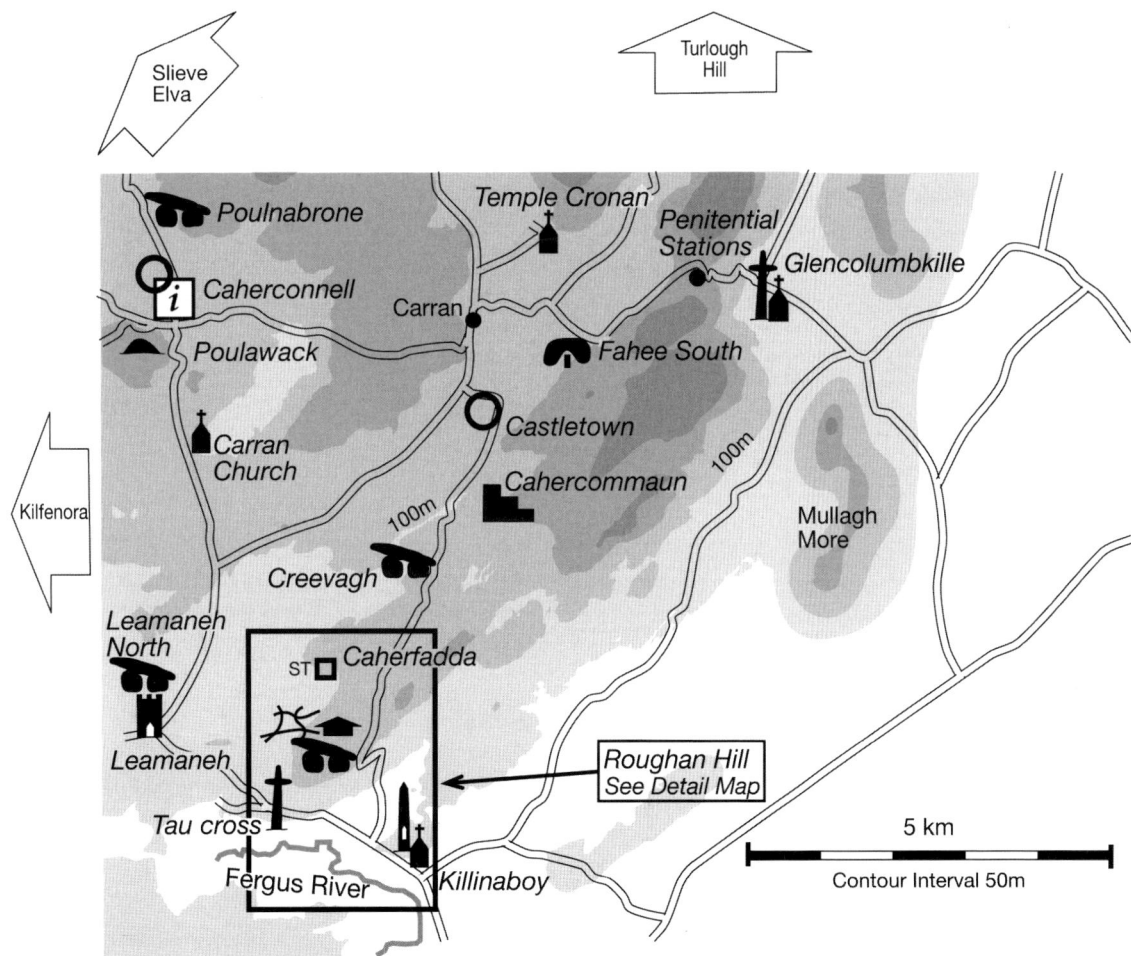

N

Slieve
Elva

Turlough
Hill

Poulnabrone

Temple Cronan

Penitential
Stations

Glencolumbkille

Caherconnell

i

Carran

Poulawack

Fahee South

Castletown

Carran
Church

Cahercommaun

Kilfenora

100m

100m

Mullagh
More

Creevagh

Leamaneh
North

ST

Caherfadda

Roughan Hill
See Detail Map

Leamaneh

5 km

Tau cross

Contour Interval 50m

Fergus River

Killinaboy

Inishmore

Aran Islands

Explorer Map F

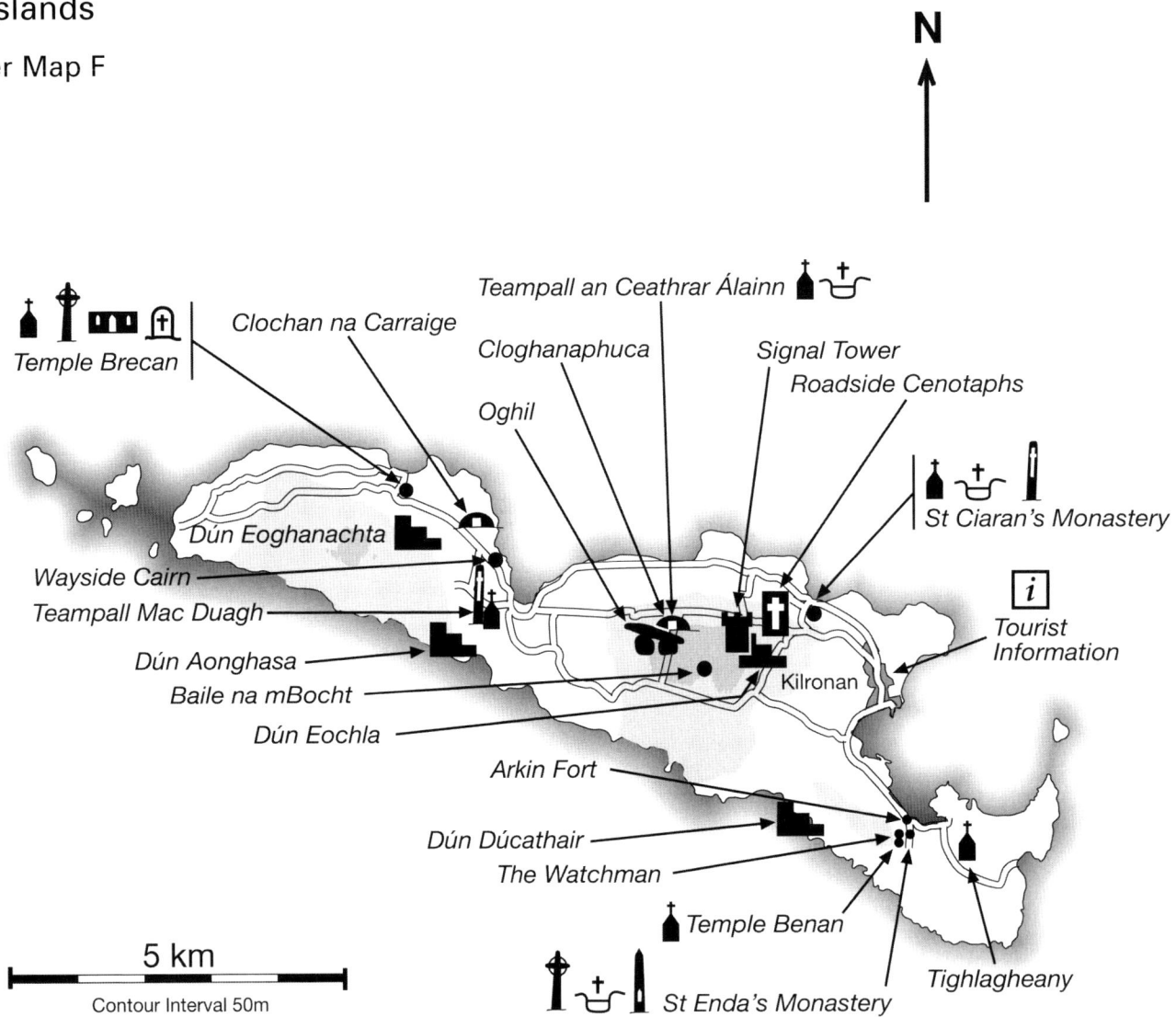

N

Temple Brecan

Clochan na Carraige

Teampall an Ceathrar Álainn

Cloghanaphuca

Signal Tower

Roadside Cenotaphs

Oghil

St Ciaran's Monastery

Dún Eoghanachta

Wayside Cairn

Teampall Mac Duagh

Dún Aonghasa

Baile na mBocht

Dún Eochla

Kilronan

Tourist Information

Arkin Fort

Dún Dúcathair

The Watchman

Temple Benan

St Enda's Monastery

Tighlagheany

5 km

Contour Interval 50m

Inishmaan
and **Inisheer**
Aran Islands

Explorer Map G

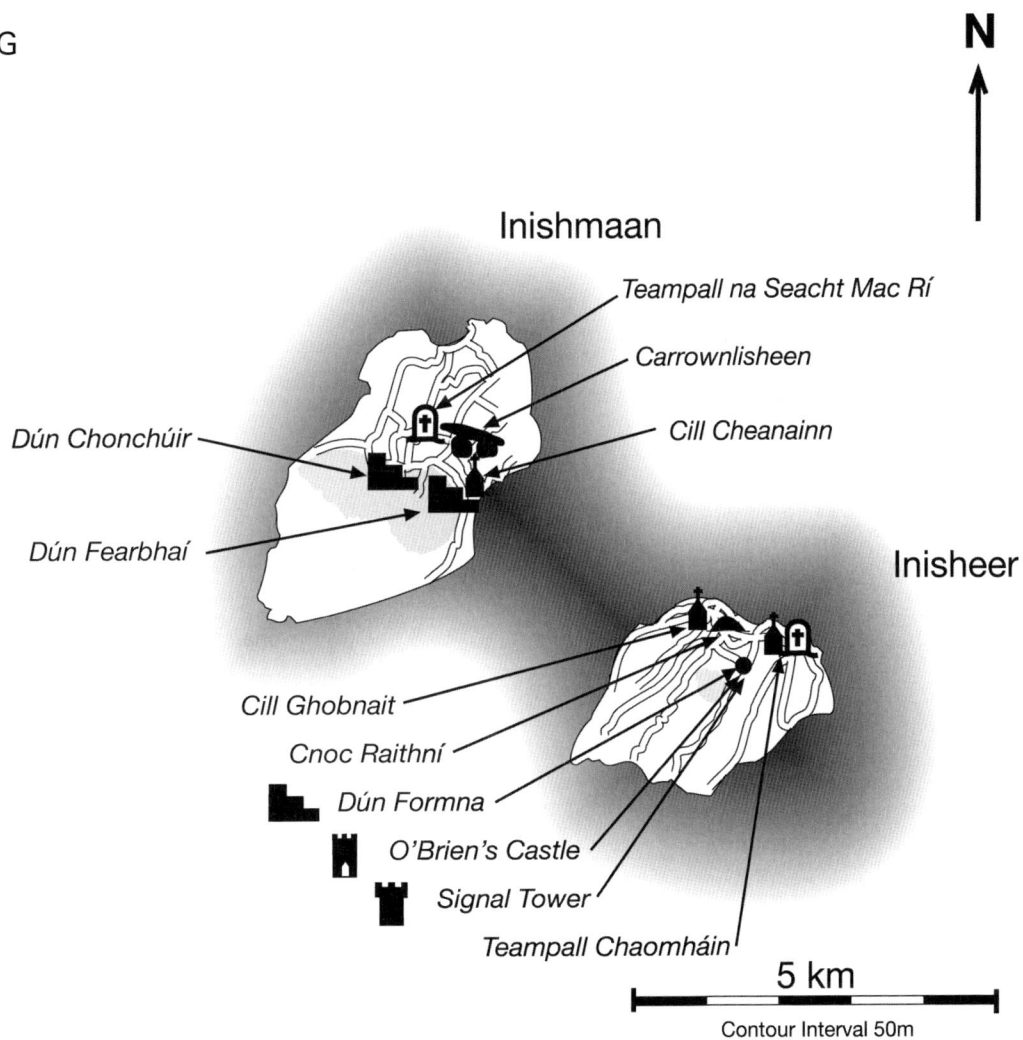

N

Inishmaan

Teampall na Seacht Mac Rí

Carrownlisheen

Dún Chonchúir

Cill Cheanainn

Dún Fearbhaí

Inisheer

Cill Ghobnait

Cnoc Raithní

Dún Formna

O'Brien's Castle

Signal Tower

Teampall Chaomháin

5 km

Contour Interval 50m

Glossary

ambry – A cupboard in the thickness of the wall, often found in tower houses and near altars in churches.

antae – The extensions found on the gable ends of some early stone churches which are thought to mimic the stout corner posts of earlier wooden churches.

antiquarian – An early scholar who described, illustrated, compared and classified antiquities. Generally refers to people in the nineteenth century and earlier.

apse – A half-circular or polygonal termination of a church or chapel.

arcade – A series of arches on pillars or columns.

articulated – When bones are found in an 'articulated' state it means they are in their anatomically correct positions even though they may no longer be held together by any soft tissue. See also 'disarticulated'.

bargeboard – A verge board or gable rafter finishing the outside of a gable below the verge or edge of the roof covering.

bartizan – A small projecting corner turret on a castle built on top of a machicolation.

batter – The outward sloping of a wall face.

bawn – The walled courtyard of a castle.

Beaker pottery – A distinctive type of Final Neolithic/Early Bronze Age pottery found over wide parts of Europe. The pots have an S-shaped profile and are decorated with many devices including incised lines, cord impressions, and comb impressions.

bracken – A widespread and often weedy fern which can form dense thickets.

bullaun stone – A stone (typically a boulder) with a large round man-made depression in it. They resemble stone mortars and are often found on early ecclesiastical sites. They may have been used to pound grains or herbs or were possibly as holy water receptacles.

cairn – A large pile of stones which often covers or contains a burial or several burials. Although cairns of widely varying dates are known and many cairns were probably used and reused over centuries or even millennia, it seems likely many cairns date to the Bronze Age.

cenotaph – A monument erected to honour a dead person whose remains lie elsewhere.

chamfer – An architectural term referring to a splayed or bevelled surface made by cutting off a square edge.

chancel – The eastern portion of a church.

Chapter House – The apartment in monasteries set apart for the daily meetings of the brethren at which a chapter of the Rule of the Order was read.

choir – The area between the nave and the presbytery in a church. The space set apart for the monks.

clochán / clocháin (plural) – A structure built and roofed entirely in stone. They typically have a beehive shape.

corbel – A stone projecting to support a beam or other stonework.

crannóg – An artificial platform built in a lake. They are typically constructed with layers of brushwood.

crozier – A staff with a crook at the end, carried by an abbot, bishop, or archbishop as a symbol of office.

dendrochronological dating – Tree-ring dating. The chronology is constructed from overlapping patterns of tree rings starting with a modern tree. It is a very precise method of dating.

diagnostic – When an artefact is 'diagnostic' it means it is characteristic of a particular time period. Diagnostic artefacts are, therefore, useful for dating sites.

disarticulated – When bones are 'disarticulated' they are no longer in their anatomically correct positions. When a megalithic tomb is filled with 'disarticulated' bones, it is filled with a jumbled mass of bones. See also 'articulated'.

femur – The 'thigh bone' which extends from the pelvis to the knee.

garderobe – A latrine.

Gaelic – In a Medieval context, it refers to the native Irish.

Gothic Style – A Medieval style of architecture which was particularly popular in the eastern part of the country. Characteristic features of the Gothic style are pointed arches, square-edged or moulded arch rings, capitals covered with foliage and windows completely framed by mouldings. In Ireland, Gothic architecture generally dates to after 1200 AD.

grykes – The deep and narrow fissures found in the limestone landscapes of the Burren and the Aran Islands.

inhumation – A burial is said to be an 'inhumation' when the body is buried without cremating it.

jamb – The side of a doorway, archway or other opening.

karstic – A limestone terrain characterised by erosional features such as grykes, sinkholes, underground streams and caves.

keep – The strongest and securest part of a castle.

leaba/leapacha (plural) – A saint's 'bed'. Typically a small stone enclosure which is (or is purported to be) the grave of a saint.

leacht/leachtanna (plural) – Small rectangular stone mounds found on many early ecclesiastical sites. Some may have been used as open-air altars and some were certainly incorporated into pilgrimage rounds. Some may mark the graves of important people, such as early saints, while others appear to be dedicated to people buried elsewhere. The word *leacht* translates as a 'grave', a 'grave mound' or a 'memorial cairn'.

lintel – A horizontal stone or beam spanning the top of an opening, often over a door or a window.

machicolation – A line of corbels projecting from a castle wall and supporting a small wall which stands proud of the castle wall. The purpose of the structure is to provide a protected place from which stones and other missiles could be dropped or fired on attackers below.

megalithic – mega = big, lithic = stone. A term used to refer generally to the many different types of tombs constructed from large stones during the Neolithic period.

midden – An accumulation of food debris and other debris. Middens typically appear as layers of dark soil on archaeological sites.

nave – The main body of the church where the congregation sits.

oratory – A small chapel set apart for private prayer.

pastoral farming – The practice of raising animals for food, as opposed to 'arable farming' which is the practice of raising plants for food.

phalange – A bone of a finger or a toe.

plantain – A low herb with broad spreading leaves and slender spikes of minute flowers. Its significance to archaeologists is that it is a weed which spreads with the practice of pastoral farming.

prehistory – That period of the past before written records. In Ireland, prehistory includes all periods up to and including the Iron Age. The historic period in Ireland begins with the start of the Early Medieval period, *c.* 400 AD, when writing and literacy were introduced.

presbytery – The eastern part of a monastic church, east of the monks' choir and extending to the sanctuary.

quern stone – A stone upon which grain is ground. The earliest quern stones were saddle-shaped and were used in conjunction with a hand-held rubbing stone. In the Iron Age bee-hive-shaped rotary querns were developed while post-Iron Age periods are characterised by flatter rotary querns.

radiocarbon dating – A method for dating organic remains (i.e., the remains of things that were once alive). Carbon is absorbed by all living organisms (plants and animals) while they are alive. In a living organism that is taking in Carbon, the isotopes of Carbon (C-14, C-12 & C-13) are present at known levels. When the organism dies, it ceases to take in fresh Carbon and the unstable isotope Carbon-14 steadily decays. The less Carbon-14 in the sample, the older the sample.

Romanesque Style – The Romanesque style of ecclesiastical architecture is characterised by the use of round arches, decorative sculpture, high-vaulted ceilings and walls divided into distinctive 'storeys', but not all of these elements appear on all Romanesque churches. Romanesque architecture had its origins during the latter eleventh century and early twelfth century on the continent and in England. In Ireland it generally dates to the twelfth century but in the west it continued in use into the early thirteenth century.

rubbing stone – A hand-held stone used in conjunction with a prehistoric saddle-shaped quern stone.

sacristy – A room in a church where the sacred vessels and vestments are kept.

souterrain – An underground structure often found within ring forts, cashels and other Early Medieval sites. They were probably used both as refuges and storage cellars.

stratigraphy – Refers to the superimposition of layers or 'strata' of soil (or other deposit) one on top of the other.

tibia – The inner and larger of the two bones of the lower leg, extending from the knee to the ankle.

trabeate – An early style of doorway on churches. It is distinguished by being topped with a horizontal lintel rather than an arch.

transept – The cross-arm of a church or any wing projecting laterally from a church.

Transitional Style – A Medieval style of architecture characteristic of the west of Ireland sometimes called the 'School of the West'. It is transitional between the Romanesque and the Gothic styles and incorporates elements of both styles.

trefoil – An ornament, symbol, or architectural form having the appearance of three divisions or leaves. Trefoil-headed windows are a feature of some Medieval buildings.

turlough – A lake which seasonally fills and drains. Turloughs are typical of karstic areas where the drainage is below ground rather than above ground.

Bibliography

The two quotes at the beginning of the book are reproduced in:
Woodward, C. 2002 *In Ruins*. London: Vintage.

General

Barry, T. 1987. *The Archaeology of Medieval Ireland*. London: Routledge.

Champion, T.C. et al 1984. *Prehistoric Europe*. London: Academic press.

Edwards, N. 1990. *The Archaeology of Early Medieval Ireland*. London: Routledge.

O'Brien, J. and P. Harbison 1996. *Ancient Ireland*. London: George Weidenfeld & Nicholson Ltd.

Ó Cróinín, D. 1995. *Early Medieval Ireland 400 – 1200*. London: Longman.

O'Keeffe, T. 2000. *Medieval Ireland: An Archaeology*. Gloucestershire: Tempus.

Waddell, J. 1998. *The Prehistoric Archaeology of Ireland*. Galway: Galway University Press.

The Landscape

Crabtree, K. 1982. Evidence for the Burren's Forest Cover. In Bell, M & S. Limburg (eds) *Archaeological Aspects of Woodland Ecology*. BAR International Series 146, 105-113.

Drew, D. 1997. The Burren, County Clare. In Aalen F.K. Whelan & M. Stout (eds.) *Atlas of the Irish Rural Landscape*, 287–298. Cork: Cork University Press.

Feehan, J. 1991. The rocks and landforms of the Burren. In O'Connell, J. and A. Korff (eds.) *The Book of the Burren*. Kinvarra: Tir Eolas.

Feehan, J. 1994. The Geology of the Aran Islands. In Waddell, J., J. O'Connell and A. Korff (eds.) *The Book of Aran*. Kinvarra: Tír Eolas.

Roden, C. 1994. The Aran Flora. In Waddell, J.J. O'Connell and A. Korff (eds.) *The Book of Aran*. Kinvarra: Tír Eolas.

Watts, W. 1984. The Holocene vegetation of the Burren, western Ireland. In Haworth, E. & J. Lund (eds.) *Lake Sediments and Environmental History, Studies in palaeoliminology and paleoecology in honour of Winifred Tutin*, 359–376. Minneapolis: University of Minnesota Press.

The Burren

Burren General

Gosling, P. 1991a. The Burren in Early Historic Times. In O'Connell, J. and A. Korff (eds.) 1991, *The Book of the Burren*. Kinvarra: Tír Eolas.

Gosling, P. 1991b. The Burren in Medieval Times. In O'Connell, J. and A. Korff (eds.) 1991, *The Book of the Burren*. Kinvarra: Tír Eolas.

Macnamara, G. 1901. Inchiquin, County Clare. *Journal of the Royal Society of Antiquaries* 11.

Swan, L. 1991. The Churches, Monasteries and Burial Grounds of the Burren. In O'Connell, J. and A. Korff (eds.) 1991, *The Book of the Burren*. Kinvarra: Tír Eolas.

Waddell, J. 1991. The First People, The Prehistoric Burren. In O'Connell, J. and A. Korff (eds.) 1991, *The Book of the Burren*. Kinvarra: Tír Eolas.

Westropp, T. 1897. Prehistoric Stone Forts of Northern Clare. *Journal of the Royal Society of Antiquaries* 7, 116–127.

Westropp, T. 1898. Prehistoric Remains in the Burren, County Clare (Carran and Kilcorney). *Journal of the Royal Society of Antiquaries* 28, 353–366.

Westropp, T. 1899a. Prehistoric Remains in the Burren, County Clare (Part II – Kilcorney and the Eastern Valleys). *Journal of the Royal Society of Antiquaries* 29, 367–384.

Westropp, T. 1900. Excursions of the Royal Society of Antiquaries of Ireland, Summer Meeting 1900. *Journal of the Royal Society of Antiquaries* 30, 273–306.

Westropp, T. 1905. Prehistoric Remains (Forts and Dolmens) Along the Borders of Burren, in the County of Clare. *Journal of the Royal Society of Antiquaries* 35, 205–239.

The First People on the Burren

Lynch, M. 2002. *A Study of a Possible Mesolithic Landscape in County Clare*. Unpublished MA thesis, National University of Ireland, Cork.

Gibbons, E. 1999. *Catalogue of Archaeological Finds from County Clare in the National Museum of Ireland*. Unpublished manuscript.

Raftery, J. 1941. Recent Acquisitions from County Clare in the National Museum. *North Munster Antiquarian Journal* 2, 170–171.

The First Farmers on the Burren

Beckett, J. and C. Jones 2002. Preliminary assessment of the bone remains at the Parknabinnia chambered tomb (Cl. 153) on Roughan Hill. *The Other Clare* 26, 5–7.

Brindley, A. and J. Lanting 1992. Radiocarbon dates from the cemetery at Poulawack, County Clare. *Journal of Irish Archaeology* 6, 13–17.

Cooney, G. 2000. *Landscapes of the Neolithic*. London: Routledge.

de Valera, R. and S. Ó Nualláin 1961. *Survey of the Megalithic Tombs of Ireland, Volume 1, County Clare*. Dublin: The Stationery Office.

Hencken, H. 1935. A Cairn at Poulawack, County Clare. *Journal of the Royal Society of Antiquaries of Ireland 65*, 191–222.

Hodder, I. 1984. Burials, Houses, Women and Men in the European Neolithic. In Miller, D. and C. Tilley (eds.) *Ideology, Power and Prehistory*. Cambridge: Cambridge University Press.

Jones, C. 2003. Neolithic beginnings on Roughan Hill and the Burren. In Armit, I. et al. (eds.) *Neolithic Settlement in Ireland and Western Britain*. Oxford: Oxbow.

Jones, C. and P. Walsh 1996. Recent Discoveries on Roughan Hill, County Clare. *Journal of the Royal Society of Antiquaries of Ireland* 126, 86–107.

Knowles, M. 1905. Kitchen Middens – County Clare. *Journal of the Limerick Field Club* 2 (1901–1904), 35–42.

Knowles, W.J. 1901. The fourth report on the prehistoric remains from the sandhills of the coast of Ireland. *Proceedings of the Royal Irish Academy 6*.

Lynch, A. 1988. Poulnabrone – a stone in time, *Archaeology Ireland* 2, 105–107.

Lynch, A. and B. Ó'Donnabháin 1994. Poulnabrone, County Clare. *The Other Clare* 18, 5–7.

Renfrew, C. 1976. Megaliths, Territories and Populations. In *Acculturation and Continuity in Atlantic Europe mainly during the Neolithic period and the Bronze Age. Papers presented at the IV Atlantic Colloquium, Ghent 1975*. Brugge: De Tempel.

Renfrew, C. 1981. The Megalith Builders of Western Europe. In Evans, J.B. Cunliffe and C. Renfrew (eds.) *Antiquity and Man: Essays in Honour of Glyn Daniel*. London: Thames and Hudson.

Ryan, M. 1981. Poulawack, County Clare: the affinities of the central burial structure. In Ó Corráin, D. (ed.) *Irish Antiquity: Essays and Studies presented to Professor M.J. O'Kelly*, 134–146. Dublin: Four Courts Press.

Shanks, M. and C. Tilley 1982. Ideology, symbolic power and ritual communication: a reinterpretation of Neolithic mortuary practices. In Hodder, I. (ed.) *Symbolic and Structural Archaeology*, 129–54. Cambridge: Cambridge University Press.

Sherratt, A. 1990. The genesis of megaliths: monumentality, ethnicity and social complexity in Neolithic north-west Europe. *World Archaeology* 22 (2).

Westropp, T. 1905. Prehistoric Remains (Forts and Dolmens) Along the Borders of Burren, in the County of Clare. *Journal of the Royal Society of Antiquaries* 35, 205–239.

Zvelebil, M. and P. Rowley-Conway 1984. Transition to Farming in Northern Europe: A Hunter-Gatherer Perspective. *Norwegian Archaeological Review* 2, 104–128.

From Neolithic to Bronze Age

de Valera, R. and S. Ó Nualláin 1961. *Survey of the Megalithic Tombs of Ireland, Volume 1, County Clare.* Dublin: The Stationery Office.

Earle, T. 1989. The Evolution of Chiefdoms. *Current Anthropology* 30 (1).

Harding, A. 1984. Aspects of Social Evolution in the Bronze Age. In Bintliff, J. (ed.) *European Social Evolution: Archaeological Perspectives.* Bradford: University of Bradford.

Jones, C. 1996. Prehistoric Farmstead at Kilnaboy. *The Other Clare (Journal of The Shannon Archaeological and Historical Society)*, 20, 17–19.

Jones, C. 1997. The Final Neolithic/Early Bronze Age on the Burren, a Brief Review of the Evidence. *The Other Clare* 21, 36–39.

Jones, C. 1998. The Discovery and Dating of the Prehistoric Landscape of Roughan Hill in County Clare. *The Journal of Irish Archaeology* 9, 27–43.

Jones, C. and A. Gilmer 1999. Roughan Hill, a Final Neolithic/Early Bronze Age landscape revealed. *Archaeology Ireland* Spring 1999.

O'Brien, W. 1999. *Sacred Ground: Megalithic Tombs in Coastal South-west Ireland.* Bronze Age Studies Monograph No. 4. Galway: Department of Archaeology, National University of Ireland, Galway.

Ó Ríordáin and G. Ó h-Iceadha 1955. Lough Gur Excavations: The Megalithic Tomb. *Journal of the Royal Society of Antiquaries of Ireland* 85, 34–50.

Sherratt, A. 1984. Social Evolution: Europe in the Later Neolithic and Copper Ages. In Bintliff, J. (ed.) *European Social Evolution: Archaeological Perspectives.* Bradford: University of Bradford.

Gold, Power and War

Bourke, L. 2001. *Crossing the Rubicon: Bronze Age Metalwork from Irish Rivers.* Bronze Age Studies Monograph No. 5. Galway: Department of Archaeology, National University of Ireland, Galway.

Bradley, R. 1990. *The passage of arms: an archaeological analysis of prehistoric hoards and votive deposits.* Cambridge: Cambridge University Press.

Bridgford, S. 1997. Mightier than the Pen? (an edgewise look at Irish Bronze Age swords). In Carmen, J. (ed.) *Material Harm, archaeological studies of war and violence.* Glasgow: Cruithne Press.

Buckley, V. (ed.) 1990. *Burnt Offerings: International Contributions to Burnt Mound Archaeology.* Dublin: Wordwell.

Burgess, C. and S. Gerloff 1981. *The Dirks and Rapiers of Great Britain and Ireland.* München: C.H. Beck'sche Verlagsbuchhandlung.

Eogan, J. 2002. Excavations at a Cairn in Coolnatullagh townland, County Clare. *North Munster Antiquarian Journal* 42, 113–150.

Harbison, P. 1969. *The Axes of the Early Bronze Age in Ireland.* München: C.H. Beck'sche Verlagsbuchhandlung.

Harding, A. 1999. Warfare: A Defining Characteristic of Bronze Age Europe? In Carman, J. and A. Harding (eds.) *Ancient Warfare.* Wiltshire: Sutton Publishing Ltd.

Kristiansen, K. 1999. The Emergence of Warrior Aristocracies in Later European Prehistory and Their Long-term History. In Carman, J. and A. Harding (eds.) *Ancient Warfare.* Wiltshire: Sutton Publishing Ltd.

Eogan, G. 1993. The Late Bronze Age: Customs, Crafts and Cults. In Shee-Twohig, E. and M. Ronayne (eds.) *Past Perceptions, The Prehistoric Archaeology of South-West Ireland.* Cork: Cork University Press.

Lucas, A. T. 1970 National Museum of Ireland: Archaeological Acquisitions in the Year 1967. *Journal of the Royal Society of Antiquaries* 100, 145–166.

Macnamara, 1901. Inchiquin, County Clare. *Journal of the Royal Society of Antiquaries* 11.

Celts?

Caufield, S. 1977. The Beehive Quern in Ireland, *Journal of the Royal Society of Antiquaries* 107, 104–138.

James, S. 1993. *Exploring the World of the Celts.* London: Thames and Hudson.

James, S. 1999. *The Atlantic Celts. Ancient People or Modern Invention?* London: British Museum Press.

Macnamara, 1901. Inchiquin, County Clare. *Journal of the Royal Society of Antiquaries* 11.

Ó Donnabháin, B. 2000. An appalling vista? The Celts and the archaeology of later prehistoric Ireland. In Desmond, A. et al. (eds.) *New Agendas in Irish Prehistory.* Dublin: Wordwell.

Raftery, B. 1983. *A Catalogue of Irish Iron Age Antiquities.* Marburg: Philipps-Universitat.

Raftery, B. 1994. *Pagan Celtic Ireland: The Enigma of the Irish Iron Age.* London: Thames and Hudson.

Waddell, J. 1995. Celts, Celticization and the Irish Bronze Age, in Waddell, J. and E. Shee-Twohig (eds), *Ireland in the Bronze Age: proceedings of the Dublin conference, April 1995.*

The Coming of Christianity

Hughes, K. and A. Hamlin 1977. *The Modern Traveller to the Early Irish Church.* London: SPCK.

Ní Ghabhláin, S. 1988. Carved Stone Head from Glencolumkille, County Clare. *Journal of the Royal Society of Antiquaries of Ireland* 118, 135–138.

Ní Ghabhláin, S. 1995a. *Church, Parish and Polity: The Medieval Diocese of Kilfenora, Ireland.* Unpublished PhD dissertation. University of California Los Angeles.

Petrie, G. 1845 *Ecclesiastical Architecture of Ireland anterior to the Anglo-Norman Invasion.* Dublin: Hodges and Smith.

Rynne, C. 1998. The Craft of the Millwright in Early Medieval Munster. In Monk, M. and J. Sheehan (eds.) *Early Medieval Munster: Archaeology, History and Society.* Cork: Cork University Press.

Sheehan, J. 1982. The Early Historic church-sites of north Clare. *North Munster Antiquarian Journal* 24, 29–47.

Westropp, T. 1900. Excursions of the Royal Society of Antiquaries of Ireland, Summer Meeting 1900. *Journal of the Royal Society of Antiquaries* 30, 273–306.

Westropp, T. 1911. A Folklore Survey of County Clare. *Folk-Lore: transactions of The Folk-Lore Society* 22(1).

Cahercommaun and the Early Medieval Chiefdoms of the Burren

Bhreathnach, E. 1999. The construction of the stone fort at Cahercommaun: a historical hypothesis. In Cotter, C. *Cahercommaun Fort, County Clare: a reassessment of its cultural context.* Discovery Programme Reports 5, 83–91.

Cotter, C. 1999. *Cahercommaun Fort, County Clare: a reassessment of its cultural context.* Discovery Programme Reports 5, 41–96.

Deevy, M. 1998. *Medieval ring brooches in Ireland: A study of jewellery, dress and society.* Dublin: Wordwell.

Fitzpatrick, M. 1999. Cathair Mór, Ballylabban, Stone Fort. In *Excavations 1999.* Dublin: Wordwell.

Gibson, B. 1990. *Tulach Commain: A View of an Irish Chiefdom.* Unpublished PhD dissertation. University of California Los Angeles.

Hencken, H. 1938. *Cahercommaun: A Stone Fort in County Clare.* Dublin: Royal Society of Antiquaries.

Macalister, R.A.S. 1945. *Corpus Inscriptionum Insularum Celticarum.* Volume 1. Dublin: Stationery Office.

Macalister, R.A.S. 1949. *Corpus Inscriptionum Insularum Celticarum.* Volume 2. Dublin: Stationery Office.

Ní Ghabhláin, S. 1995a. *Church, Parish and Polity: The Medieval Diocese of Kilfenora, Ireland.* Unpublished PhD dissertation. University of California Los Angeles.

O'Conor, K. 1998. *The Archaeology of Medieval Rural Settlement in Ireland.* Discovery Programme Monographs 3. Dublin: Royal Irish Academy.

Ó Floinn, R. 1999. The Date of some metalwork from Cahercommaun reassessed. In Cotter, C. *Cahercommaun Fort, County Clare: a reassessment of its cultural context.* Discovery Programme Reports 5, 73–82.

Stout, M. 1997. *The Irish Ringfort*. Dublin: Four Courts Press.

Medieval Churches and Society on the Burren

Cronin, R. 1998. Late High Crosses in Munster: Tradition and Novelty in Twelfth-Century Irish Art. In Monk, M. and J. Sheehan (eds.) *Early Medieval Munster: Archaeology, History and Society*. Cork: Cork University Press.

De Poar, L. 1956. The Limestone Crosses of Clare and Aran. *Journal of the Galway Archaeological and Historical Society* 26 (3&4), 53–71.

Harbison, P. 1992. *The High Crosses of Ireland*. Bonn.

Henry, F. 1970. *Irish Art in the Romanesque Period (1020–1170 AD)*. London: Methuen & Co. Ltd.

Leask, H. 1955. *Irish Churches and Monastic Buildings, Vol. 1. The first phases and the Romanesque*. Dundalk: Dundalgan Press.

Leask, H. 1960. *Irish Churches and Monastic Buildings, Vol. 2. Gothic Architecture to A.D. 1400*. Dundalk: Dundalgan Press.

Ní Ghabhláin, S. 1995a. *Church, Parish and Polity: The Medieval Diocese of Kilfenora, Ireland*. Unpublished PhD dissertation. University of California Los Angeles.

Ní Ghabhláin, S. 1995b. Church and community in Medieval Ireland: the diocese of Kilfenora. *Journal of the Royal Society of Antiquaries* 125, 61–84.

Ní Ghabhláin, S. 1996. The Origin of Medieval parishes in Gaelic Ireland: the evidence from Kilfenora. *Journal of the Royal Society of Antiquaries* 126, 37–61.

Stalley, R. 1975. Corcomroe Abbey, some observations on its architectural history. *Journal of the Royal Society of Antiquaries* 105, 25–46.

Stalley, R. 1987. *The Cistercian Monasteries of Ireland*. New Haven: Yale University Press.

Relics and Pilgrimage on the Burren

Bourke, C. 2000. The bells of Saints Caillin and Cuana: two twelfth-century cups. In *Seanchas, Studies in Early and Medieval Irish Archaeology, History and Literature in honour of Francis J. Byrne*. Dublin: Four Courts Press.

Harbison, P. 1976. The double-armed cross on the church gable at Killinaboy, County Clare. *North Munster Antiquarian Journal* 18, 3–12.

Harbison, P. 1991. *Pilgrimage in Ireland*. Syracuse: Syracuse University Press.

Harbison, P. 2000. An ancient pilgrimage 'Relic-Road' in north Clare? *The Other Clare* 24, 55–59.

Kelly, E. 1996. *Sheela-na-Gigs, Origins and Functions*. Dublin: Town House and Country House.

Lucas, A. 1986. The Social Role of Relics and Reliquaries in Ancient Ireland. *Journal of the Royal Society of Antiquaries* 116, 5–37.

Macnamara, G. 1899. The ancient stone crosses of Ui-Fearmaic, County Clare. *Journal of the Royal Society of Antiquaries* 29.

O'Farrell, F. 1984. The Cross in the Field, Kilfenora – part of a Founder's Tomb? *North Munster Antiquarian Journal* 26, 8–13.

O'Floinn, R. 1991. Ecclesiastical objects of the Early Medieval period from County Clare. *The Other Clare* 15, 12–14.

Petrie, G. 1845 *Ecclesiastical Architecture of Ireland anterior to the Anglo-Norman Invasion.* Dublin.

Rynne, E. 1967. The Tau-Cross at Kilnaboy: Pagan or Christian? In Rynne, E. (ed.) *North Munster Studies, essays in commemoration of Monsignor Michael Moloney.* Limerick: The Thomond Archaeological Society.

Rynne, E. 2000. The Kilshanny Bell. In Ó Murchadha, C. (ed.) *County Clare Studies: Essays in Memory of Gerald O'Connell, Seán Ó Murchadha, Thomas Coffey and Pat Flynn.* Ennis: The Clare Archaeological and Historical Society.

Westropp, T. 1894. Churches with Round Towers in Northern Clare (Part I). *Journal of the Royal Society of Antiquaries* 24, 25–34.

The Tower Houses of the Burren

Cronin, R. 1997. *The tower houses of north-west Clare.* Unpublished MA dissertation. National University of Ireland, Galway.

FitzPatrick, E. 2004. *Royal Inauguration in Gaelic Ireland, c. 1100–1600. A Cultural Landscape Study.* Woodbridge: Boydell and Brewer Press.

FitzPatrick, E. 1997. The Historic Assembly Sites of Tulach Ui Dheadhaidh and Carn Mhic Tail. *The Other Clare* 21, 17–19.

Gernon, L. 1620. Quote reproduced in Leask, H. 1986. *Irish Castles and Castellated Houses.* Dundalk: Dundalgan Press Ltd.

Gibson, B. 1990. *Tulach Commain: A View of an Irish Chiefdom.* Unpublished PhD dissertation. University of California Los Angeles.

le Gouz, B. 1644. Quote reproduced in Westropp, T. 1899b Notes on the lesser castles or 'peel towers' of the County Clare. *Proceedings of the Royal Irish Academy* 5, 348–363.

O'Conor, K. 1998. *The Archaeology of Medieval Rural Settlement in Ireland.* Discovery Programme Monographs 3. Dublin: Royal Irish Academy.

Leask, H. 1986. *Irish Castles and Castellated Houses*. Dundalk: Dundalgan Press Ltd.

McNeill, T. 1997. *Castles in Ireland: Feudal Power in a Gaelic World*. London: Routledge.

Sweetman, D. 1999. *The Medieval Castles of Ireland*. Cork: The Collins Press.

Westropp, T. 1899b Notes on the lesser castles or 'peel towers' of the County Clare. *Proceedings of the Royal Irish Academy 5, 348–363*.

Westropp, T. 1900. Excursions of the Royal Society of Antiquaries of Ireland, Summer Meeting 1900. *Journal of the Royal Society of Antiquaries 30, 273–306.*

Nineteenth-Century Military Fortifications on the Burren

Kerrigan, P. 1995. *Castles and Fortifications in Ireland 1485–1945*. Cork: The Collins Press.

The Aran Islands

Aran Islands General

Barry, J.G. 1886. Aran of the Saints. *Journal of the Royal Society of Antiquaries 17, 488–94.*

Cooke, J. 1903. *Wakeman's Handbook of Irish Antiquities*, 3rd ed. Dublin: Hodges & Figgis & Co. Ltd.

Gosling, P. 1993. *Archaeological Inventory of County Galway*. Dublin: The Stationery Office.

Haddon, A.C. and C.R. Browne 1893. The Ethnography of the Aran Islands, County Galway. *Proceedings of the Royal Irish Academy 18, 768–829.*

Macalister, R.A.S. 1921. *Ireland in Pre-Celtic Times*. Dublin: Maunsel and Roberts Ltd.

Ó hEithir, B. and R. Ó hEithir (eds) 1991. *An Aran Reader*. Dublin: The Lilliput Press.

O'Flaherty, R. 1684. *A Chorographical Description of West or H-Iar Connaught*. Edited by J. Hardiman 1846. Dublin.

Pouchin Mould, D. 1972. *The Aran Islands*. Newton Abbot: David & Charles.

Robinson, T. 1986. *Stones of Aran: Pilgrimage*. Penguin Books Ltd.

Robinson, T. 1995. *Stones of Aran: Labyrinth*. Dublin: The Lilliput Press Ltd.

Robinson, T. 1996. *Oileáin Árann, A Companion to the map of the Aran Islands*. Roundstone: Folding Landscapes.

Westropp, T. 1895. Aran Islands. *Journal of the Royal Society of Antiquaries 25, 250–278.*

Westropp 1905. *Illustrated Guide to the Northern, Western, and Southern Islands, and Coast of Ireland*. Royal Society of Antiquaries of Ireland. Dublin.

Waddell, J. 1994. The Archaeology of the Aran Islands. In Waddell, J., J. O'Connell and A. Korff (eds.) *The Book of Aran*. Kinvarra: Tír Eolas.

Wilde, W. 1861. *A Descriptive Catalogue of the Antiquities of Animal Materials and Bronze in the Museum of the Royal Irish Academy*. Dublin: Hodges, Smith, & Co.

The Colonisation and Early Settlement of the Aran Islands

De Valera, R. and S. Ó Nualláin 1972. *Survey of the Megalithic Tombs of Ireland, Volume III, County Galway etc.* Dublin: Stationery Office.

Murphy, D. 1888. On two sepulchral urns found, in June, 1885, in the south island of Arran. *Proceedings of the Royal Irish Academy* 12, 476–79.

O'Connell, M. and K. Molloy 2001. Farming and Woodland Dynamics in Ireland During the Neolithic. *Proceedings of the Royal Irish Academy* 101B, 99–128.

The Late Bronze Age Chiefdom of Dún Aonghasa

Cotter, C. 1993. Western Stone Fort Project, Interim Report. In *Discovery Programme Reports, Volume 1*, 1–19. Dublin: Royal Irish Academy.

Cotter, C. 1995a. Western Stone Fort Project, Interim Report. In *Discovery Programme Reports, Volume 2*, 1–11. Dublin: Royal Irish Academy.

Cotter, C. 1996. Western Stone Fort Project, Interim Report. In *Discovery Programme Reports, Volume 4*, 1–14. Dublin: Royal Irish Academy.

Westropp, T. 1899c. Dun Aenghus, Aran. *Journal of the Royal Society of Antiquaries* 29, 66–67.

Westropp, T. 1910a. A study of the fort of Dun Aengusa in Inishmore, Aran Isles, Galway Bay: its plan, growth and records. *Proceedings of the Royal Irish Academy* 28C, 1–46.

The Stone Forts of the Aran Islands

Cotter, C. 1993. Western Stone Fort Project, Interim Report. In *Discovery Programme Reports, Volume 1*, 1–19. Dublin: Royal Irish Academy.

Cotter, C 1995a. Western Stone Fort Project, Interim Report. In *Discovery Programme Reports, Volume 2*, 1–11. Dublin: Royal Irish Academy.

Cotter, C. 1995b. 'Dún Eoghanachta', Eoghanacht, Inis Mór. In *Excavations Bulletin 1995*. Dublin: Wordwell.

Cotter, C. 1996. Western Stone Fort Project, Interim Report. In *Discovery Programme Reports, Volume 4*, 1–14. Dublin: Royal Irish Academy.

Westropp, T. 1899c. Dun Aenghus, Aran. *Journal of the Royal Society of Antiquaries* 29, 66–67.

Westropp, T. 1910a. A study of the fort of Dun Aengusa in Inishmore, Aran Isles, Galway Bay: its plan, growth and records. *Proceedings of the Royal Irish Academy* 28C, 1–46.

Westropp, T. 1910b. A study of the early forts and stone huts in Inishmore, Aran Isles, Galway Bay. *Proceedings of the Royal Irish Academy* 28C, 174–200.

Windele, J. 1854. Quote is reproduced in Westropp, T. 1910a. A study of the fort of Dun Aengusa in Inishmore, Aran Isles, Galway Bay: its plan, growth and records. *Proceedings of the Royal Irish Academy* 28C, 1–46.

Life Outside the Forts

Goulden, J. 1955. Killnamanagh: The Lost Church of Aran. *Journal of the Galway Archaeological and Historical Society*, 29 (1&2), 35–40.

Kinahan, G. 1869. Notes on some of the ancient villages in the Aran Isles, County of Galway. *Proceedings of the Royal Irish Academy* 10, 25–30.

Waddell, J. 1988. J.R.W. Goulden's excavations on Inishmore, Aran, 1953–1955. *Journal of the Galway Archaeological and Historical Society* 41, 37–59.

Christianity and Pilgrimage on the Aran Islands

Berger, R. 1992. Radiocarbon dating mortar in Ireland. *Radiocarbon* 34, 880–89.

Berger, R. 1995. Radiocarbon Dating of Early Medieval Irish Monuments. *Proceedings of the Royal Irish Academy* 95, 159–74.

Crawford, H. 1923. Carvings from Aran Churches. *Journal of the Royal Society of Antiquaries* 53, 99–100.

De Poar, L. 1956. The Limestone Crosses of Clare and Aran. *Journal of the Galway Archaeological and Historical Society* 26 (3&4), 53–71.

Goulden, J. 1955. Killnamanagh: The Lost Church of Aran. *Journal of the Galway Archaeological and Historical Society*, 29 (1&2), 35–40.

Haddon and Browne 1893. The Ethnography of the Aran Islands, County Galway. *Proceedings of the Royal Irish Academy* 18, 768–829.

Harbison, P. 1991. *Pilgrimage in Ireland*. Syracuse: Syracuse University Press.

Harbison, P. 1992. *The High Crosses of Ireland*. Bonn.

Henry, F. 1970. *Irish Art in the Romanesque Period (1020–1170 AD)*. London: Methuen & Co. Ltd.

Higgins, J. 1987. *The Early Christian Cross Slabs, Pillar Stones and Related Monuments of County Galway, Ireland*. British Archaeological Reports, International Series 375. Oxford.

Leask, H. 1955. *Irish Churches and Monastic Buildings, Vol. 1. The first phases and the Romanesque*. Dundalk: Dundalgan Press.

Leask, H. 1960. *Irish Churches and Monastic Buildings, Vol. 2. Gothic Architecture to A.D. 1400.* Dundalk: Dundalgan Press.

Lucas, A. 1986. The Social Role of Relics and Reliquaries in Ancient Ireland. *Journal of the Royal Society of Antiquaries* 116, 5–37.

Macalister, R.A.S. 1922. The Cross-inscribed 'Holed Stone' at Mainistir Chiaráin, Aran Island. *Journal of the Royal Society of Antiquaries* 52, 177.

Macalister, R.A.S. 1945. *Corpus Inscriptionum Insularum Celticarum.* Volume 1. Dublin: Stationery Office.

Macalister, R.A.S. 1949. *Corpus Inscriptionum Insularum Celticarum.* Volume 2. Dublin: Stationery Office.

Manning, C. 1985. Archaeological excavations at two church sites on Inishmore, Aran Islands. *Journal of the Royal Society of Antiquaries* 115, 96–120.

Ní Ghabhláin, S. 2003. *Excavations at Mainistir Chiaráin (Teampaill Chiaráin), Inis Mór.* Unpublished manuscript.

Ní Ghabhláin, S. and J. Moran 1997. *Excavations at Mainistir Chiaráin 96E081.* Unpublished manuscript.

O'Flaherty, R. 1684. *A Chorographical Description of West or H-Iar Connaught.* Edited by J. Hardiman 1846. Dublin.

O'Sullivan, A. 1983. Saint Brecan of Clare, *Celtica* 15, 128–39.

Petrie, G. 1845 *Ecclesiastical Architecture of Ireland anterior to the Anglo-Norman Invasion.* Dublin.

Waddell, J. 1972. An Archaeological Survey of Temple Brecan, Aran. *Journal of the Galway Archaeological and Historical Society* 33, 1–27.

Waddell, J. 1981. An Unpublished High Cross on Aran, County Galway. *Journal of the Royal Society of Antiquaries* 111, 29–35.

Westropp, T. 1895. Aran Islands. *Journal of the Royal Society of Antiquaries* 25, 250–278.

Power Struggles on the Aran Islands

Canny, N. 1989. Early Modern Ireland c.1500–1700. In Foster, R. (ed.) *The Oxford Illustrated History of Ireland.* Oxford: Oxford University Press.

Manning, C. 1985. Archaeological excavations at two church sites on Inishmore, Aran Islands. *Journal of the Royal Society of Antiquaries* 115, 96–120.

Walsh, P. 1994. Arkin Fort: The Military History of a Garrison Outpost on Inis Mór. In Waddell, J., J. O'Connell and A. Korff (eds.) *The Book of Aran.* Kinvarra: Tír Eolas.

Archaeology of the Eighteenth and Nineteenth Centuries

Brady, G. 1866. Quote reproduced in Robinson, T. 1991. *Mementos of Mortality. The Cenotaphs and Funerary Cairns of Árainn (Inishmore, County Galway)*. Roundstone: Folding Landscapes.

Kerrigan, P. 1995. *Castles and Fortifications in Ireland 1485–1945*. Cork: The Collins Press.

Robinson, T. 1991. *Mementos of Mortality. The Cenotaphs and Funerary Cairns of Árainn (Inishmore, County Galway)*. Roundstone: Folding Landscapes.

Index

Also Available from The Collins Press

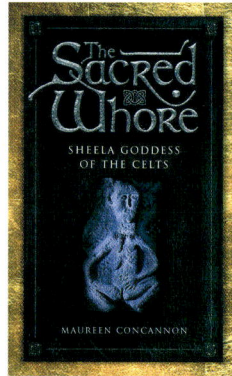

The Sacred Whore: Sheela Goddess of the Celts
Maureen Concannon

There has recently been a growing awareness of ancient carved stone images of naked female figures. Unnoticed and ignored for centuries, they are being rediscovered on early churches, medieval castles and bishops' tombs. This is the story of these mysterious carvings, their history, location and psychological significance. Called Sheela na gigs, they are found at early monastic settlements in Ireland, Scotland, Wales, England and pilgrim routes on the continent set up by Irish missionaries. Anthropology, archaeology, mythology, history and psychology are combined in this book.

ISBN: 1-903464-52-8 • Price: €20.00 PB • 2004

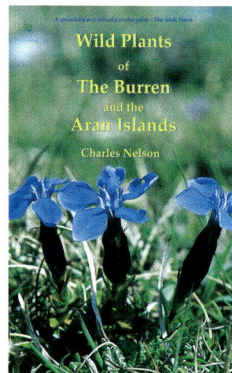

Wild Plants of the Burren and Aran Islands
Charles E. Nelson

The Burren and Aran Islands are renowned for the beauty of their natural flora. Charles Nelson has selected 120 of the most widely occurring plus a number of special plants. Introduced with background information on the plants and how to use the guide, photographs are grouped according to flower colour and the pages colour coded. Plants are described using the common English name, followed by the name in Irish and then the Latin (botanical) name.

ISBN: 1-898256-70-5 • Price: €14.95 PB • Full colour • Reissue 2004

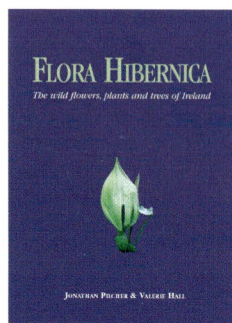

Flora Hibernica: The Wild Flowers, Plants and Trees of Ireland
Jonathan Pilcher and Valerie Hall

Where did the humble daisy originate? Is it true dandelions and nettles were here before we were? What should you do if you come face to face with a giant hogweed? Why are the Irish obsessed with fuschia, and what is the result of our earlier obsession with rhododendron? What are the plants that make our forty shades of green? Where do they grow? *Flora Hibernica* answers these and many more questions.

ISBN: 1-903464-51-X • Price: €25.00 PB • Full colour • 2004